HEROES

GODSEND

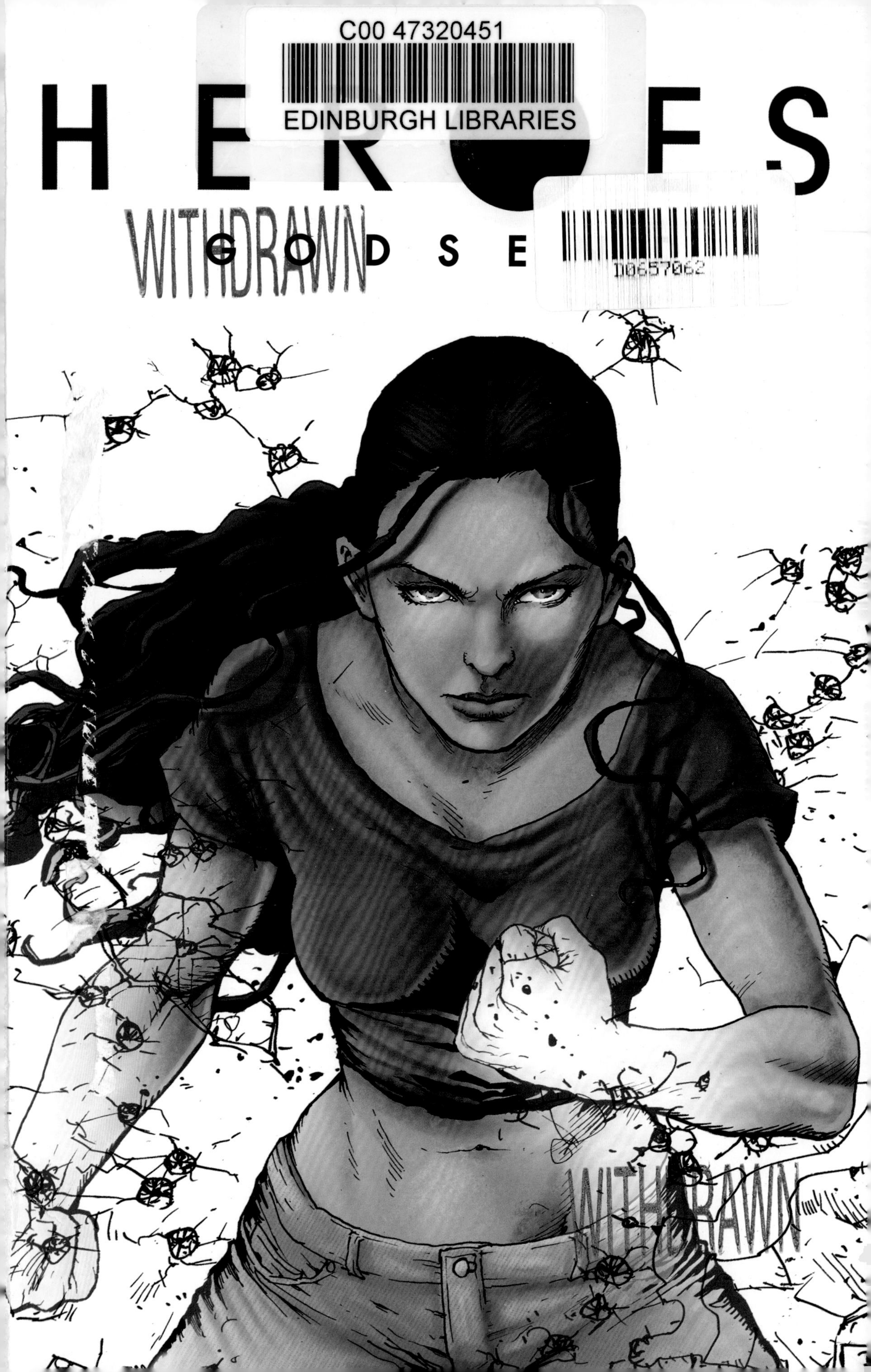

GODSEND

WRITTEN BY
Joey Falco

ARTWORK BY
Roy Allan Martinez

COLORS BY
Ester Salguero

LETTERING BY
Jim Campbell

Farah Nazan is one of the toughest characters in the *Heroes Reborn Event Series* – but what made her that way? *Heroes Godsend* explores her shocking past – and how her encounters with other *Heroes* characters shaped her life...

Special thanks to:
Tim Kring, James Middleton, and all of the *Heroes Reborn* crew. Liz Umeda, Jason McNaughton, Vernon Sanders, and all at NBCUniversal. Also, Eduardo Alpuente and Alberto Garrido of the Infinitoons Agency.

Heroes: Godsend
ISBN: 9781782767763

Collecting *Heroes: Godsend* #1 to 5.
Published by Titan Comics, a division of Titan Publishing Group, Ltd, 144 Southwark Street, London SE1 0UP, UK.
Heroes Reborn: Event Series is a trademark and copyright of Universal Television. Licensed by Universal Studios Licensing LLC 2016 All Rights Reserved.
No portion of this graphic novel may be reproduced, stored in a retrieval system or transmitted in any form or by any means,

10 9 8 7 6 5 4 3 2 1

First printed in China in November 2016

A CIP catalogue record for this title is available from the British Library.

www.titan-comics.com

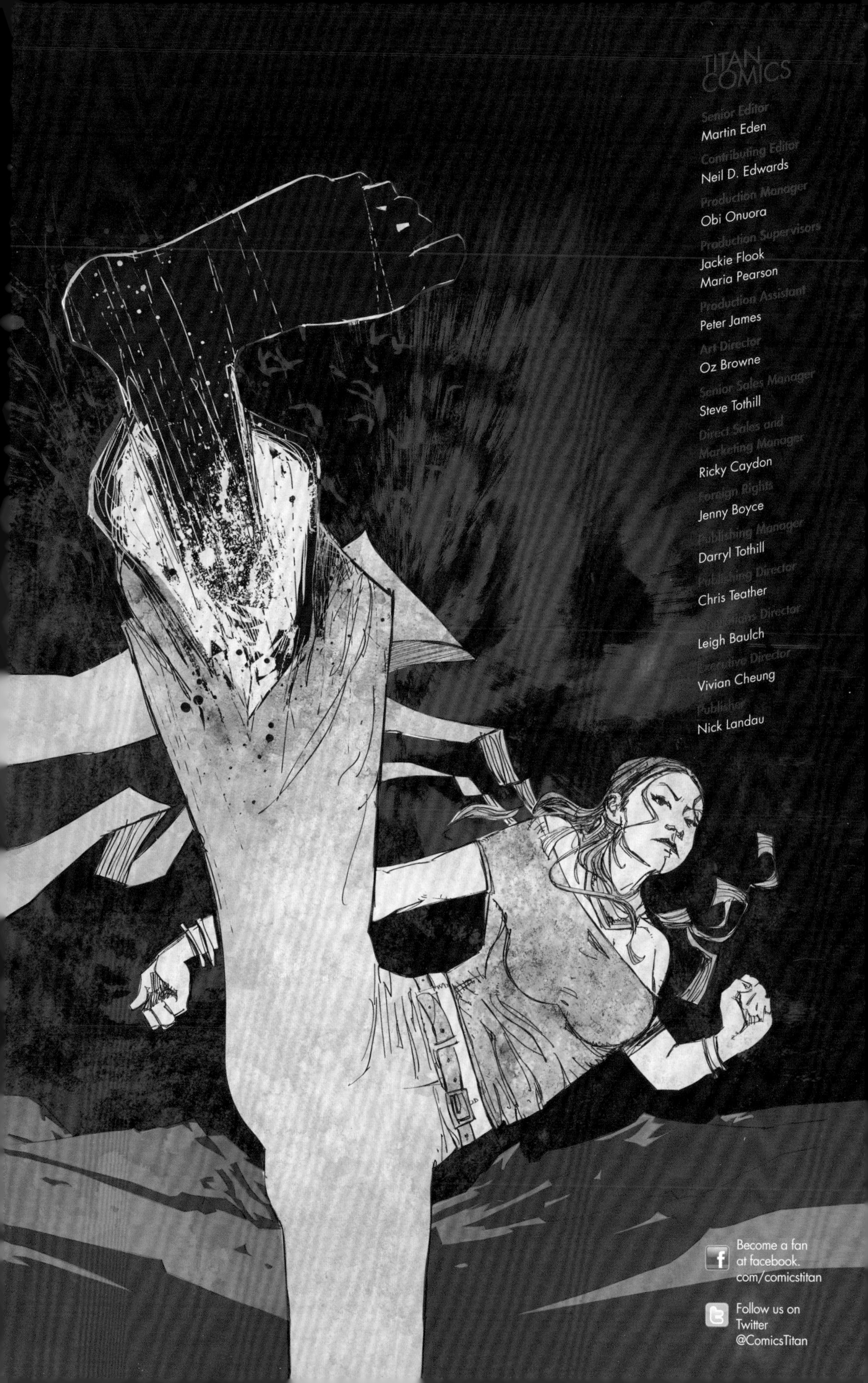

TITAN COMICS

Senior Editor
Martin Eden

Contributing Editor
Neil D. Edwards

Production Manager
Obi Onuora

Production Supervisors
Jackie Flook
Maria Pearson

Production Assistant
Peter James

Art Director
Oz Browne

Senior Sales Manager
Steve Tothill

Direct Sales and Marketing Manager
Ricky Caydon

Foreign Rights
Jenny Boyce

Publishing Manager
Darryl Tothill

Publishing Director
Chris Teather

Operations Director
Leigh Baulch

Executive Director
Vivian Cheung

Publisher
Nick Landau

FOREWORD
By actress Nazneen D. Contractor

Photo by Joe DeAngelis

Farah Nazan is going down as the most favorite character I've ever played. Through her, I tapped into so many facets of the woman the wonderful and talented writer Joey Falco created.

Farah is a daughter, student, warrior, nurturer and, for good measure, a superhero. She is one of the first female Muslim superheroes on the big and small screens. As a true hero, she always puts the well-being of others first. She's not afraid of fighting for what she believes in, and she will sacrifice herself, and all she has, for what matters most.

In this comic book, you see Farah's powers emerge from her desire to "disappear" from society, post-9/11. But ironically, it is through her power of camouflage that she gains her voice and becomes a protector of her Muslim community in Astoria, New York. Farah's inner hero was born in the crucible of fear,

persecution and doubt. From this emerges a woman stronger, self-realized, and determined.

I love her origin story. I was fortunate enough to read all about it shortly into my filming of *Heroes Reborn* and thus was able to fuel many of my scenes with the complex and beautiful back-story that is *Heroes Godsend*. Origin stories are always special, as one gets to experience the birth or rebirth of a character. Through *Heroes Godsend*, the reader gets a first-hand look at Farah's rebirth from a young, orphaned woman into a fully-fledged superhero.

She's the first superhero I've ever portrayed. I never had a stunt double on set, so I got to thoroughly enjoy all the action sequences we shot.

I truly hope you enjoy this comic story – it is so very dear to me and I hope it inspires and encourages your inner Hero.

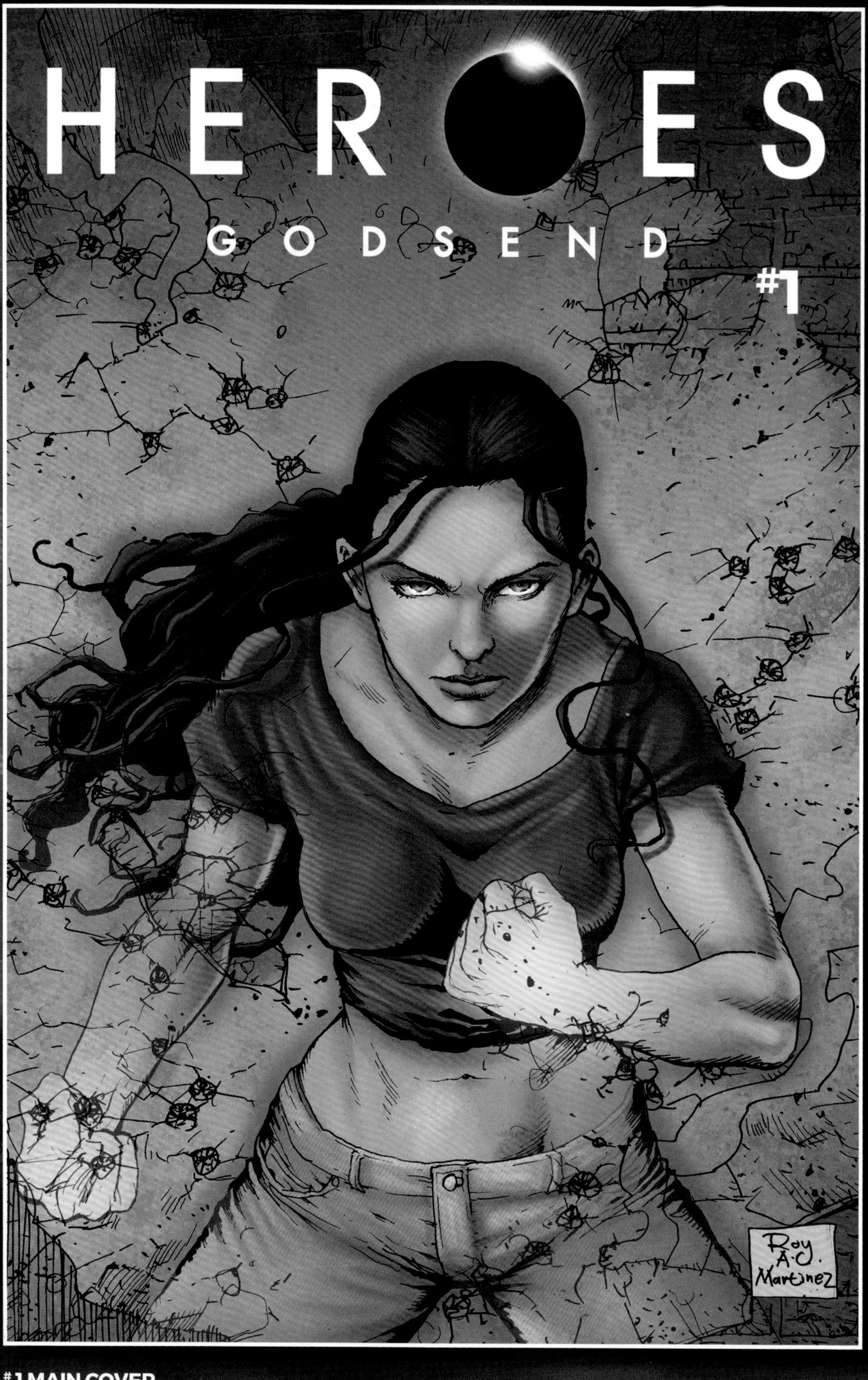
HEROES
GODSEND
#1
Roy A.C. Martinez

#1 MAIN COVER
ARTWORK BY ROY ALLAN MARTINEZ

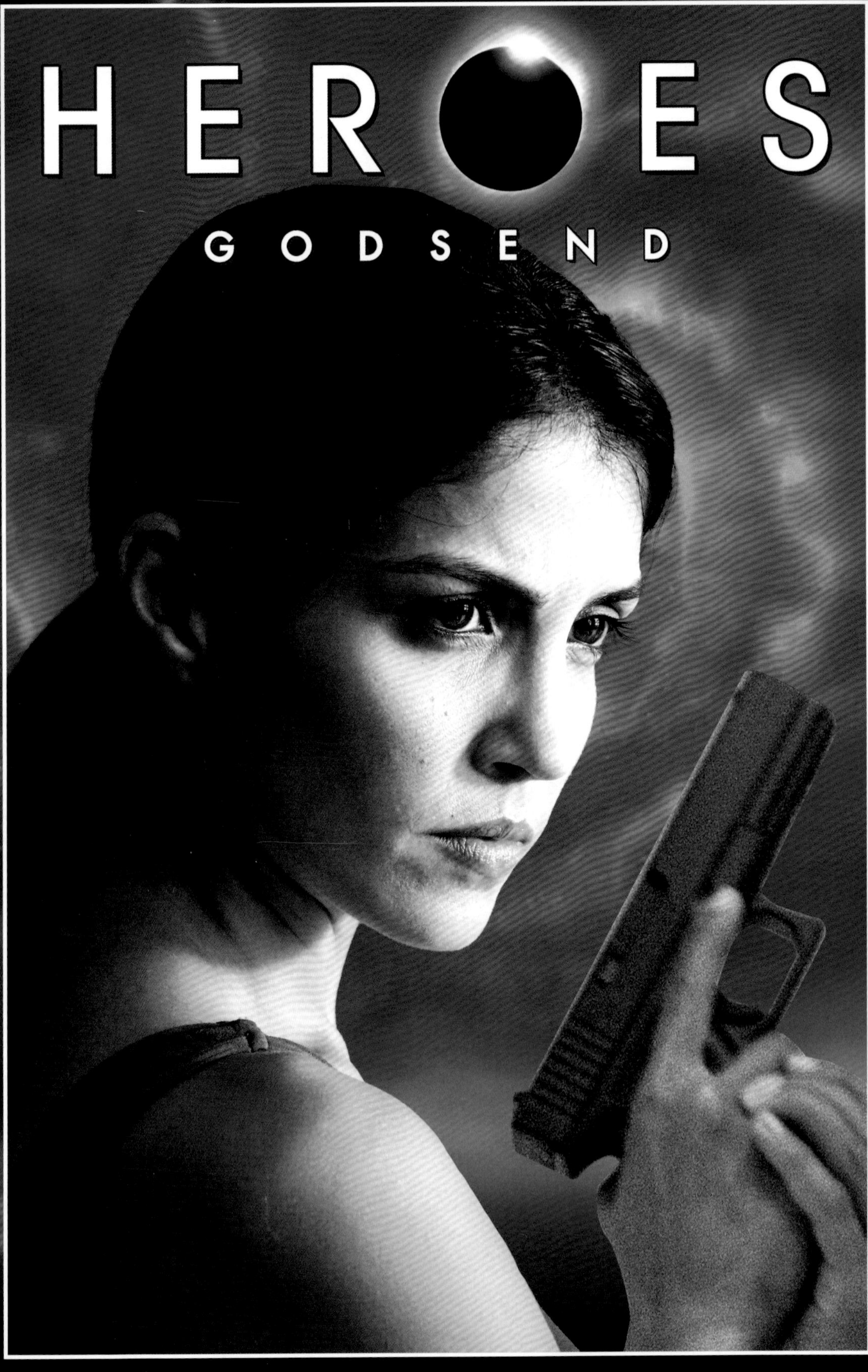
HEROES
GODSEND

1 VARIANT COVER
PHOTO COVER COMPOSITION BY ROB FARMER

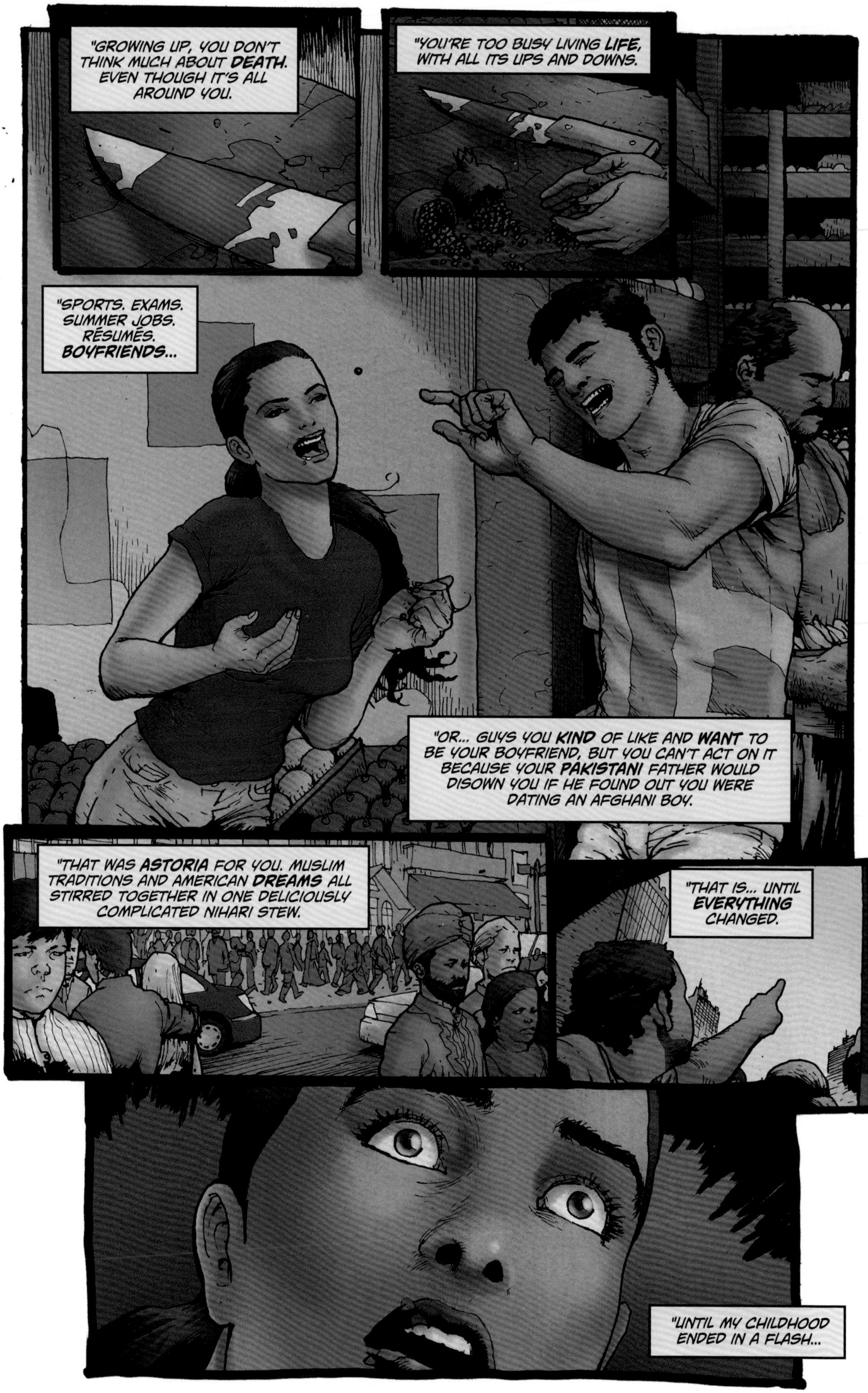
"GROWING UP, YOU DON'T THINK MUCH ABOUT DEATH. EVEN THOUGH IT'S ALL AROUND YOU.
"YOU'RE TOO BUSY LIVING LIFE, WITH ALL ITS UPS AND DOWNS.
"SPORTS. EXAMS. SUMMER JOBS. RÉSUMÉS. BOYFRIENDS...
"OR... GUYS YOU KIND OF LIKE AND WANT TO BE YOUR BOYFRIEND, BUT YOU CAN'T ACT ON IT BECAUSE YOUR PAKISTANI FATHER WOULD DISOWN YOU IF HE FOUND OUT YOU WERE DATING AN AFGHANI BOY.
"THAT WAS ASTORIA FOR YOU. MUSLIM TRADITIONS AND AMERICAN DREAMS ALL STIRRED TOGETHER IN ONE DELICIOUSLY COMPLICATED NIHARI STEW.
"THAT IS... UNTIL EVERYTHING CHANGED.
"UNTIL MY CHILDHOOD ENDED IN A FLASH...

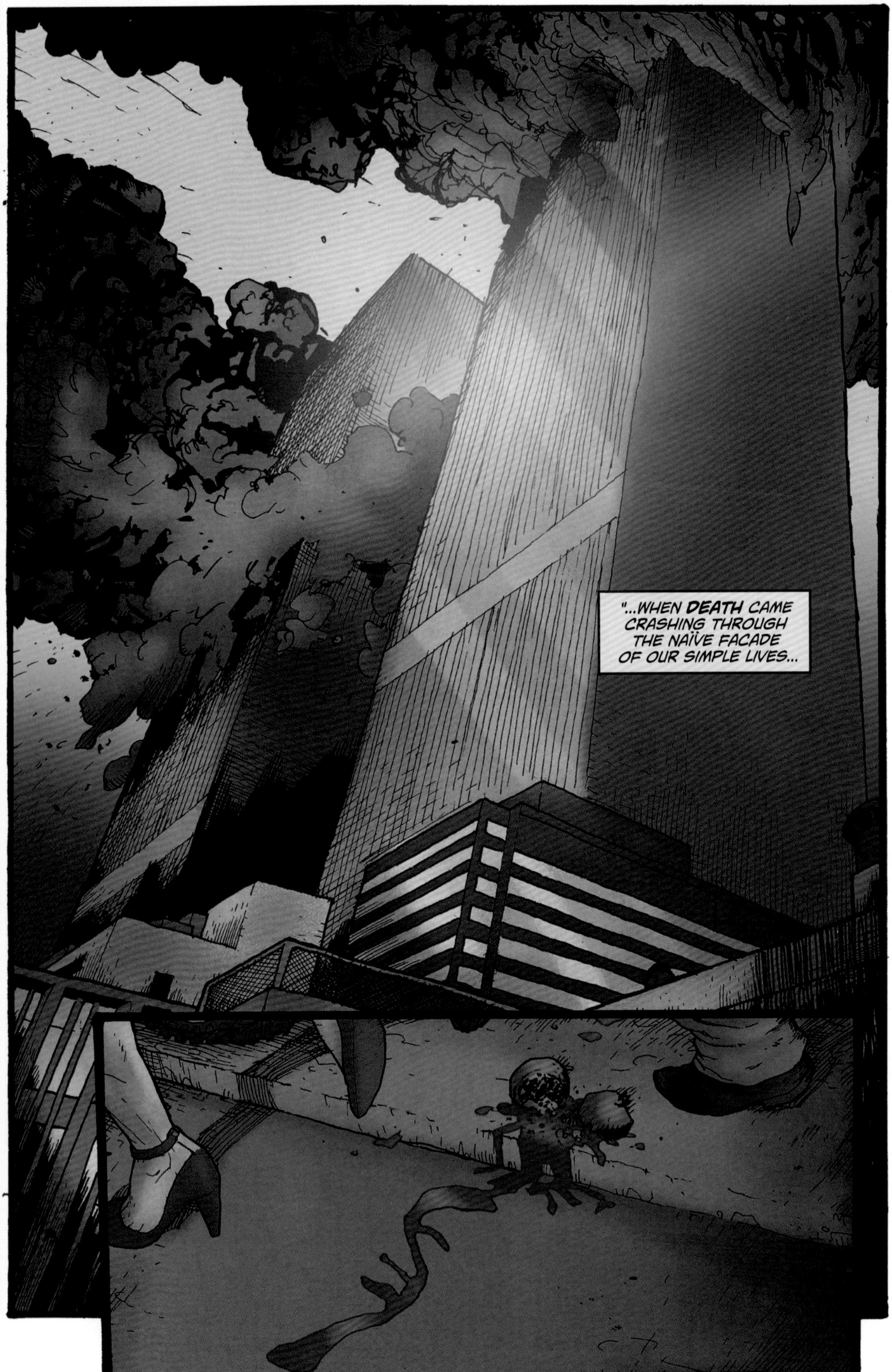
"...WHEN DEATH CAME CRASHING THROUGH THE NAÏVE FACADE OF OUR SIMPLE LIVES...

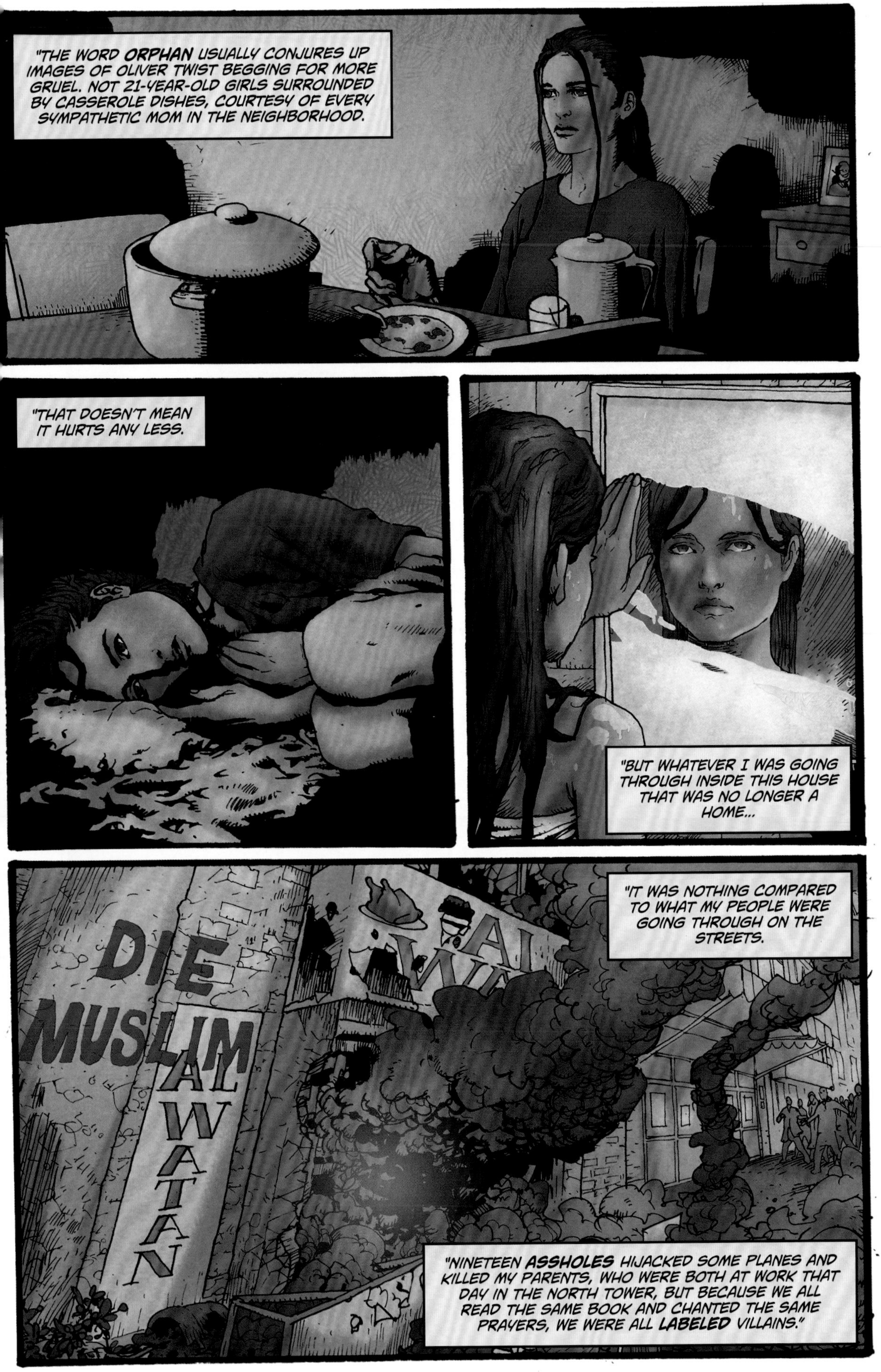
"THE WORD ORPHAN USUALLY CONJURES UP IMAGES OF OLIVER TWIST BEGGING FOR MORE GRUEL. NOT 21-YEAR-OLD GIRLS SURROUNDED BY CASSEROLE DISHES, COURTESY OF EVERY SYMPATHETIC MOM IN THE NEIGHBORHOOD.
"THAT DOESN'T MEAN IT HURTS ANY LESS.
"BUT WHATEVER I WAS GOING THROUGH INSIDE THIS HOUSE THAT WAS NO LONGER A HOME...
"IT WAS NOTHING COMPARED TO WHAT MY PEOPLE WERE GOING THROUGH ON THE STREETS.
DIE MUSLIM
AL WATAN
"NINETEEN ASSHOLES HIJACKED SOME PLANES AND KILLED MY PARENTS, WHO WERE BOTH AT WORK THAT DAY IN THE NORTH TOWER, BUT BECAUSE WE ALL READ THE SAME BOOK AND CHANTED THE SAME PRAYERS, WE WERE ALL LABELED VILLAINS."

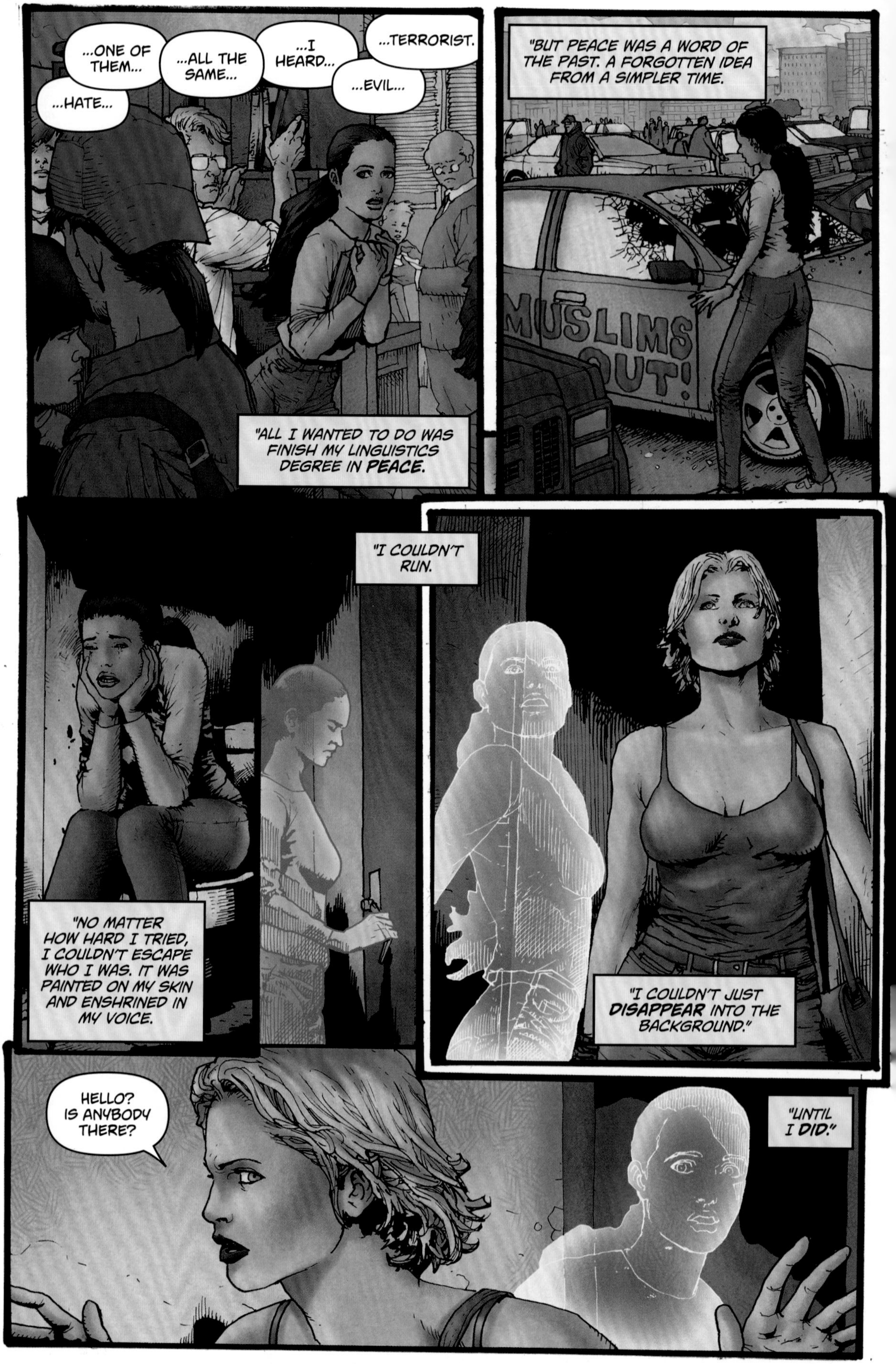
...HATE...
...ONE OF THEM...
...ALL THE SAME...
...I HEARD...
...EVIL...
...TERRORIST.
"ALL I WANTED TO DO WAS FINISH MY LINGUISTICS DEGREE IN PEACE.
"BUT PEACE WAS A WORD OF THE PAST. A FORGOTTEN IDEA FROM A SIMPLER TIME.
MUSLIMS OUT!
"I COULDN'T RUN.
"NO MATTER HOW HARD I TRIED, I COULDN'T ESCAPE WHO I WAS. IT WAS PAINTED ON MY SKIN AND ENSHRINED IN MY VOICE.
"I COULDN'T JUST DISAPPEAR INTO THE BACKGROUND."
HELLO? IS ANYBODY THERE?
"UNTIL I DID."

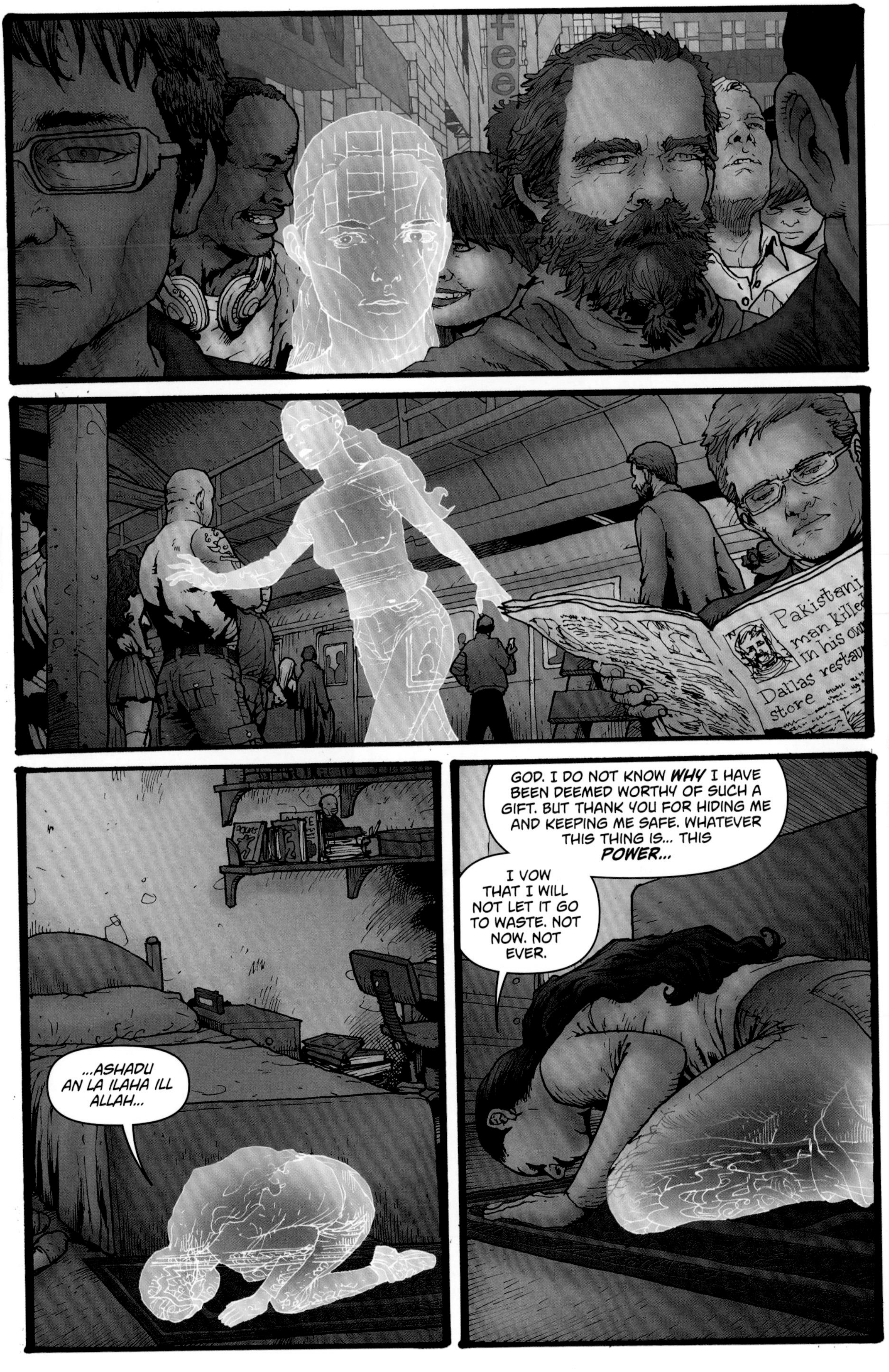
Pakistani
man kille
in his ow
Dallas resta
store
...ASHADU AN LA ILAHA ILL ALLAH...
GOD. I DO NOT KNOW *WHY* I HAVE BEEN DEEMED WORTHY OF SUCH A GIFT. BUT THANK YOU FOR HIDING ME AND KEEPING ME SAFE. WHATEVER THIS THING IS... THIS ***POWER...***
I VOW THAT I WILL NOT LET IT GO TO WASTE. NOT NOW. NOT EVER.

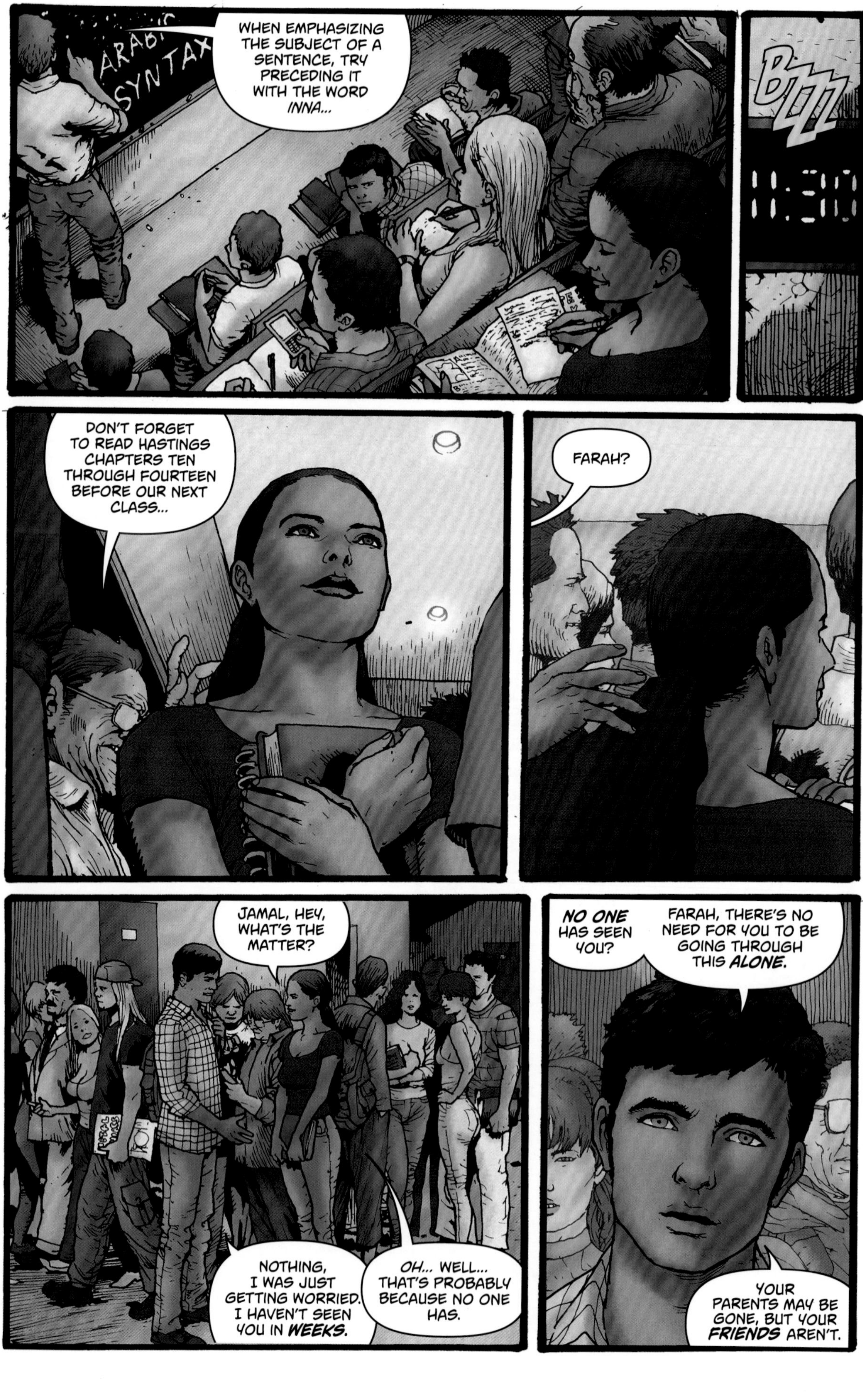

ARABIC SYNTAX
WHEN EMPHASIZING THE SUBJECT OF A SENTENCE, TRY PRECEDING IT WITH THE WORD *INNA*...
BZZZ
11:30
DON'T FORGET TO READ HASTINGS CHAPTERS TEN THROUGH FOURTEEN BEFORE OUR NEXT CLASS...
FARAH?
JAMAL, HEY, WHAT'S THE MATTER?
NOTHING, I WAS JUST GETTING WORRIED. I HAVEN'T SEEN YOU IN ***WEEKS***.
OH... WELL... THAT'S PROBABLY BECAUSE NO ONE HAS.
NO ONE HAS SEEN YOU?
FARAH, THERE'S NO NEED FOR YOU TO BE GOING THROUGH THIS ***ALONE***.
YOUR PARENTS MAY BE GONE, BUT YOUR ***FRIENDS*** AREN'T.

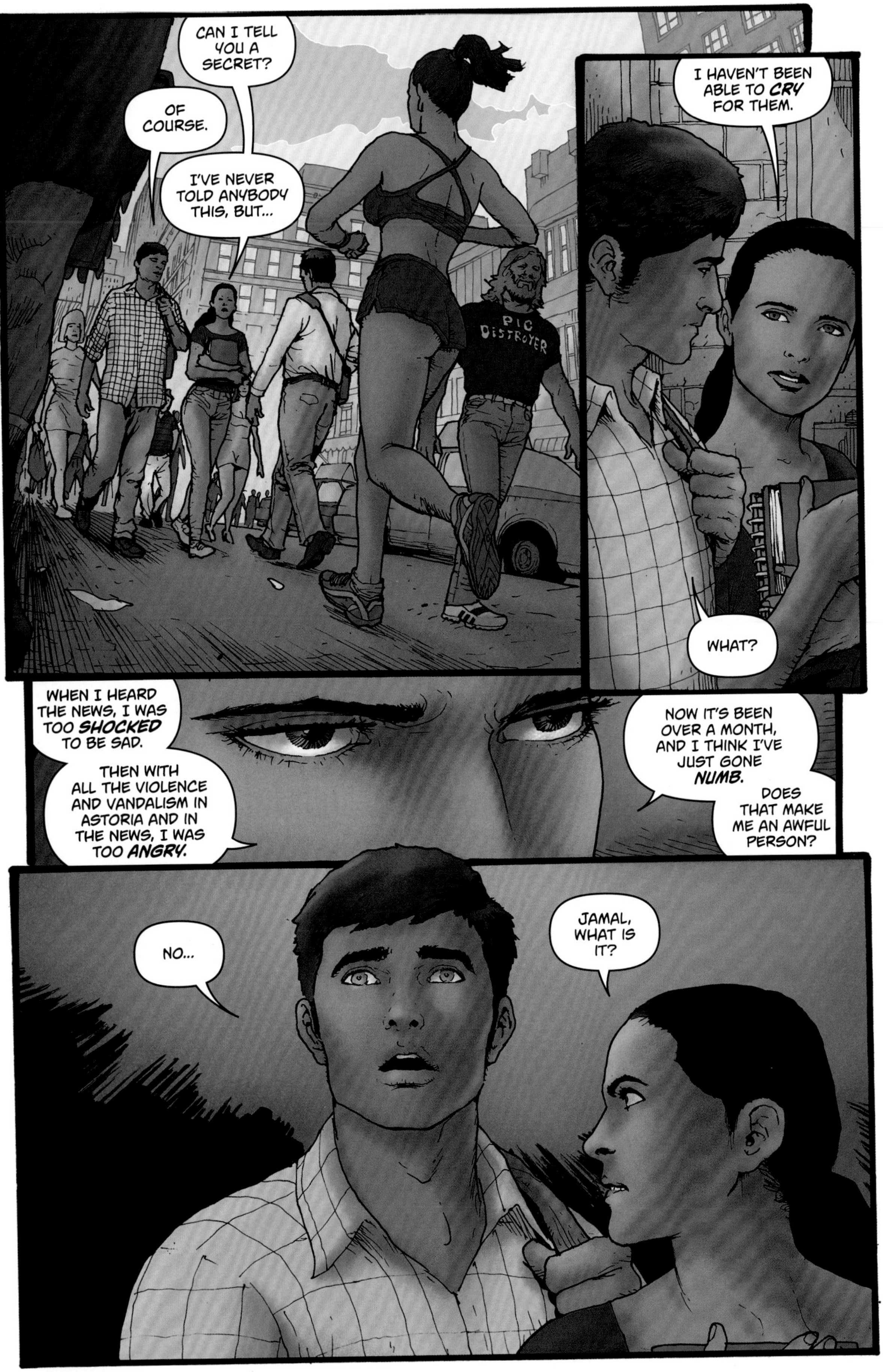
CAN I TELL YOU A SECRET?
OF COURSE.
I'VE NEVER TOLD ANYBODY THIS, BUT...
PIG DISTROYER
I HAVEN'T BEEN ABLE TO CRY FOR THEM.
WHAT?
WHEN I HEARD THE NEWS, I WAS TOO SHOCKED TO BE SAD.
THEN WITH ALL THE VIOLENCE AND VANDALISM IN ASTORIA AND IN THE NEWS, I WAS TOO ANGRY.
NOW IT'S BEEN OVER A MONTH, AND I THINK I'VE JUST GONE NUMB.
DOES THAT MAKE ME AN AWFUL PERSON?
NO...
JAMAL, WHAT IS IT?

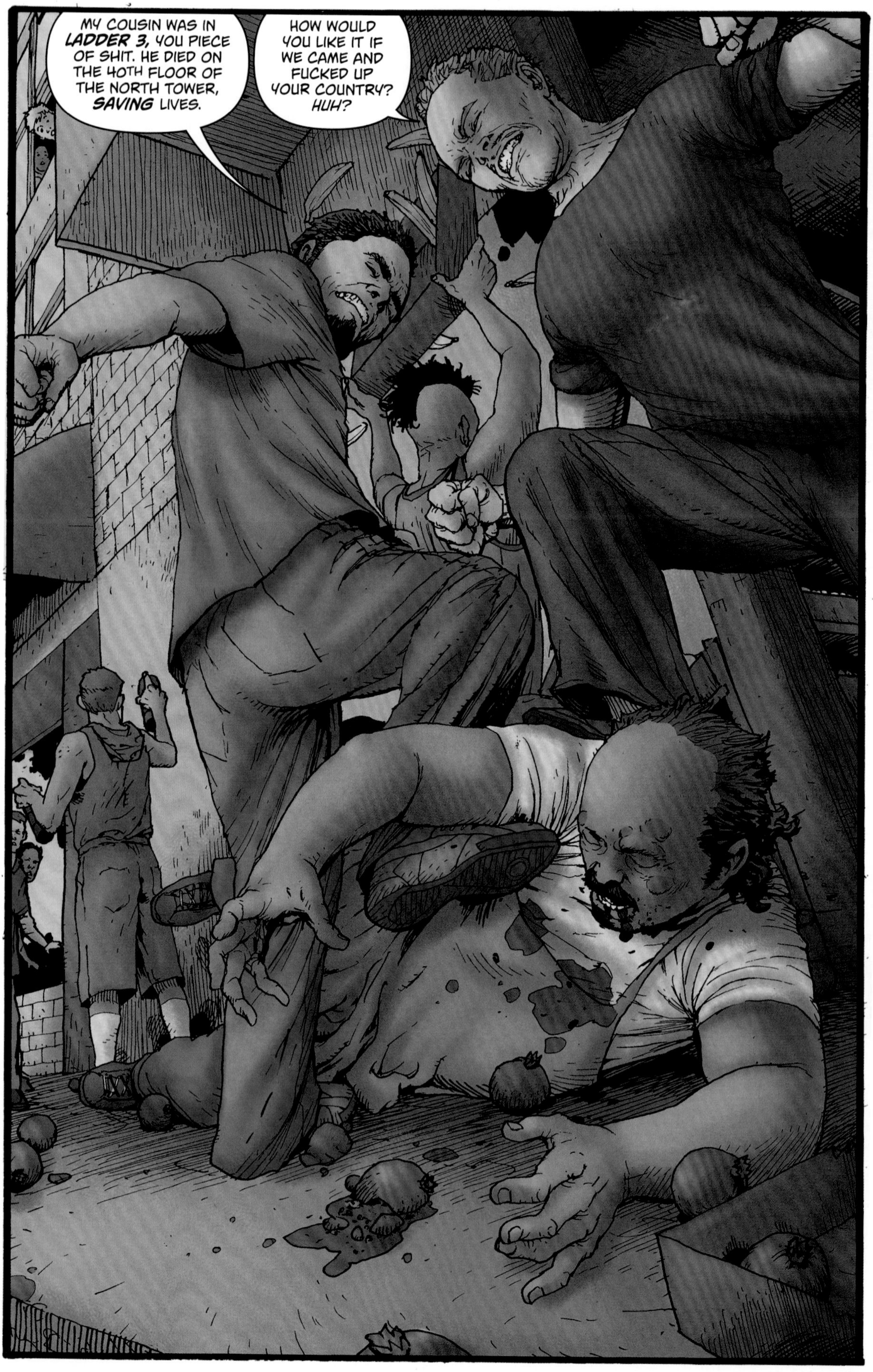
MY COUSIN WAS IN **LADDER 3,** YOU PIECE OF SHIT. HE DIED ON THE 40TH FLOOR OF THE NORTH TOWER, **SAVING** LIVES.
HOW WOULD YOU LIKE IT IF WE CAME AND FUCKED UP YOUR COUNTRY? HUH?

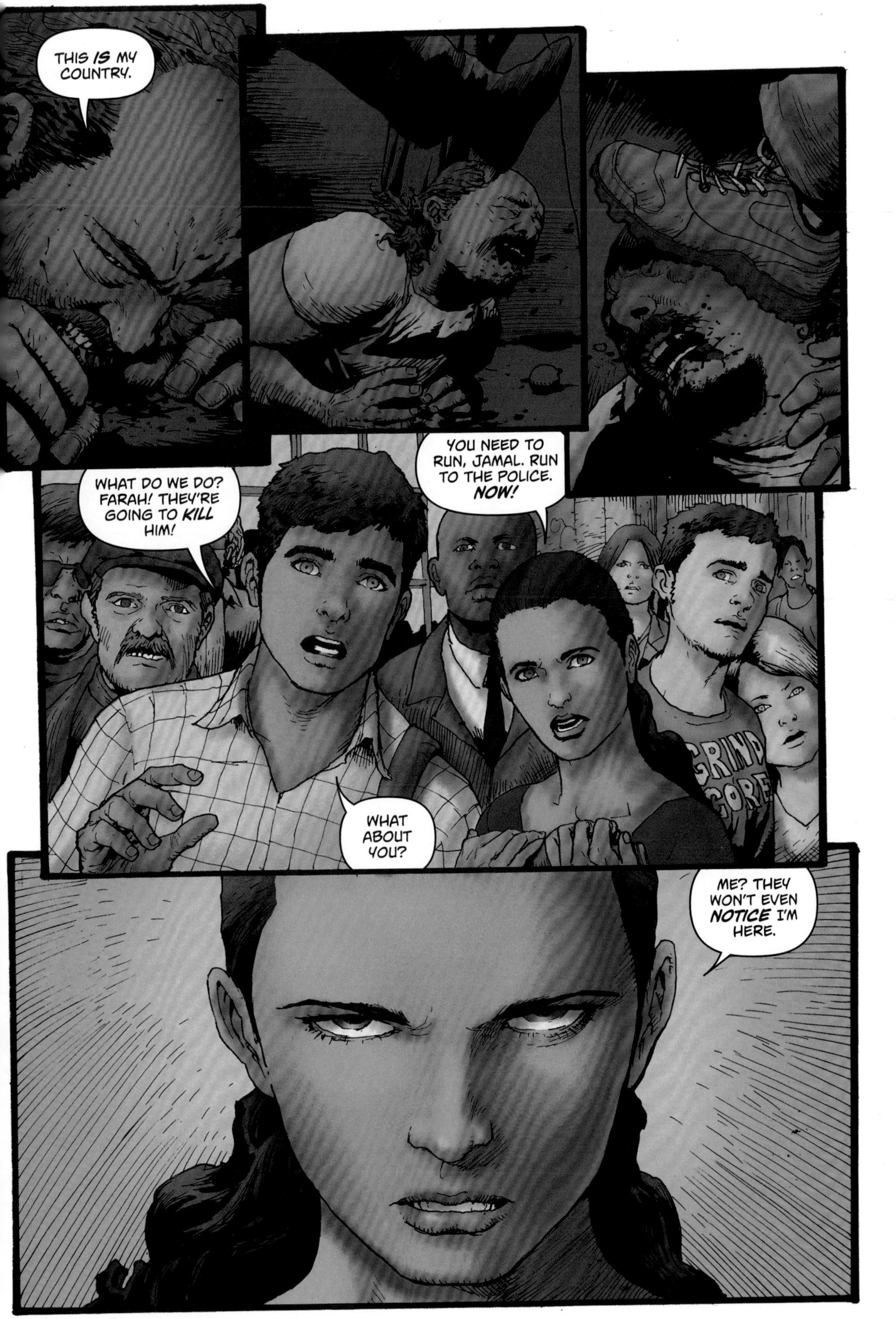
THIS *IS* MY COUNTRY.
WHAT DO WE DO? FARAH! THEY'RE GOING TO *KILL* HIM!
YOU NEED TO RUN, JAMAL. RUN TO THE POLICE. *NOW!*
WHAT ABOUT YOU?
GRIND CORE
ME? THEY WON'T EVEN *NOTICE* I'M HERE.

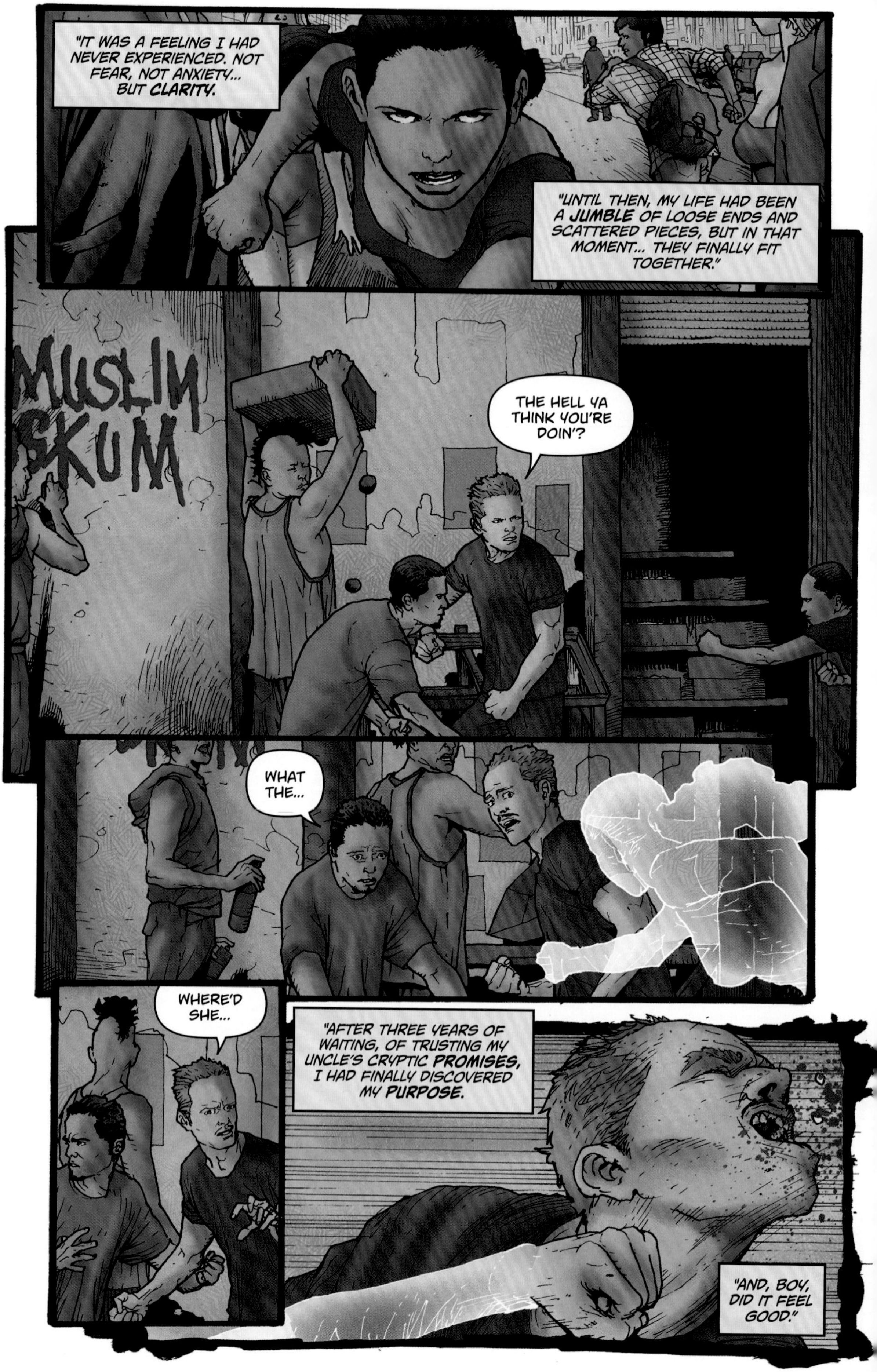
"IT WAS A FEELING I HAD NEVER EXPERIENCED. NOT FEAR, NOT ANXIETY... BUT CLARITY.
"UNTIL THEN, MY LIFE HAD BEEN A JUMBLE OF LOOSE ENDS AND SCATTERED PIECES, BUT IN THAT MOMENT... THEY FINALLY FIT TOGETHER."
MUSLIM SKUM
THE HELL YA THINK YOU'RE DOIN'?
WHAT THE...
WHERE'D SHE...
"AFTER THREE YEARS OF WAITING, OF TRUSTING MY UNCLE'S CRYPTIC PROMISES, I HAD FINALLY DISCOVERED MY PURPOSE.
"AND, BOY, DID IT FEEL GOOD."

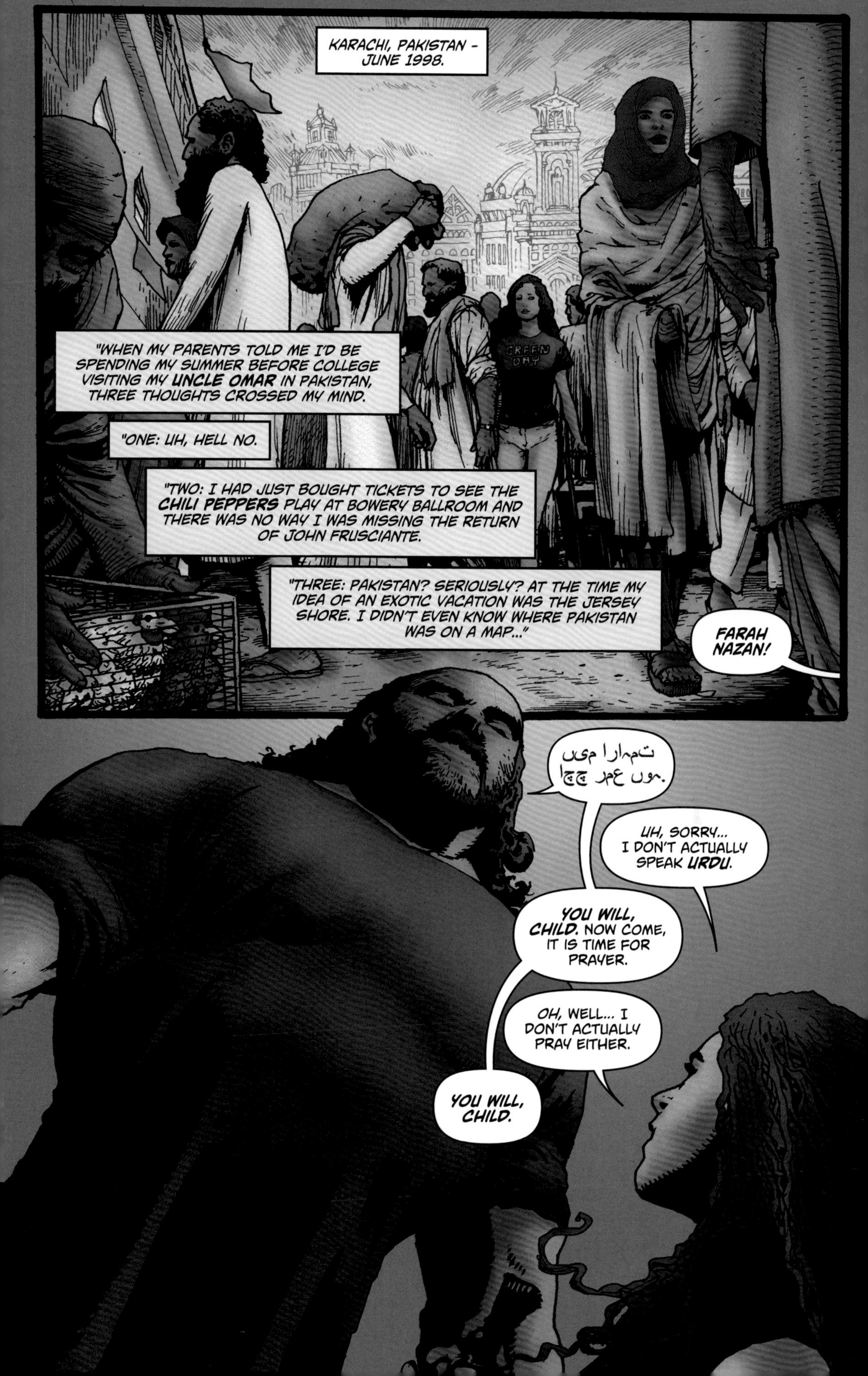
KARACHI, PAKISTAN - JUNE 1998.
"WHEN MY PARENTS TOLD ME I'D BE SPENDING MY SUMMER BEFORE COLLEGE VISITING MY UNCLE OMAR IN PAKISTAN, THREE THOUGHTS CROSSED MY MIND.
"ONE: UH, HELL NO.
"TWO: I HAD JUST BOUGHT TICKETS TO SEE THE CHILI PEPPERS PLAY AT BOWERY BALLROOM AND THERE WAS NO WAY I WAS MISSING THE RETURN OF JOHN FRUSCIANTE.
"THREE: PAKISTAN? SERIOUSLY? AT THE TIME MY IDEA OF AN EXOTIC VACATION WAS THE JERSEY SHORE. I DIDN'T EVEN KNOW WHERE PAKISTAN WAS ON A MAP..."
FARAH NAZAN!
UH, SORRY... I DON'T ACTUALLY SPEAK URDU.
YOU WILL, CHILD. NOW COME, IT IS TIME FOR PRAYER.
OH, WELL... I DON'T ACTUALLY PRAY EITHER.
YOU WILL, CHILD.

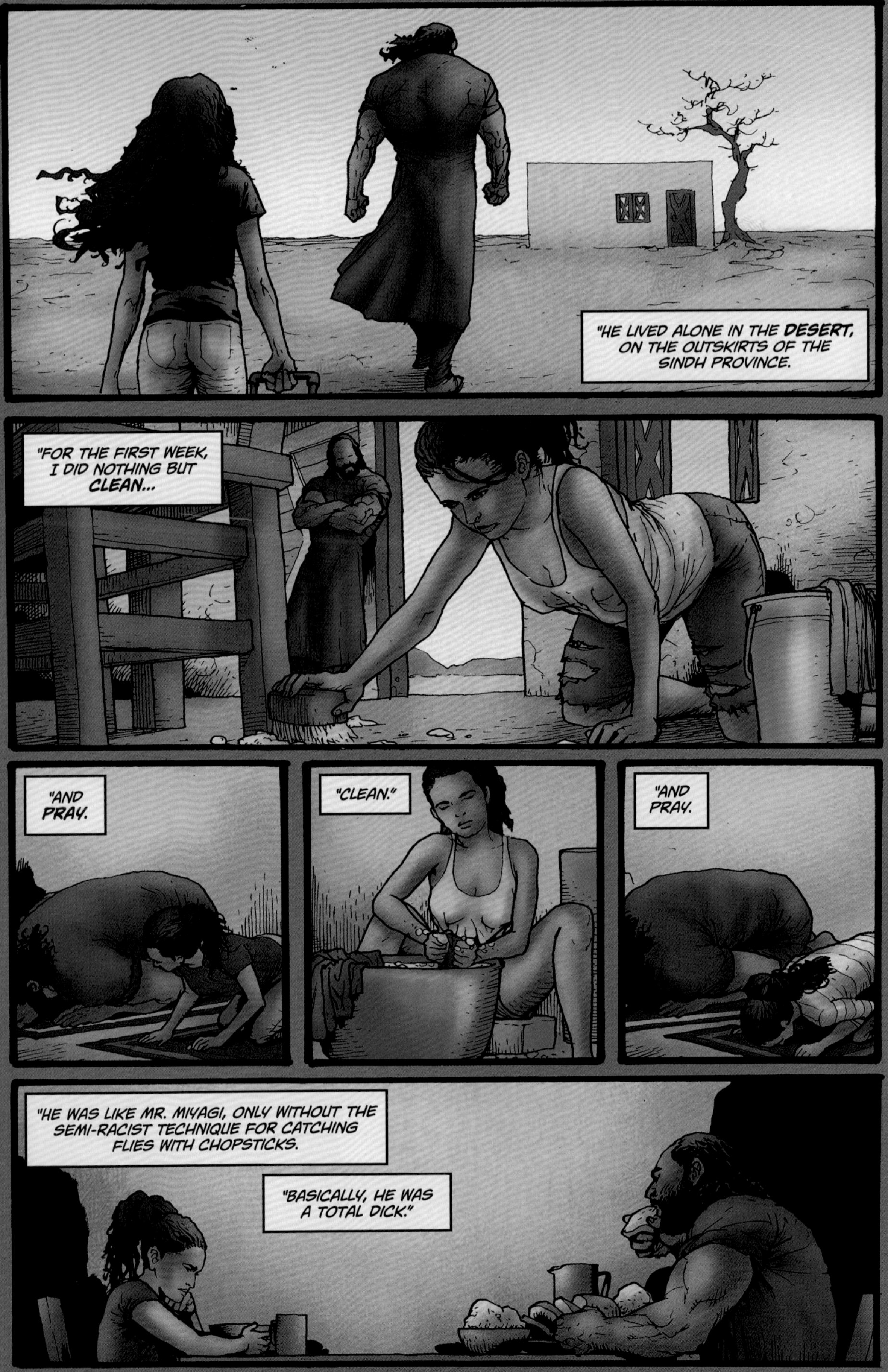
"HE LIVED ALONE IN THE DESERT, ON THE OUTSKIRTS OF THE SINDH PROVINCE.
"FOR THE FIRST WEEK, I DID NOTHING BUT CLEAN...
"AND PRAY.
"CLEAN."
"AND PRAY.
"HE WAS LIKE MR. MIYAGI, ONLY WITHOUT THE SEMI-RACIST TECHNIQUE FOR CATCHING FLIES WITH CHOPSTICKS.
"BASICALLY, HE WAS A TOTAL DICK."

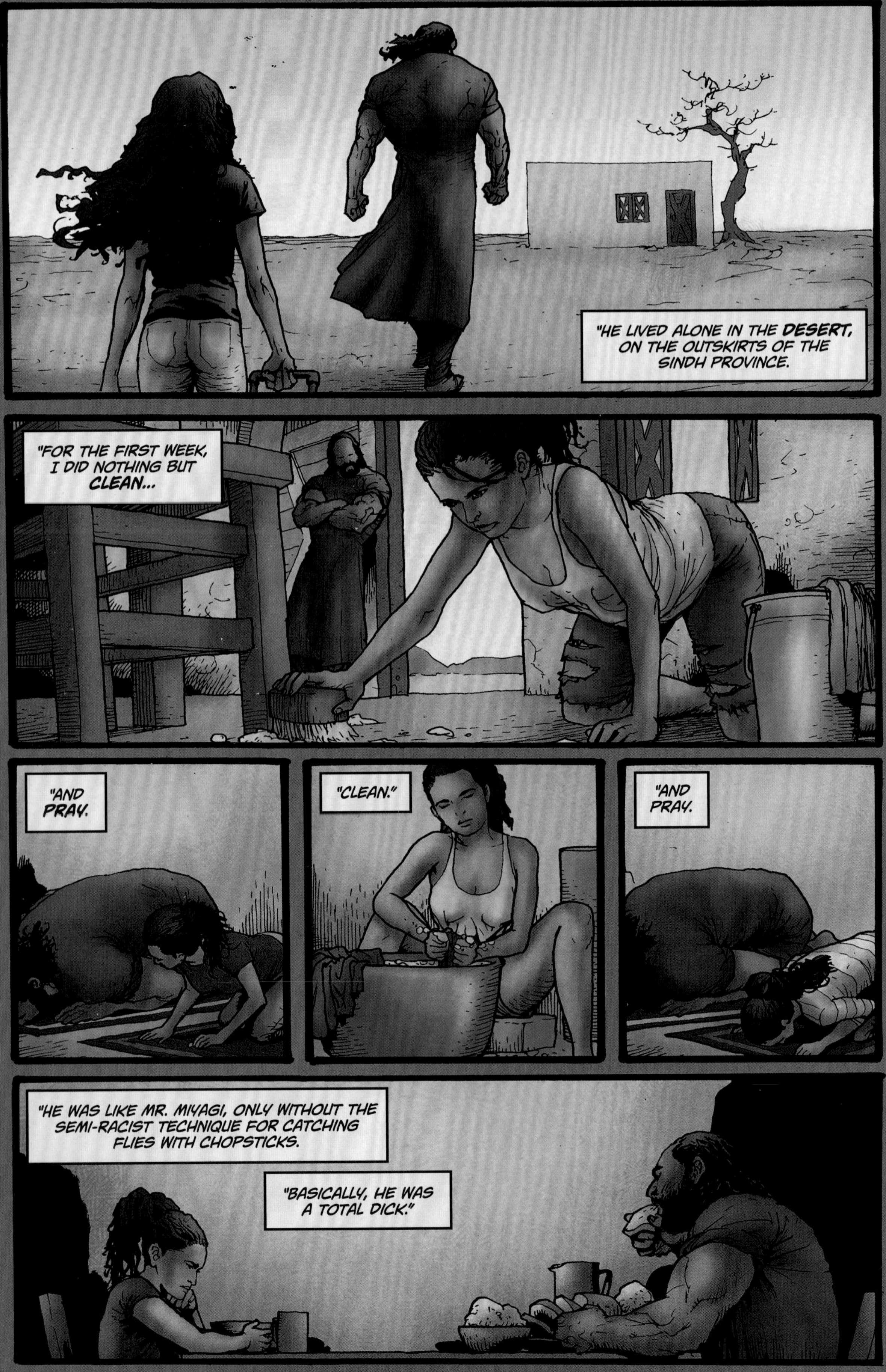
"HE LIVED ALONE IN THE DESERT, ON THE OUTSKIRTS OF THE SINDH PROVINCE.
"FOR THE FIRST WEEK, I DID NOTHING BUT CLEAN...
"AND PRAY.
"CLEAN."
"AND PRAY.
"HE WAS LIKE MR. MIYAGI, ONLY WITHOUT THE SEMI-RACIST TECHNIQUE FOR CATCHING FLIES WITH CHOPSTICKS.
"BASICALLY, HE WAS A TOTAL DICK."

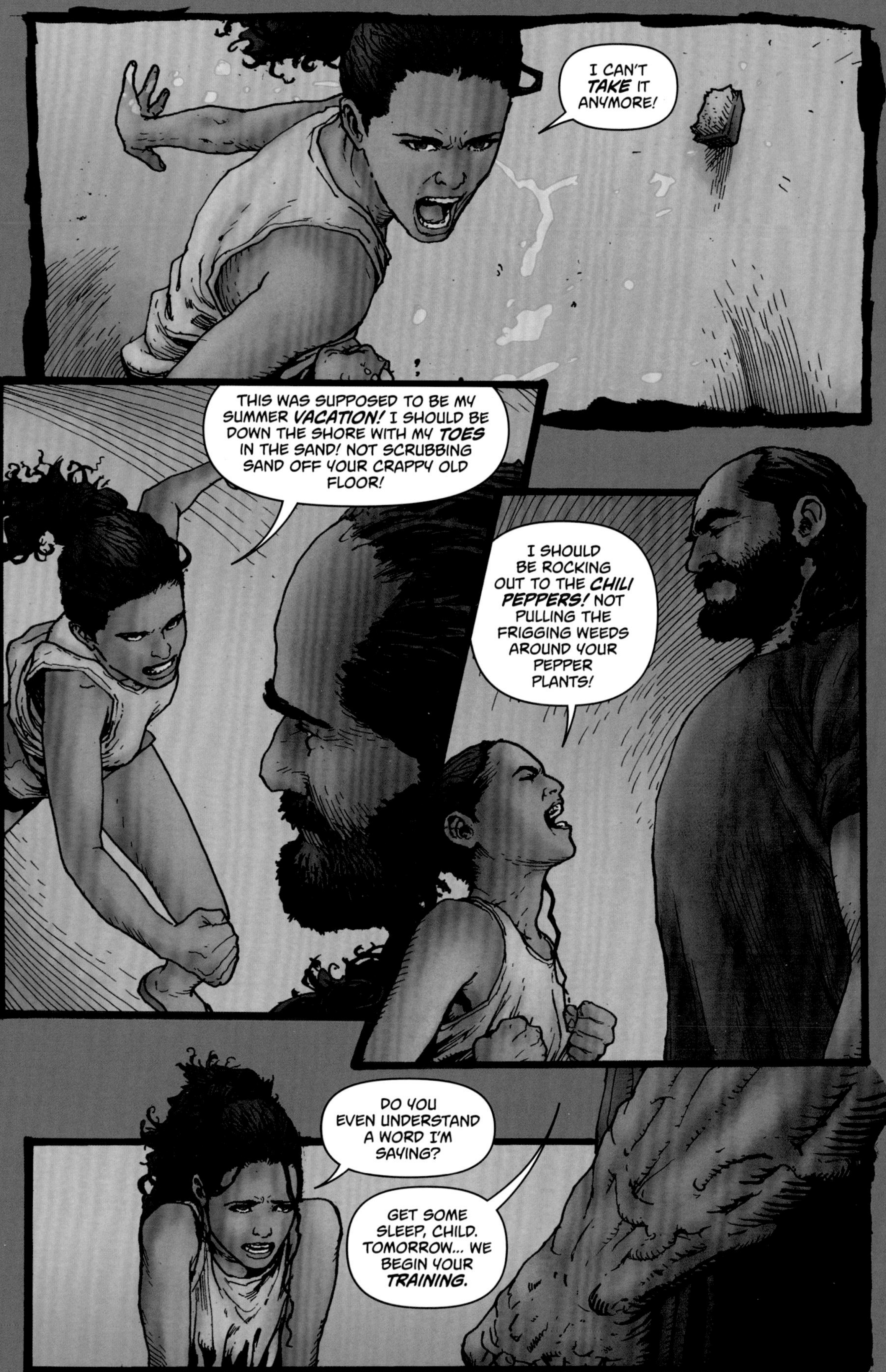
I CAN'T TAKE IT ANYMORE!
THIS WAS SUPPOSED TO BE MY SUMMER VACATION! I SHOULD BE DOWN THE SHORE WITH MY TOES IN THE SAND! NOT SCRUBBING SAND OFF YOUR CRAPPY OLD FLOOR!
I SHOULD BE ROCKING OUT TO THE CHILI PEPPERS! NOT PULLING THE FRIGGING WEEDS AROUND YOUR PEPPER PLANTS!
DO YOU EVEN UNDERSTAND A WORD I'M SAYING?
GET SOME SLEEP, CHILD. TOMORROW... WE BEGIN YOUR TRAINING.

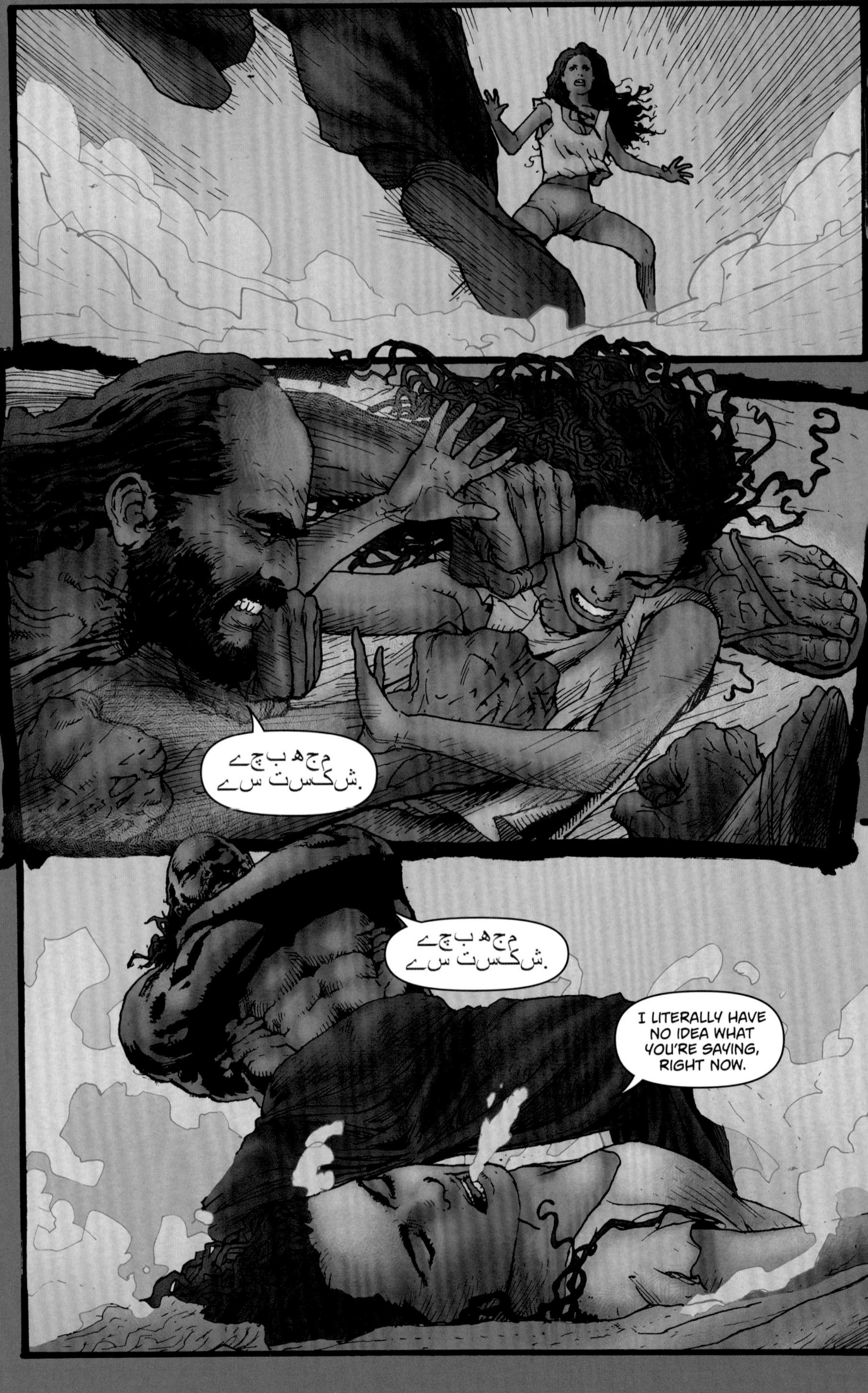
مجھ بچے
شکست سے.
مجھ بچے
شکست سے.
I LITERALLY HAVE NO IDEA WHAT YOU'RE SAYING, RIGHT NOW.

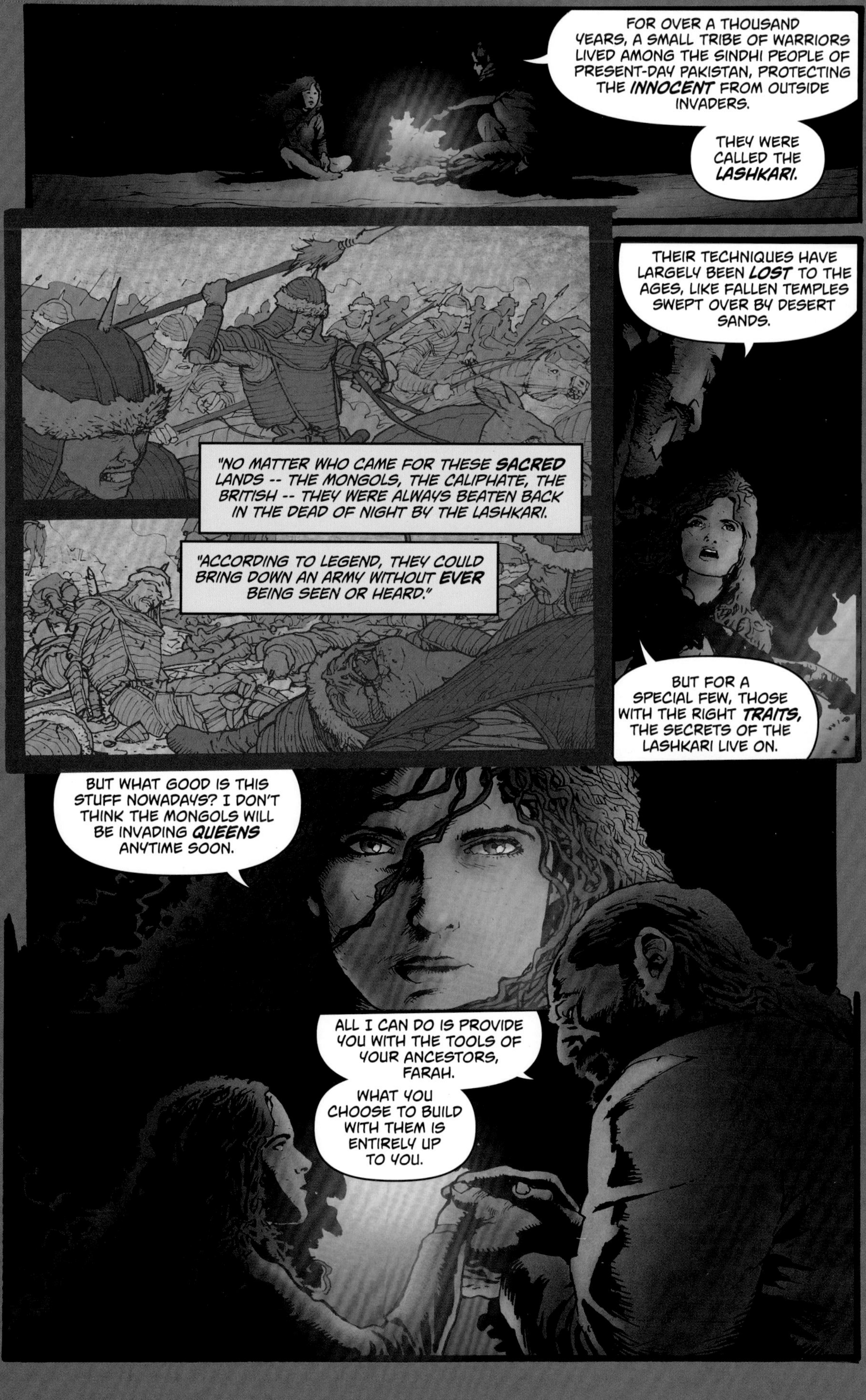
FOR OVER A THOUSAND YEARS, A SMALL TRIBE OF WARRIORS LIVED AMONG THE SINDHI PEOPLE OF PRESENT-DAY PAKISTAN, PROTECTING THE *INNOCENT* FROM OUTSIDE INVADERS.
THEY WERE CALLED THE *LASHKARI*.
"NO MATTER WHO CAME FOR THESE *SACRED* LANDS -- THE MONGOLS, THE CALIPHATE, THE BRITISH -- THEY WERE ALWAYS BEATEN BACK IN THE DEAD OF NIGHT BY THE LASHKARI.
"ACCORDING TO LEGEND, THEY COULD BRING DOWN AN ARMY WITHOUT *EVER* BEING SEEN OR HEARD."
THEIR TECHNIQUES HAVE LARGELY BEEN *LOST* TO THE AGES, LIKE FALLEN TEMPLES SWEPT OVER BY DESERT SANDS.
BUT FOR A SPECIAL FEW, THOSE WITH THE RIGHT *TRAITS*, THE SECRETS OF THE LASHKARI LIVE ON.
BUT WHAT GOOD IS THIS STUFF NOWADAYS? I DON'T THINK THE MONGOLS WILL BE INVADING *QUEENS* ANYTIME SOON.
ALL I CAN DO IS PROVIDE YOU WITH THE TOOLS OF YOUR ANCESTORS, FARAH.
WHAT YOU CHOOSE TO BUILD WITH THEM IS ENTIRELY UP TO YOU.

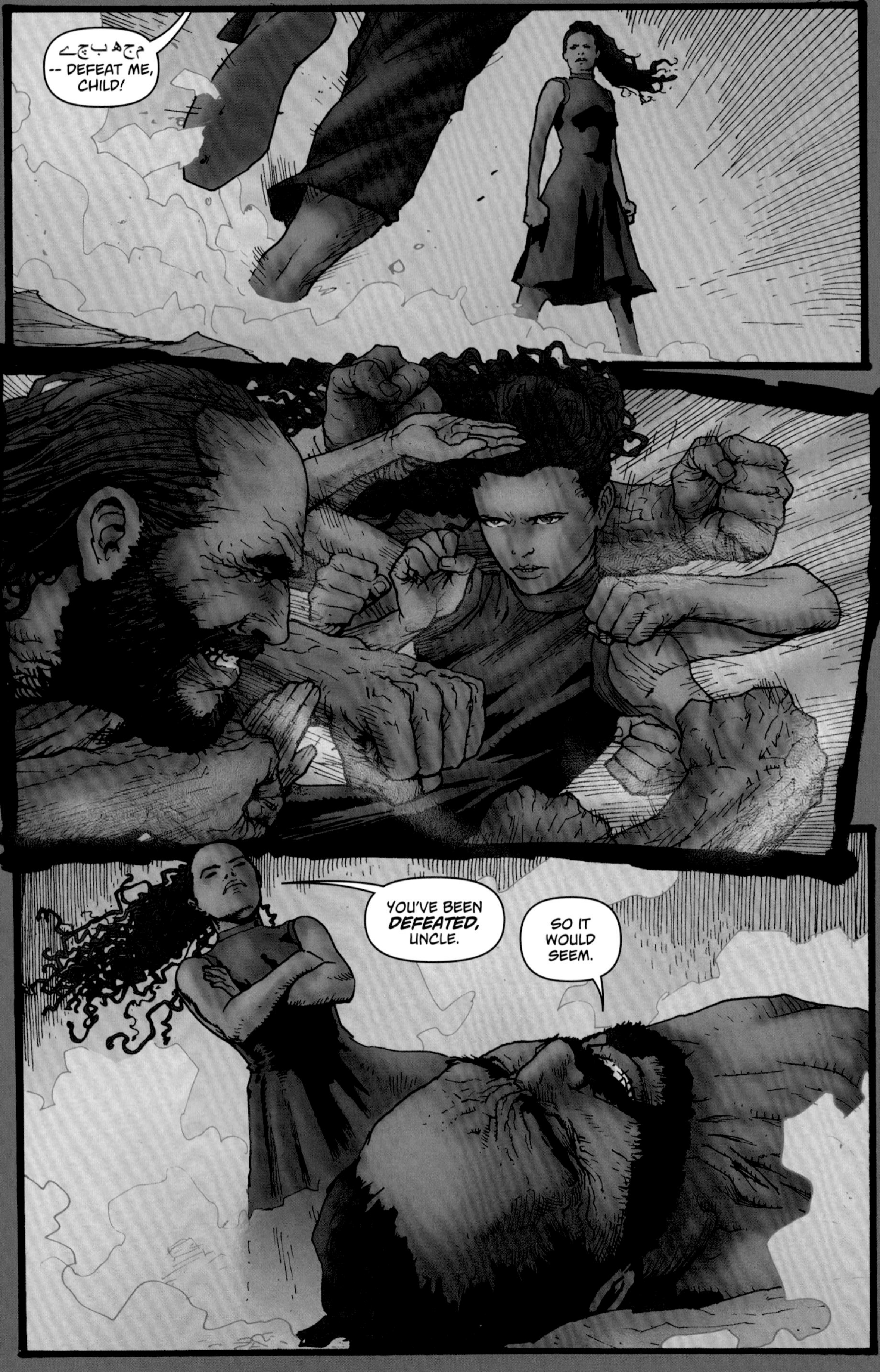
م ج ھ ب چ ے
-- DEFEAT ME, CHILD!
YOU'VE BEEN **DEFEATED,** UNCLE.
SO IT WOULD SEEM.

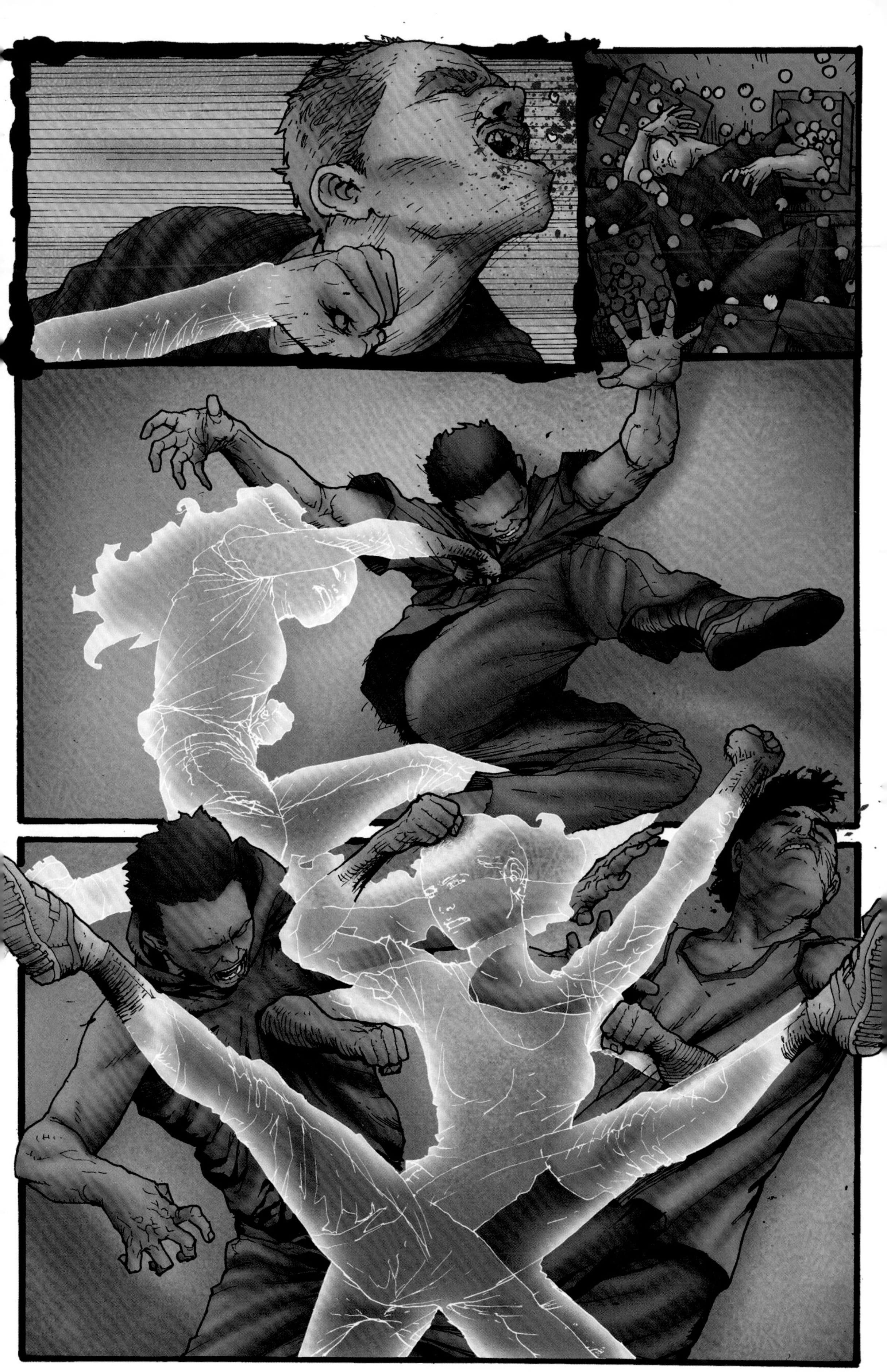

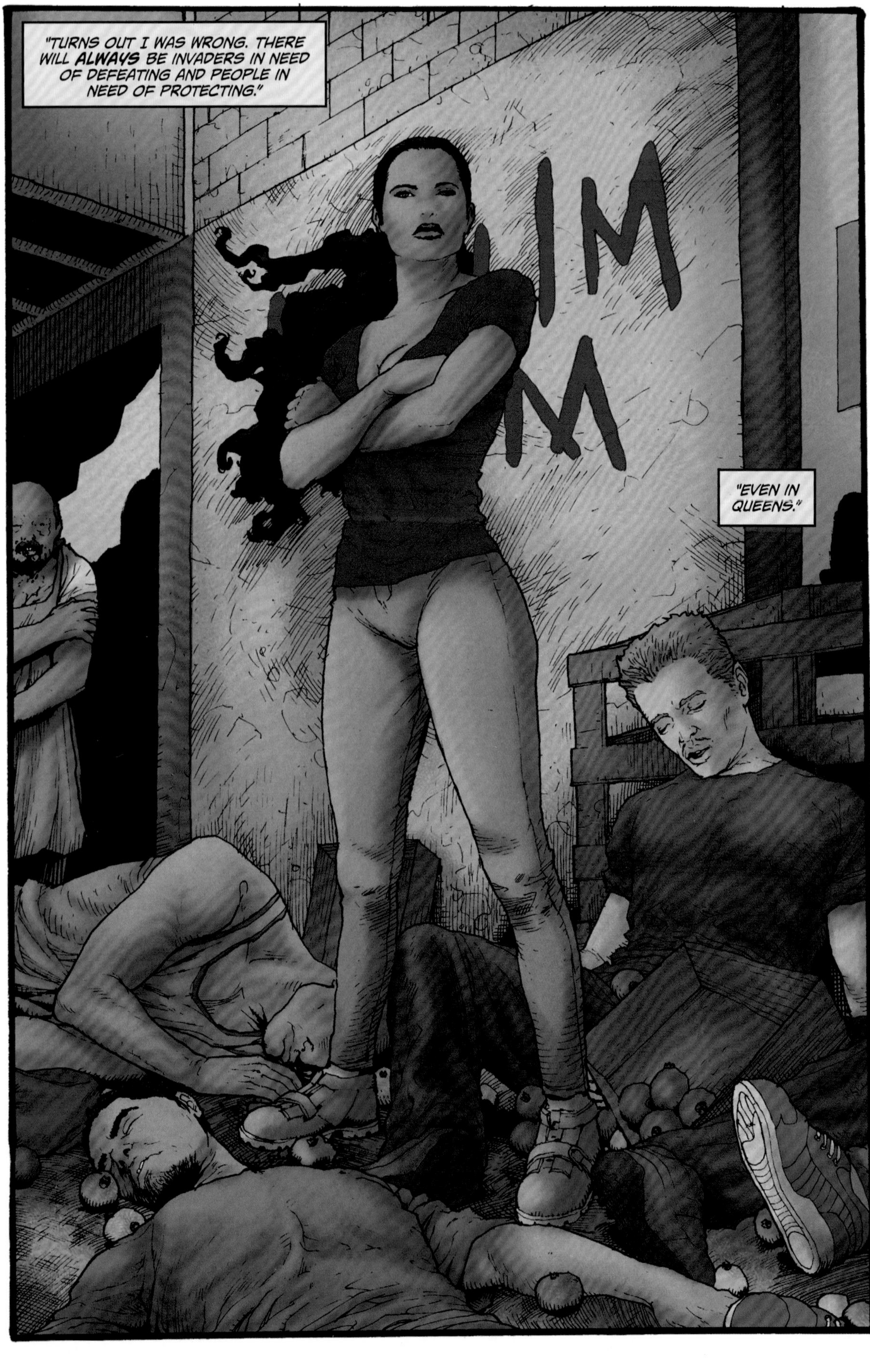
"TURNS OUT I WAS WRONG. THERE WILL ALWAYS BE INVADERS IN NEED OF DEFEATING AND PEOPLE IN NEED OF PROTECTING."
"EVEN IN QUEENS."

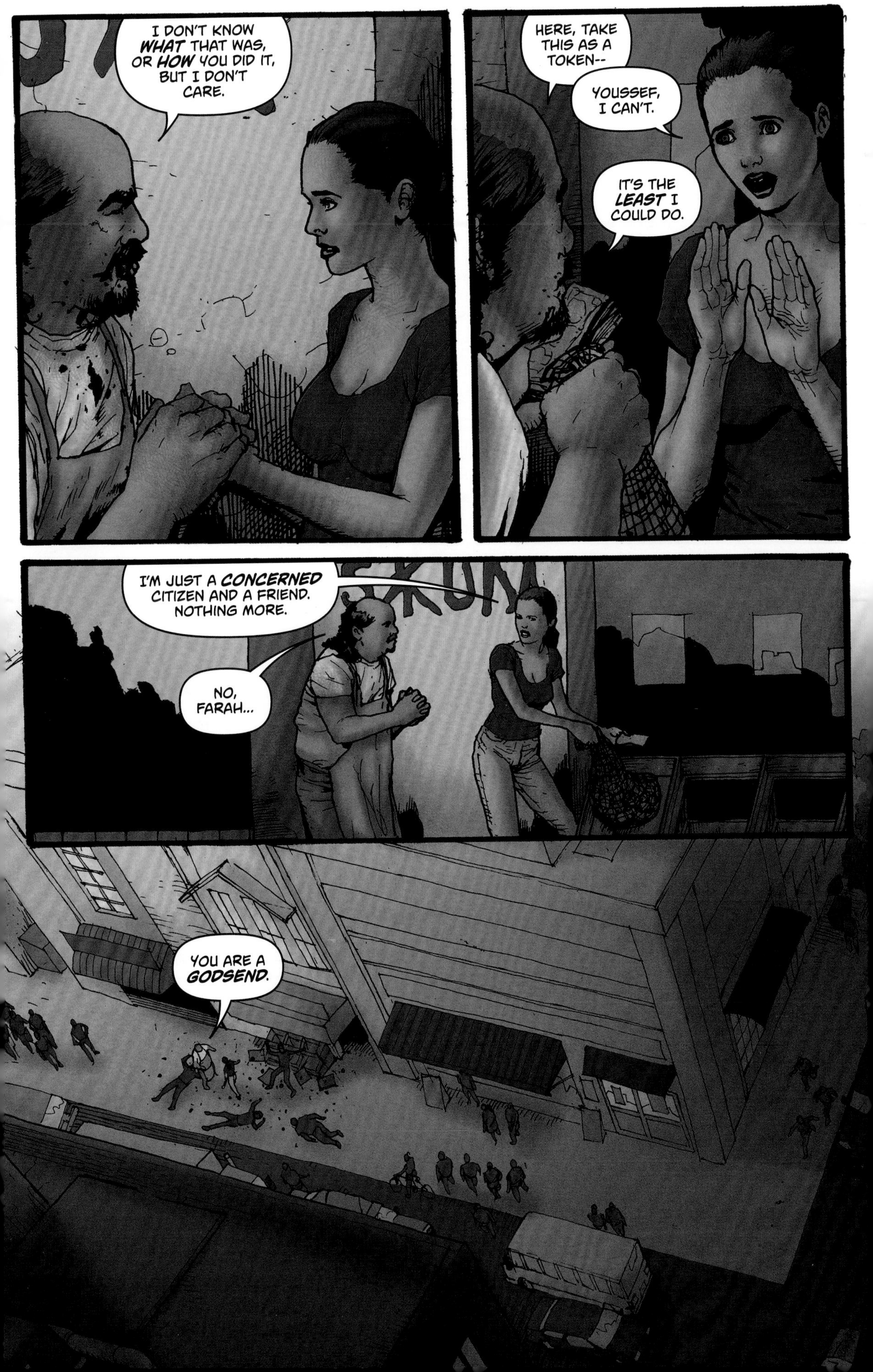
I DON'T KNOW *WHAT* THAT WAS, OR *HOW* YOU DID IT, BUT I DON'T CARE.
HERE, TAKE THIS AS A TOKEN--
YOUSSEF, I CAN'T.
IT'S THE *LEAST* I COULD DO.
I'M JUST A *CONCERNED* CITIZEN AND A FRIEND. NOTHING MORE.
NO, FARAH...
YOU ARE A *GODSEND*.

SIR, WHAT HAPPENED HERE? WHO TOOK DOWN THESE MEN?

FARAH! WHAT THE HELL DID I MISS?

IT WAS THE GODSEND.

IT WAS NOTHING. NO ONE SAW A THING.

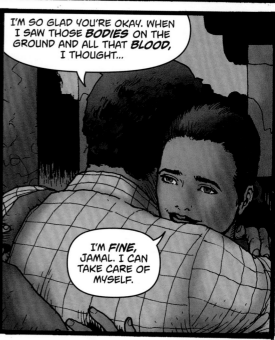

I'M SO GLAD YOU'RE OKAY. WHEN I SAW THOSE BODIES ON THE GROUND AND ALL THAT BLOOD, I THOUGHT...

I'M FINE, JAMAL. I CAN TAKE CARE OF MYSELF.

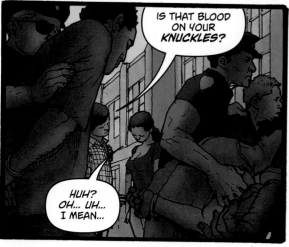

IS THAT BLOOD ON YOUR KNUCKLES?

HUH? OH... UH... I MEAN...

BLOOD? NO, OF COURSE IT'S NOT BLOOD.

IT'S ONLY POMEGRANATE JUICE.

ONE WEEK LATER...

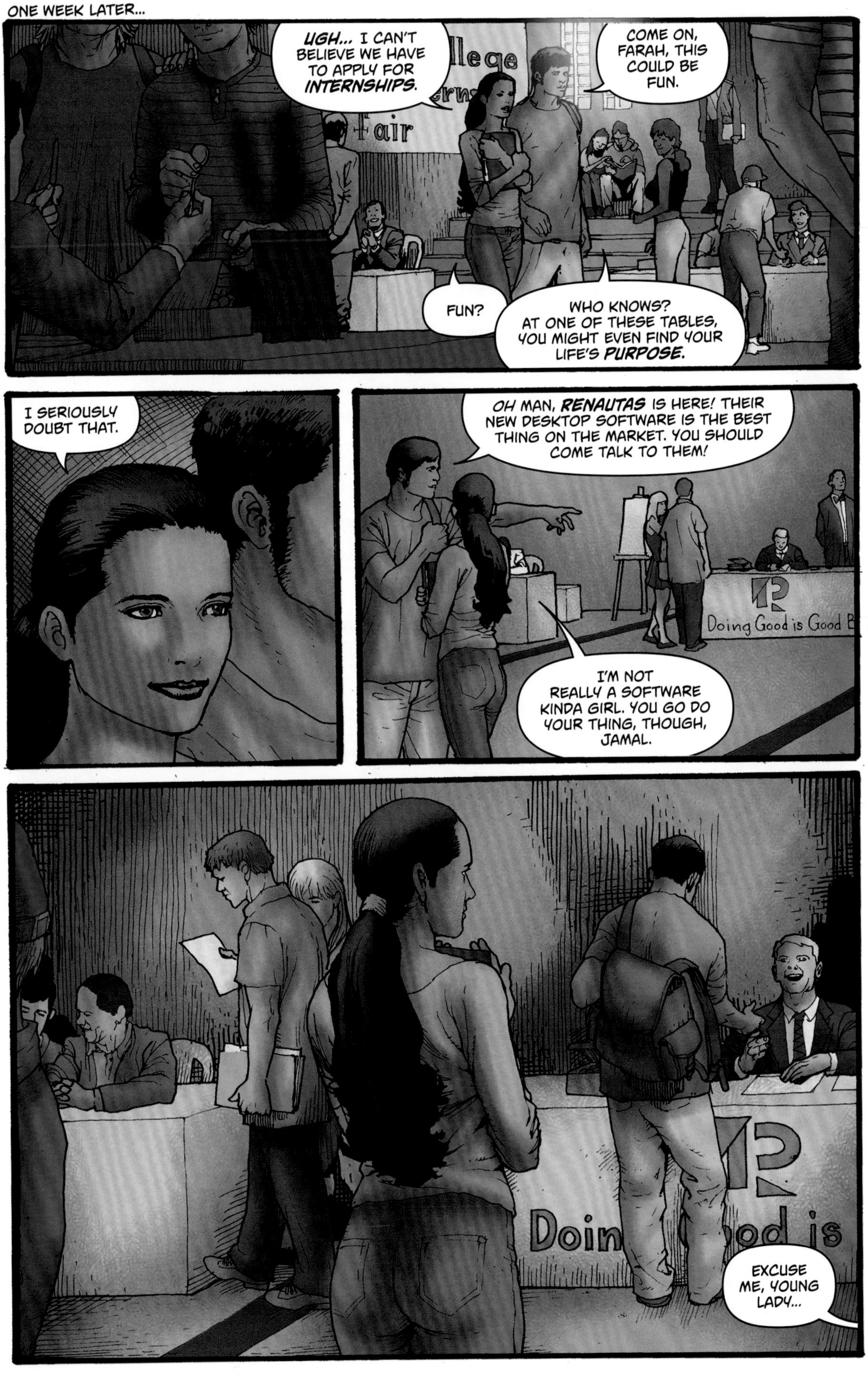

UGH... I CAN'T BELIEVE WE HAVE TO APPLY FOR INTERNSHIPS.
COME ON, FARAH, THIS COULD BE FUN.
College
Fair
FUN?
WHO KNOWS? AT ONE OF THESE TABLES, YOU MIGHT EVEN FIND YOUR LIFE'S PURPOSE.
I SERIOUSLY DOUBT THAT.
OH MAN, RENAUTAS IS HERE! THEIR NEW DESKTOP SOFTWARE IS THE BEST THING ON THE MARKET. YOU SHOULD COME TALK TO THEM!
Doing Good is Good B
I'M NOT REALLY A SOFTWARE KINDA GIRL. YOU GO DO YOUR THING, THOUGH, JAMAL.
Doin ood is
EXCUSE ME, YOUNG LADY...

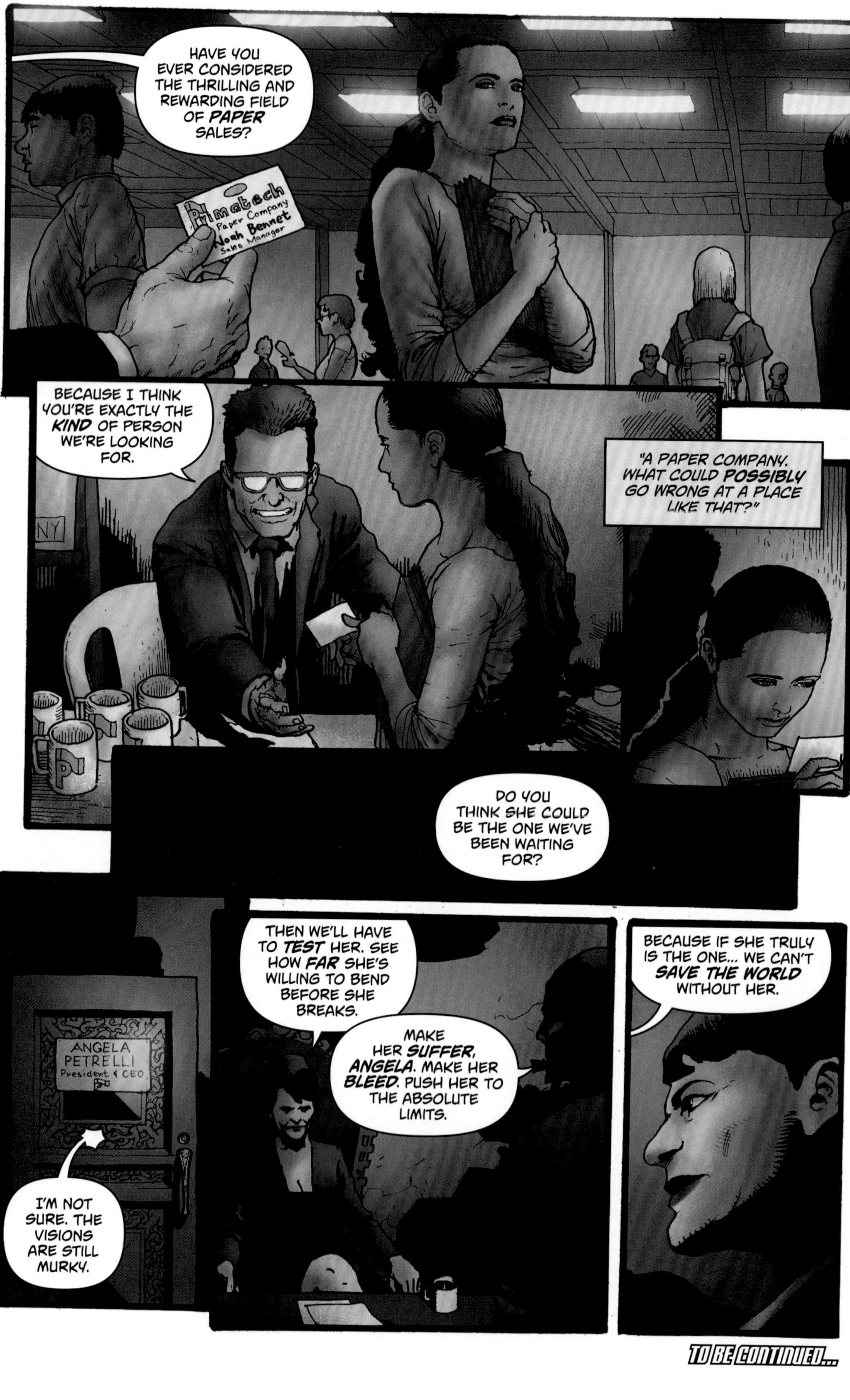
HAVE YOU EVER CONSIDERED THE THRILLING AND REWARDING FIELD OF PAPER SALES?
Primatech Paper Company Noah Bennet Sales Manager
BECAUSE I THINK YOU'RE EXACTLY THE KIND OF PERSON WE'RE LOOKING FOR.
"A PAPER COMPANY. WHAT COULD POSSIBLY GO WRONG AT A PLACE LIKE THAT?"
DO YOU THINK SHE COULD BE THE ONE WE'VE BEEN WAITING FOR?
ANGELA PETRELLI President & CEO
I'M NOT SURE. THE VISIONS ARE STILL MURKY.
THEN WE'LL HAVE TO TEST HER. SEE HOW FAR SHE'S WILLING TO BEND BEFORE SHE BREAKS.
MAKE HER SUFFER, ANGELA. MAKE HER BLEED. PUSH HER TO THE ABSOLUTE LIMITS.
BECAUSE IF SHE TRULY IS THE ONE... WE CAN'T SAVE THE WORLD WITHOUT HER.
TO BE CONTINUED...

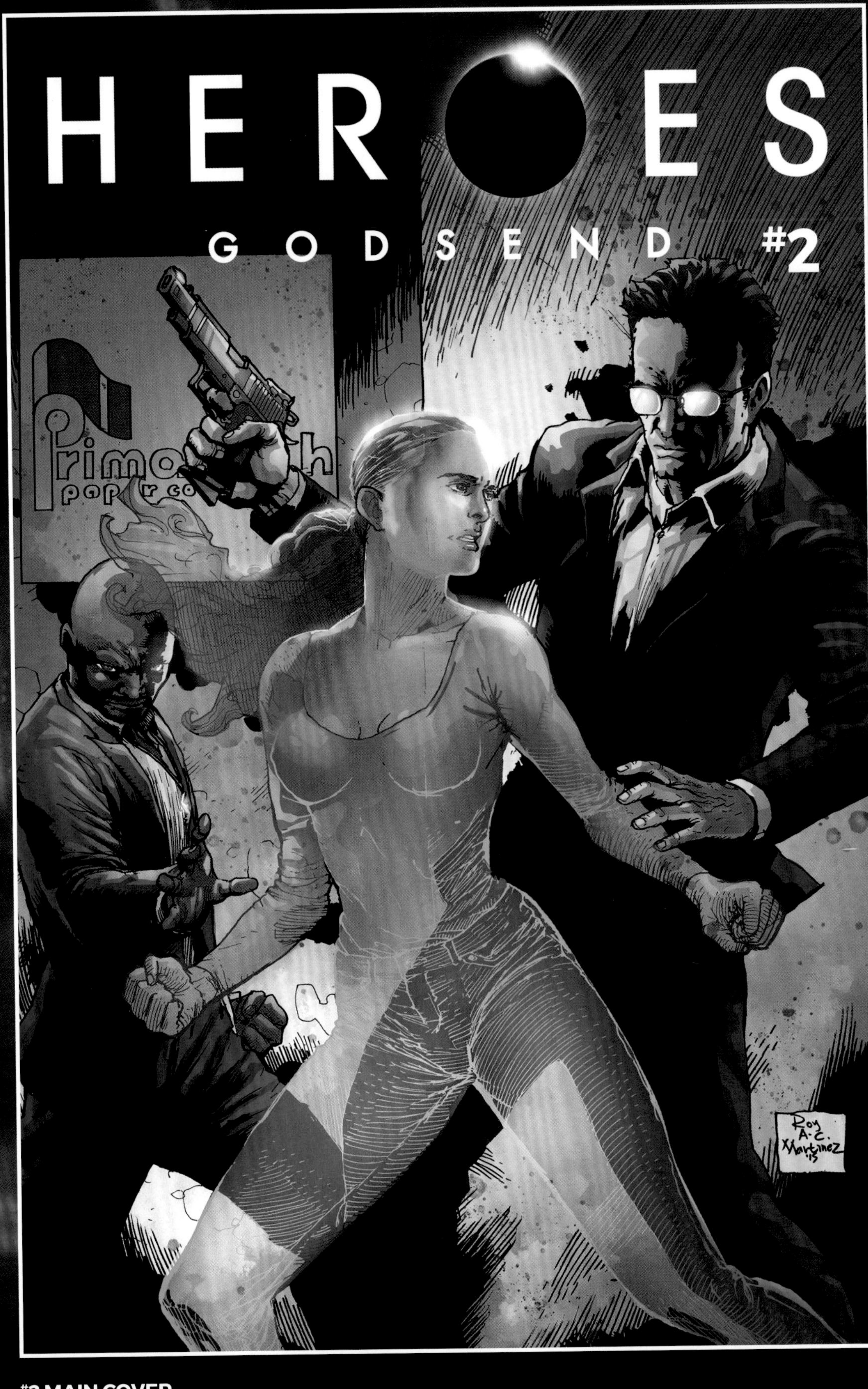
HEROES
GODSEND #2
Primo
pap r co
Roy A.C. Martinez '15

#2 MAIN COVER
ARTWORK BY ROY ALLAN MARTINEZ

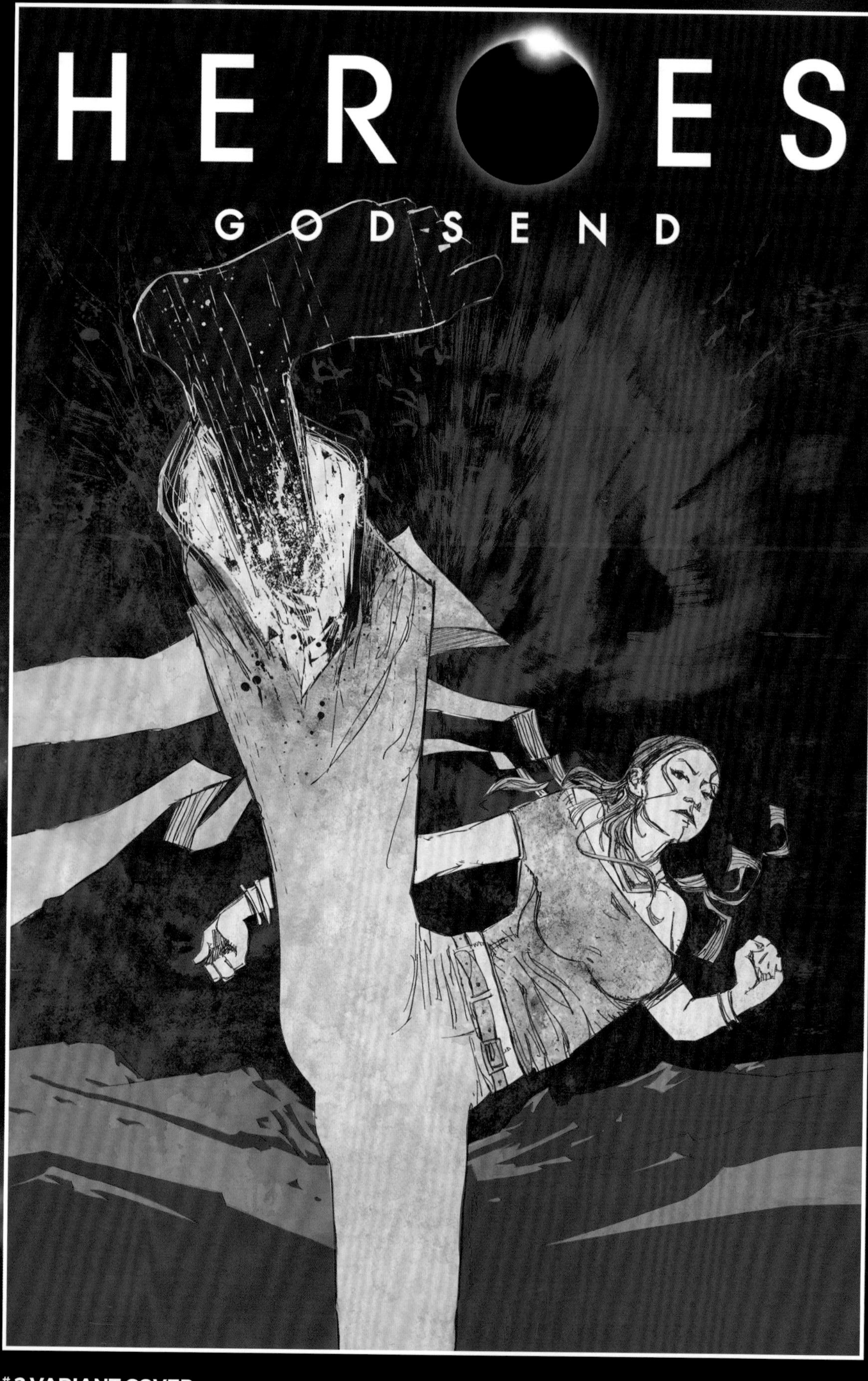
HEROES
GODSEND

 # 2 VARIANT COVER
ARTWORK BY FELIX RUIZ

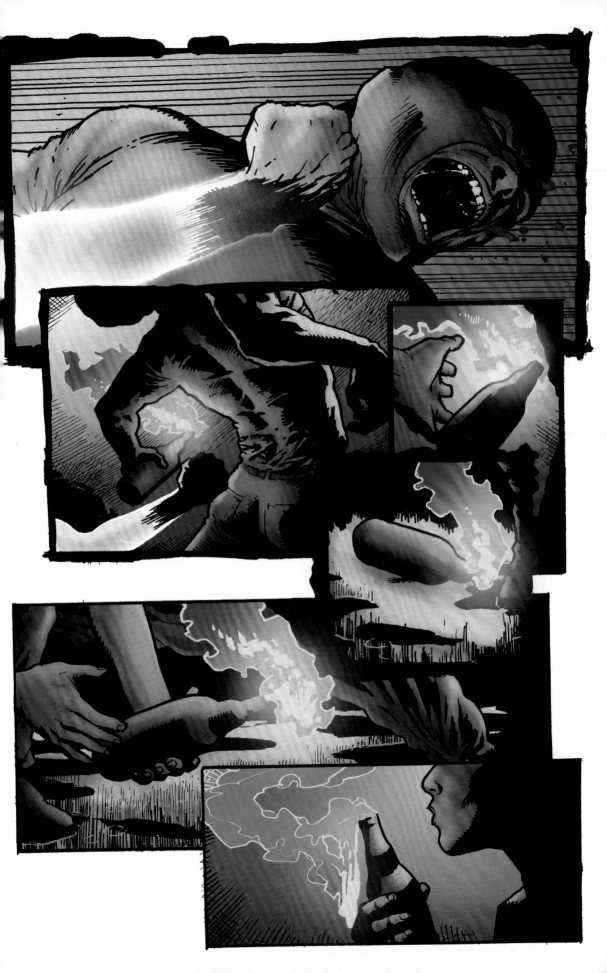

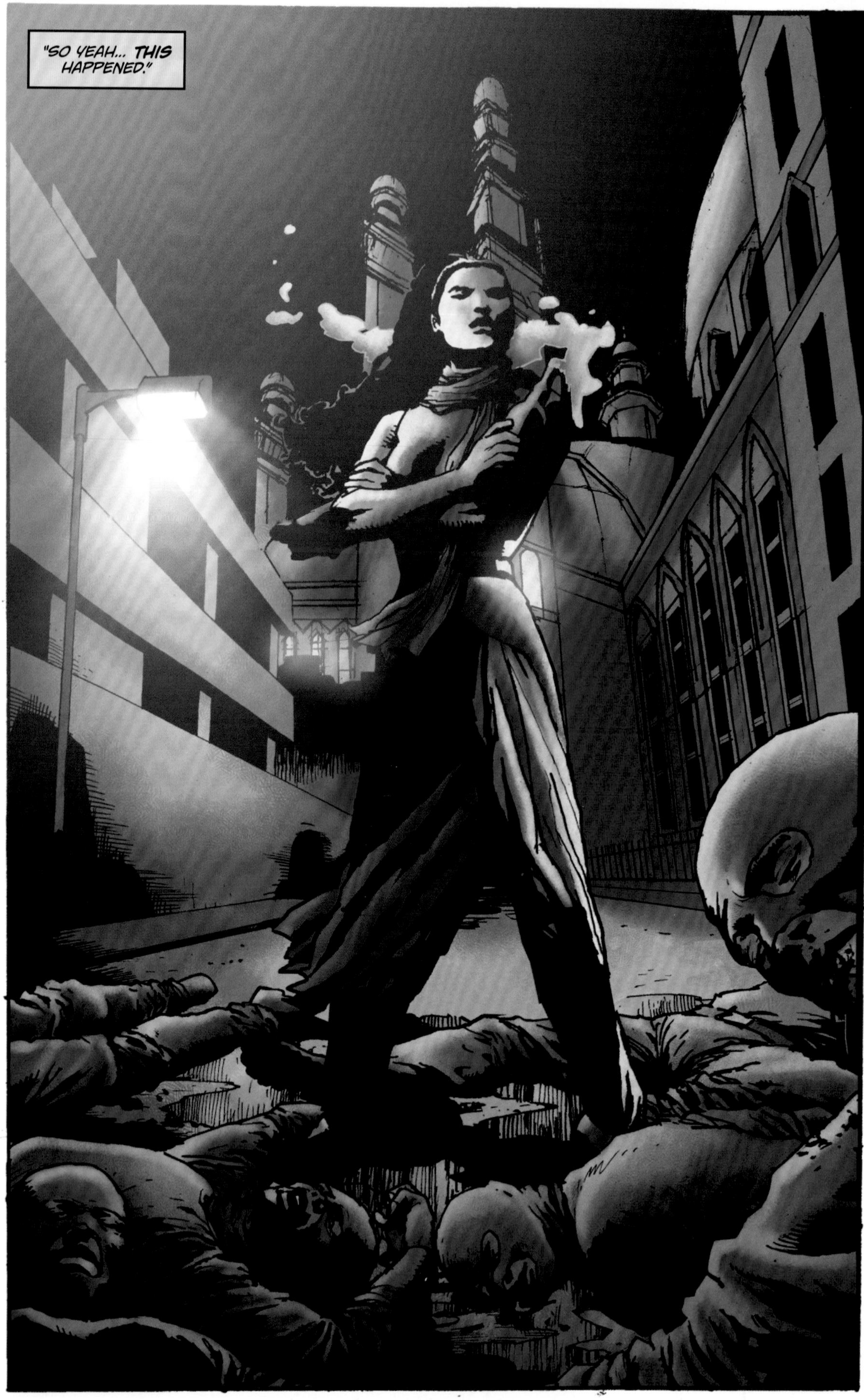
"SO YEAH... THIS HAPPENED."

"IN THE SIX MONTHS AFTER SEPTEMBER 11TH, THE NUMBER OF **HATE CRIMES** AGAINST MUSLIMS IN AMERICA ROSE 2,000 PERCENT.

"ARSON. VANDALISM. ASSAULT.

"EVEN **MURDER**.

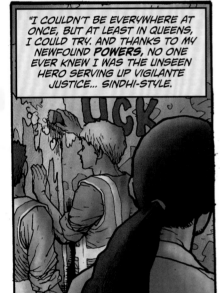

"I COULDN'T BE EVERYWHERE AT ONCE, BUT AT LEAST IN QUEENS, I COULD TRY. AND THANKS TO MY NEWFOUND **POWERS**, NO ONE EVER KNEW I WAS THE UNSEEN HERO SERVING UP VIGILANTE JUSTICE... SINDHI-STYLE.

"EXCEPT FOR YOUSSEF, OF COURSE. BUT HE WASN'T GOING TO RAT OUT HIS **FAVORITE** CUSTOMER.

"ESPECIALLY NOT AFTER THE MEDIA STARTED CALLING ME 'GODSEND,' A NAME THAT **HE** CAME UP WITH.

the Queens Herald

Godsend Nabs Arsonist

"AS HE WAS **QUICK** TO REMIND EVERYONE WHO EVER PASSED BY HIS STORE."

the prefered fruit porveyor of Godsend™

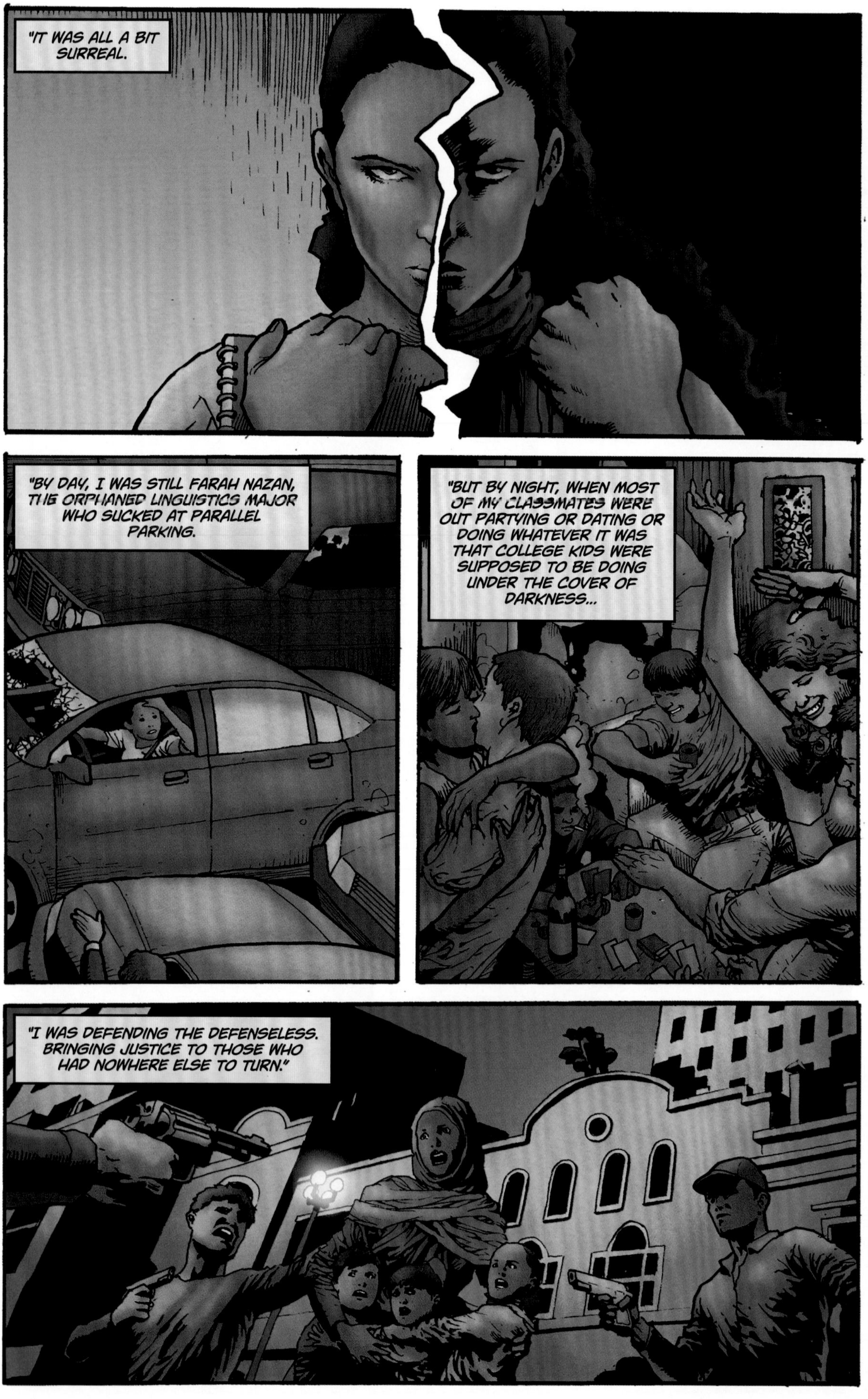
"IT WAS ALL A BIT SURREAL.
"BY DAY, I WAS STILL FARAH NAZAN, THE ORPHANED LINGUISTICS MAJOR WHO SUCKED AT PARALLEL PARKING.
"BUT BY NIGHT, WHEN MOST OF MY CLASSMATES WERE OUT PARTYING OR DATING OR DOING WHATEVER IT WAS THAT COLLEGE KIDS WERE SUPPOSED TO BE DOING UNDER THE COVER OF DARKNESS...
"I WAS DEFENDING THE DEFENSELESS. BRINGING JUSTICE TO THOSE WHO HAD NOWHERE ELSE TO TURN."

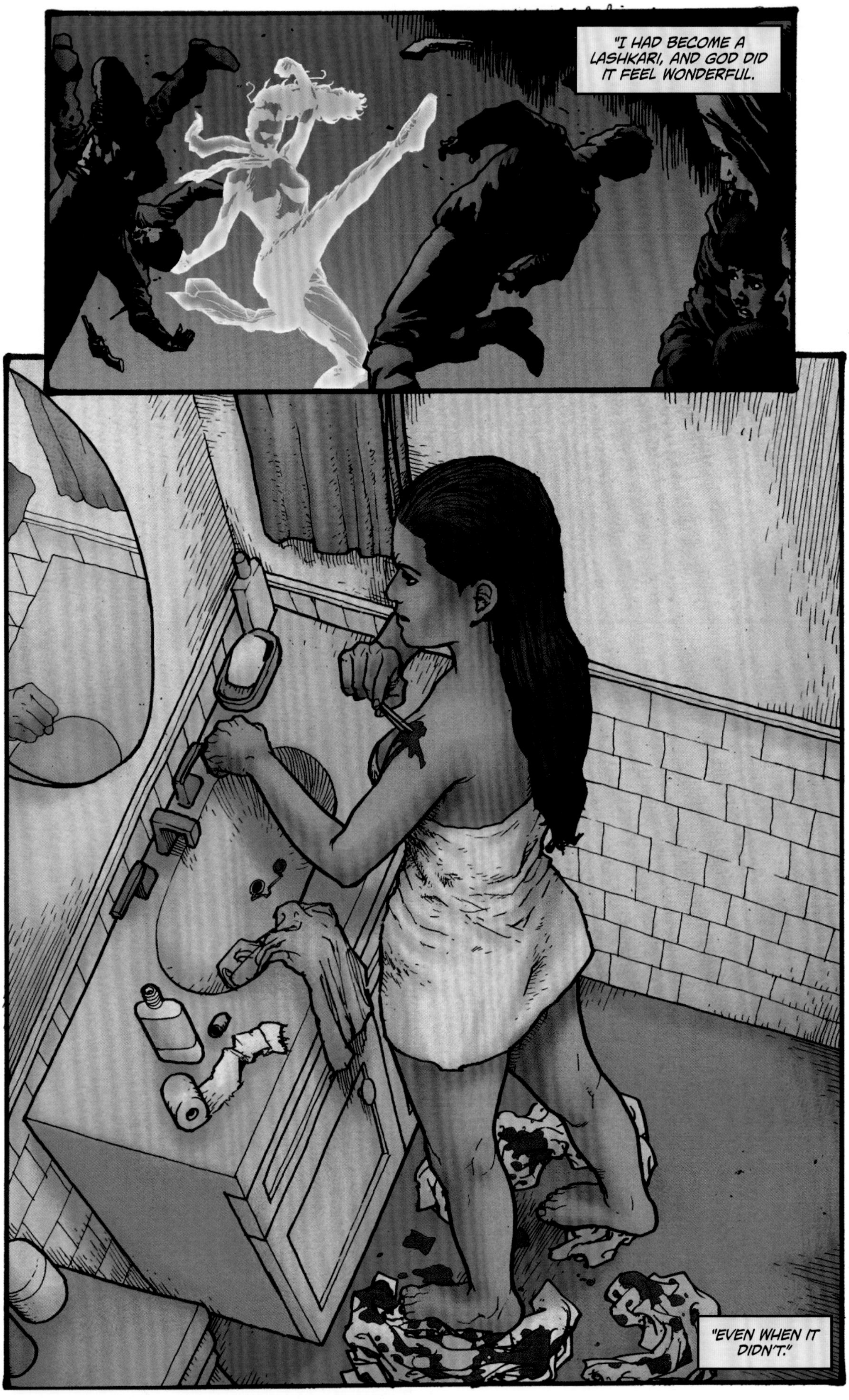
"I HAD BECOME A LASHKARI, AND GOD DID IT FEEL WONDERFUL.
"EVEN WHEN IT DIDN'T."

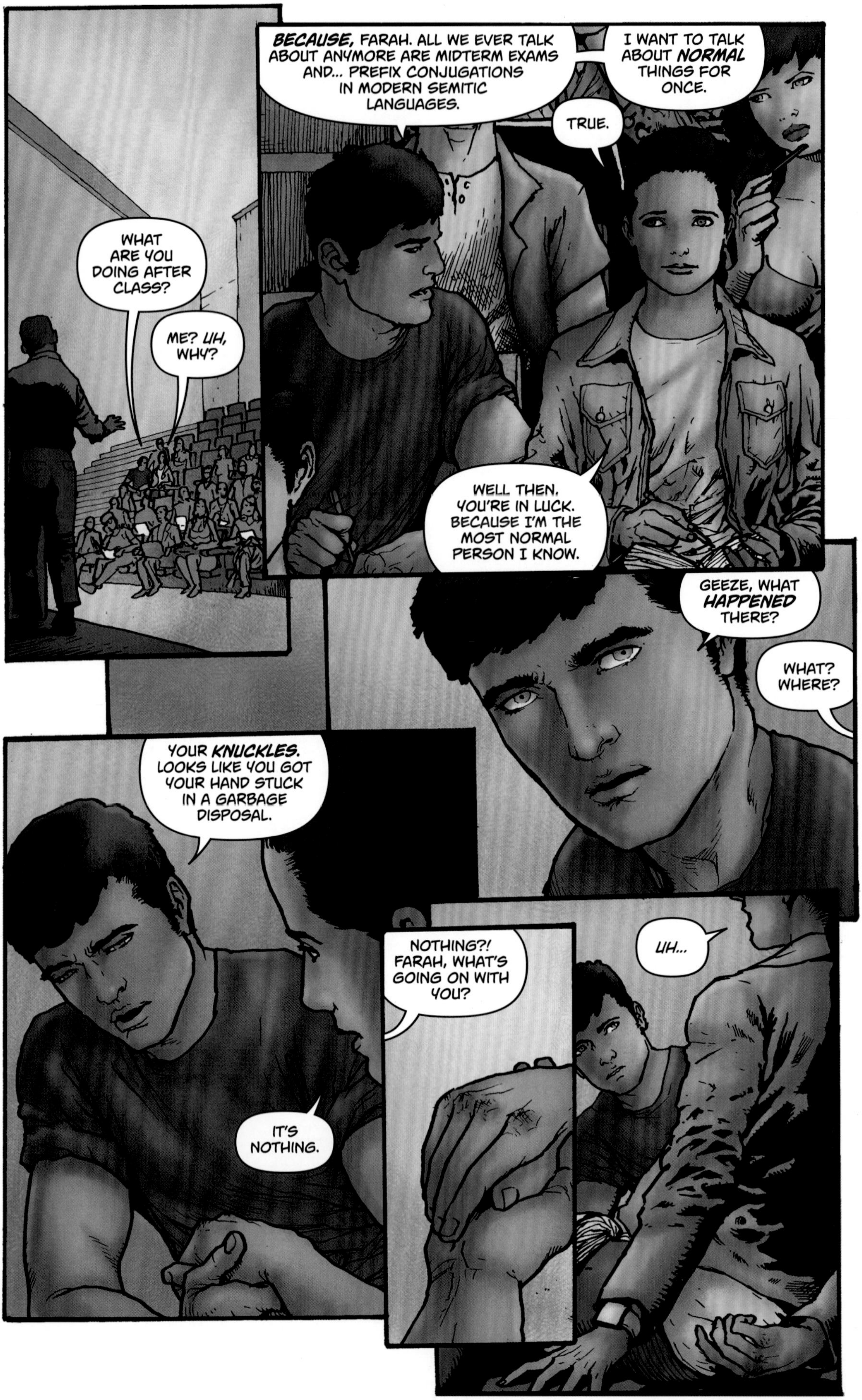
WHAT ARE YOU DOING AFTER CLASS?
ME? UH, WHY?
BECAUSE, FARAH. ALL WE EVER TALK ABOUT ANYMORE ARE MIDTERM EXAMS AND... PREFIX CONJUGATIONS IN MODERN SEMITIC LANGUAGES.
I WANT TO TALK ABOUT NORMAL THINGS FOR ONCE.
TRUE.
WELL THEN. YOU'RE IN LUCK. BECAUSE I'M THE MOST NORMAL PERSON I KNOW.
GEEZE, WHAT HAPPENED THERE?
WHAT? WHERE?
YOUR KNUCKLES. LOOKS LIKE YOU GOT YOUR HAND STUCK IN A GARBAGE DISPOSAL.
IT'S NOTHING.
NOTHING?! FARAH, WHAT'S GOING ON WITH YOU?
UH...

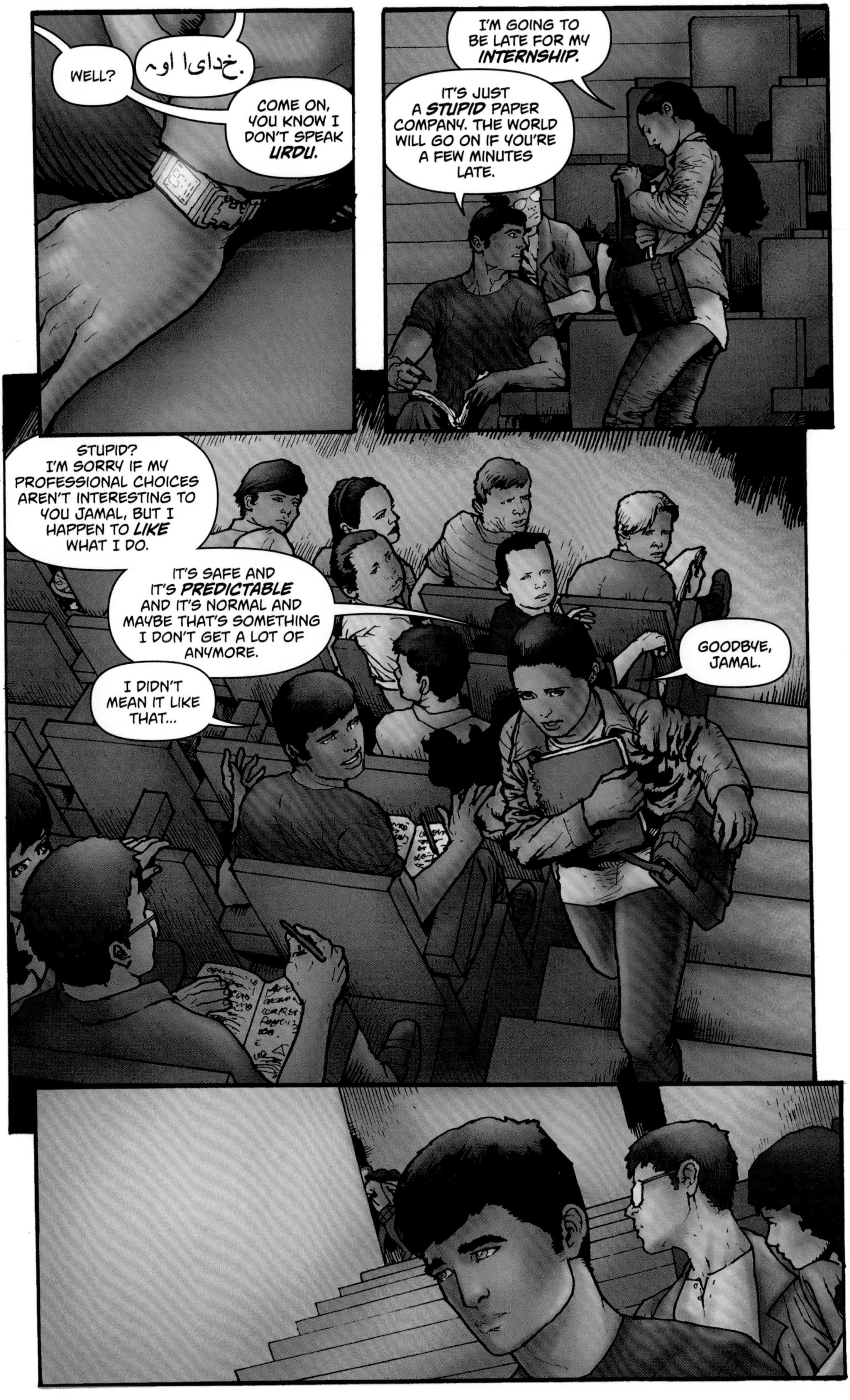
WELL?
خدای اوہ.
COME ON, YOU KNOW I DON'T SPEAK URDU.
I'M GOING TO BE LATE FOR MY INTERNSHIP.
IT'S JUST A STUPID PAPER COMPANY. THE WORLD WILL GO ON IF YOU'RE A FEW MINUTES LATE.
STUPID? I'M SORRY IF MY PROFESSIONAL CHOICES AREN'T INTERESTING TO YOU JAMAL, BUT I HAPPEN TO LIKE WHAT I DO.
IT'S SAFE AND IT'S PREDICTABLE AND IT'S NORMAL AND MAYBE THAT'S SOMETHING I DON'T GET A LOT OF ANYMORE.
I DIDN'T MEAN IT LIKE THAT...
GOODBYE, JAMAL.

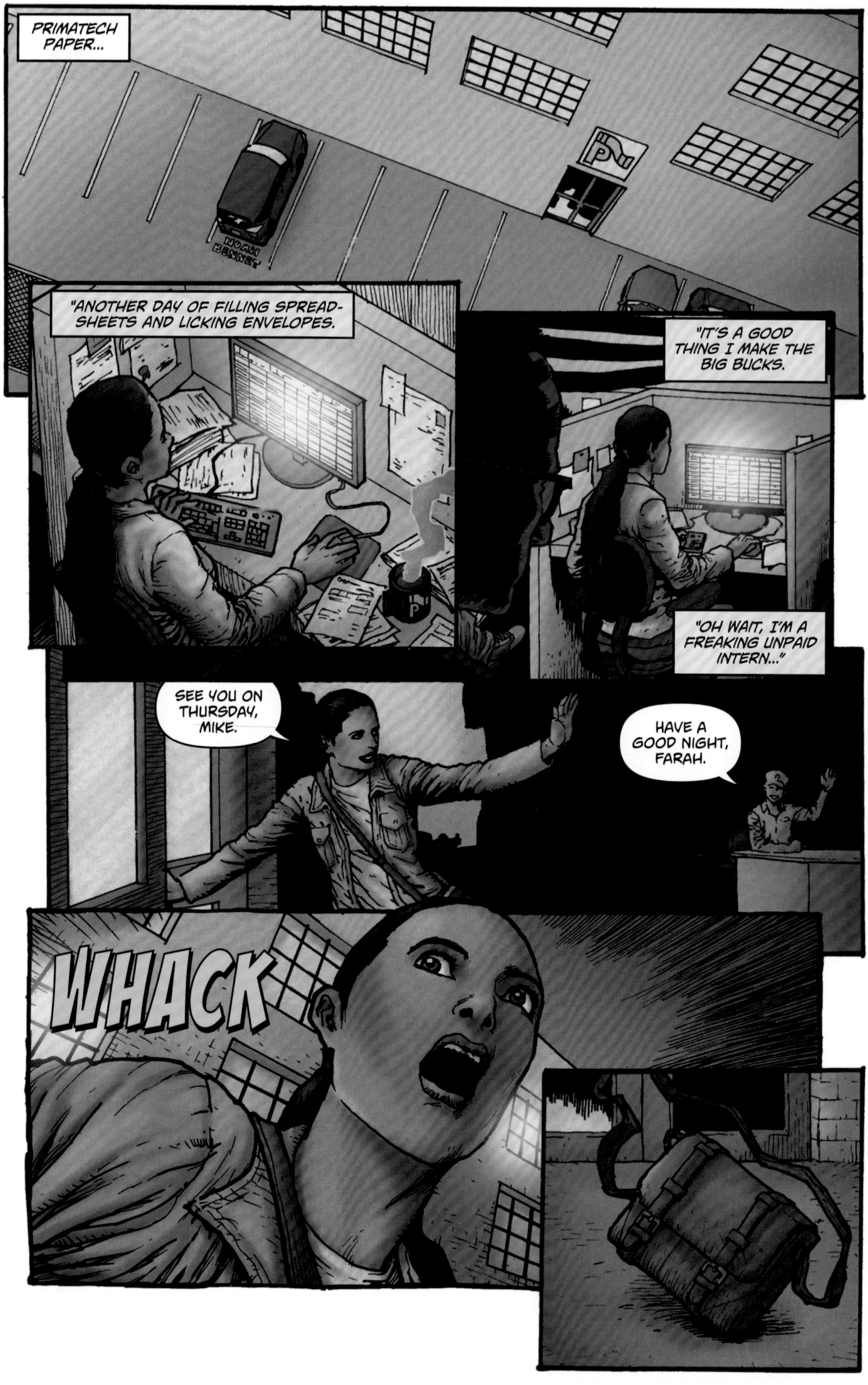
PRIMATECH PAPER...
NOAH BENNET
"ANOTHER DAY OF FILLING SPREAD-SHEETS AND LICKING ENVELOPES.
"IT'S A GOOD THING I MAKE THE BIG BUCKS.
"OH WAIT, I'M A FREAKING UNPAID INTERN..."
SEE YOU ON THURSDAY, MIKE.
HAVE A GOOD NIGHT, FARAH.
WHACK

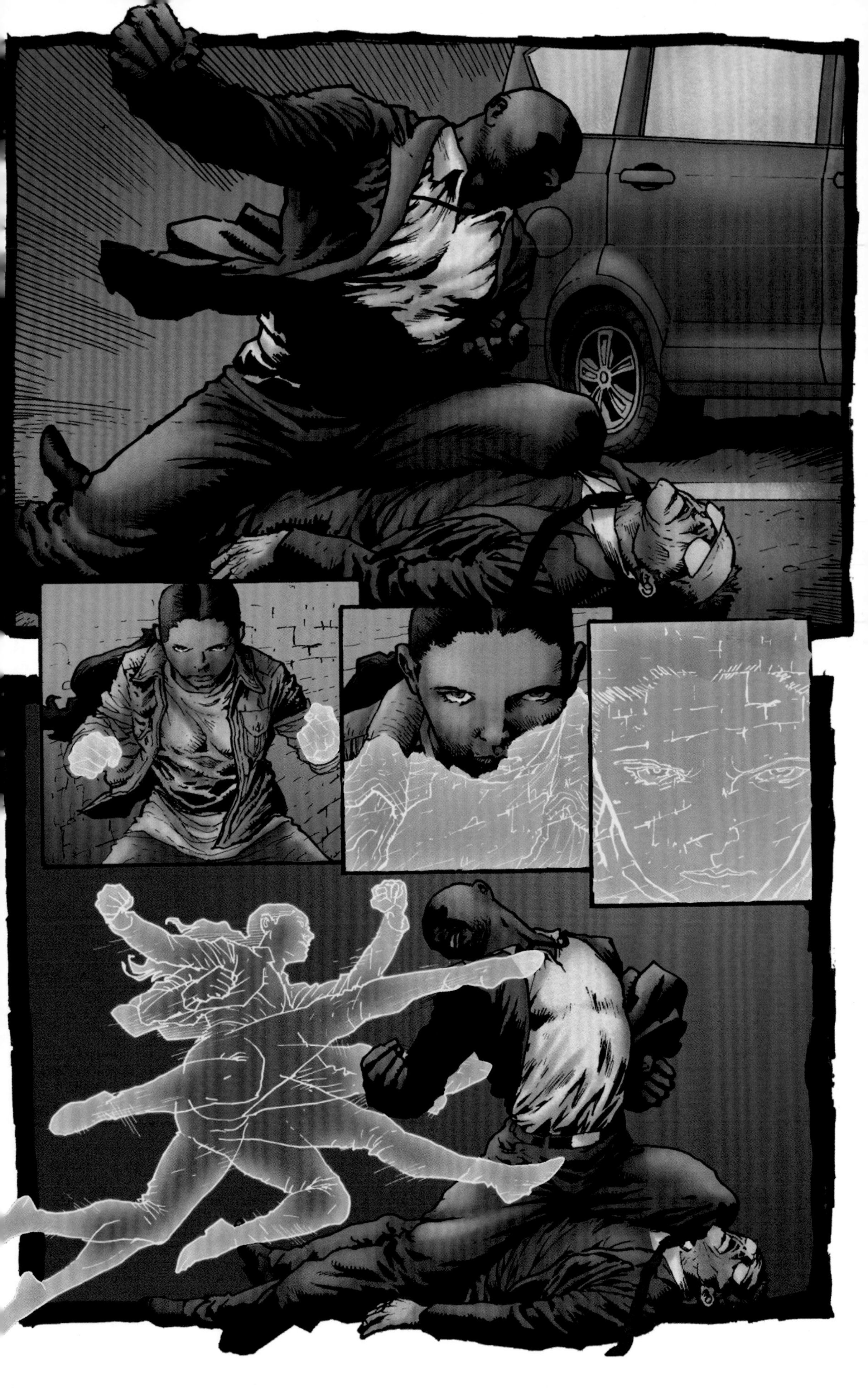

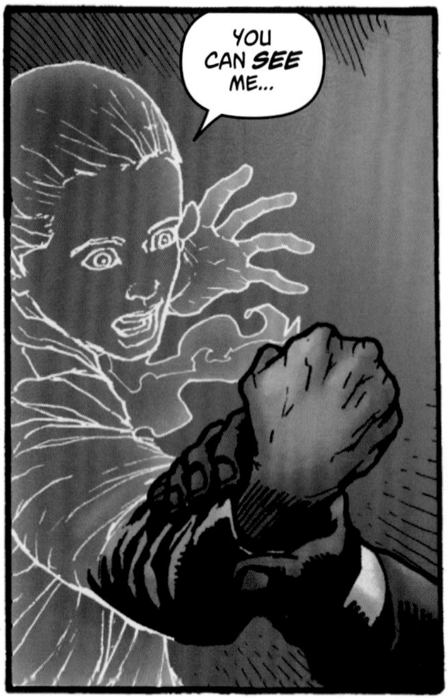
YOU CAN SEE ME...

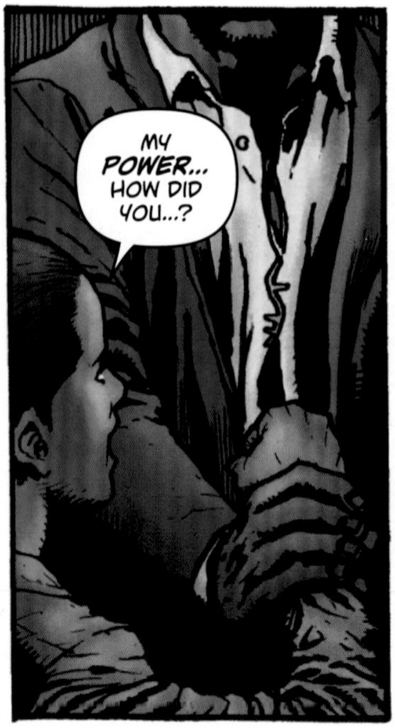
MY POWER... HOW DID YOU...?

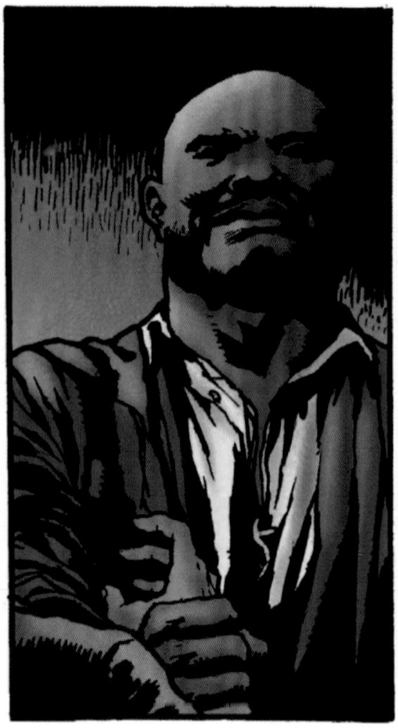

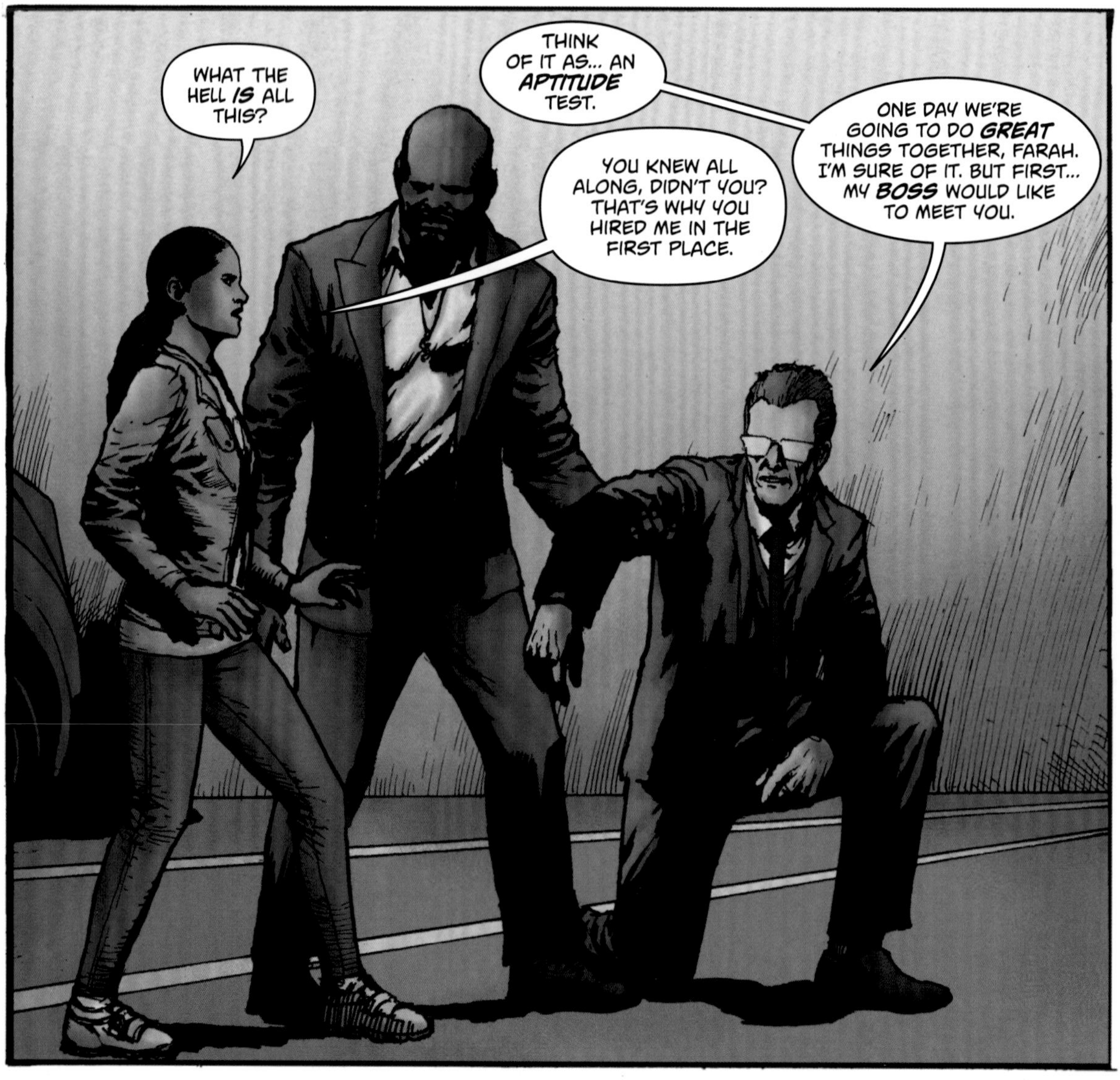
WHAT THE HELL IS ALL THIS?
THINK OF IT AS... AN APTITUDE TEST.
YOU KNEW ALL ALONG, DIDN'T YOU? THAT'S WHY YOU HIRED ME IN THE FIRST PLACE.
ONE DAY WE'RE GOING TO DO GREAT THINGS TOGETHER, FARAH. I'M SURE OF IT. BUT FIRST... MY BOSS WOULD LIKE TO MEET YOU.

GET IN.

THIS IS STARTING TO GET REALLY WEIRD.

OH...

...YOU DON'T KNOW THE HALF OF IT.

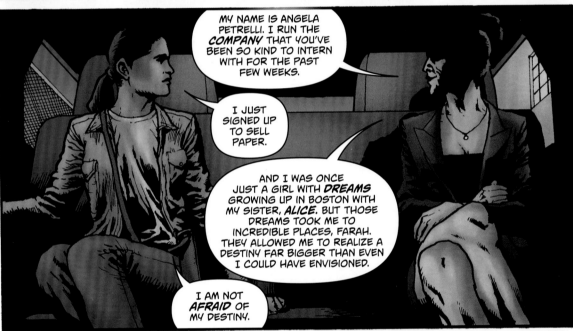

MY NAME IS ANGELA PETRELLI. I RUN THE *COMPANY* THAT YOU'VE BEEN SO KIND TO INTERN WITH FOR THE PAST FEW WEEKS.

I JUST SIGNED UP TO SELL PAPER.

AND I WAS ONCE JUST A GIRL WITH *DREAMS* GROWING UP IN BOSTON WITH MY SISTER, *ALICE*. BUT THOSE DREAMS TOOK ME TO INCREDIBLE PLACES, FARAH. THEY ALLOWED ME TO REALIZE A DESTINY FAR BIGGER THAN EVEN I COULD HAVE ENVISIONED.

I AM NOT *AFRAID* OF MY DESTINY.

YOU *WILL* BE.

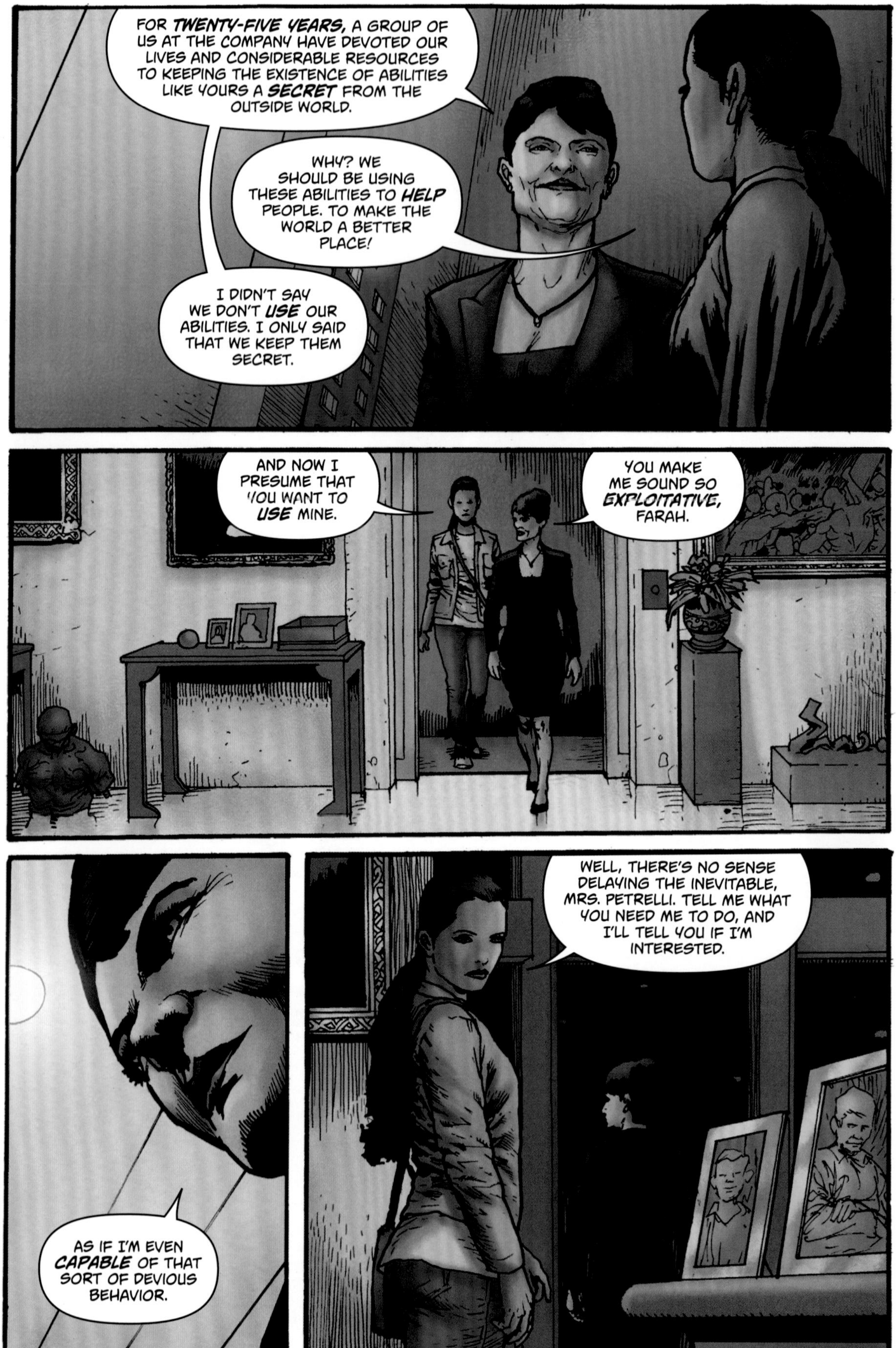

FOR TWENTY-FIVE YEARS, A GROUP OF US AT THE COMPANY HAVE DEVOTED OUR LIVES AND CONSIDERABLE RESOURCES TO KEEPING THE EXISTENCE OF ABILITIES LIKE YOURS A SECRET FROM THE OUTSIDE WORLD.
WHY? WE SHOULD BE USING THESE ABILITIES TO HELP PEOPLE. TO MAKE THE WORLD A BETTER PLACE!
I DIDN'T SAY WE DON'T USE OUR ABILITIES. I ONLY SAID THAT WE KEEP THEM SECRET.
AND NOW I PRESUME THAT YOU WANT TO USE MINE.
YOU MAKE ME SOUND SO EXPLOITATIVE, FARAH.
AS IF I'M EVEN CAPABLE OF THAT SORT OF DEVIOUS BEHAVIOR.
WELL, THERE'S NO SENSE DELAYING THE INEVITABLE, MRS. PETRELLI. TELL ME WHAT YOU NEED ME TO DO, AND I'LL TELL YOU IF I'M INTERESTED.

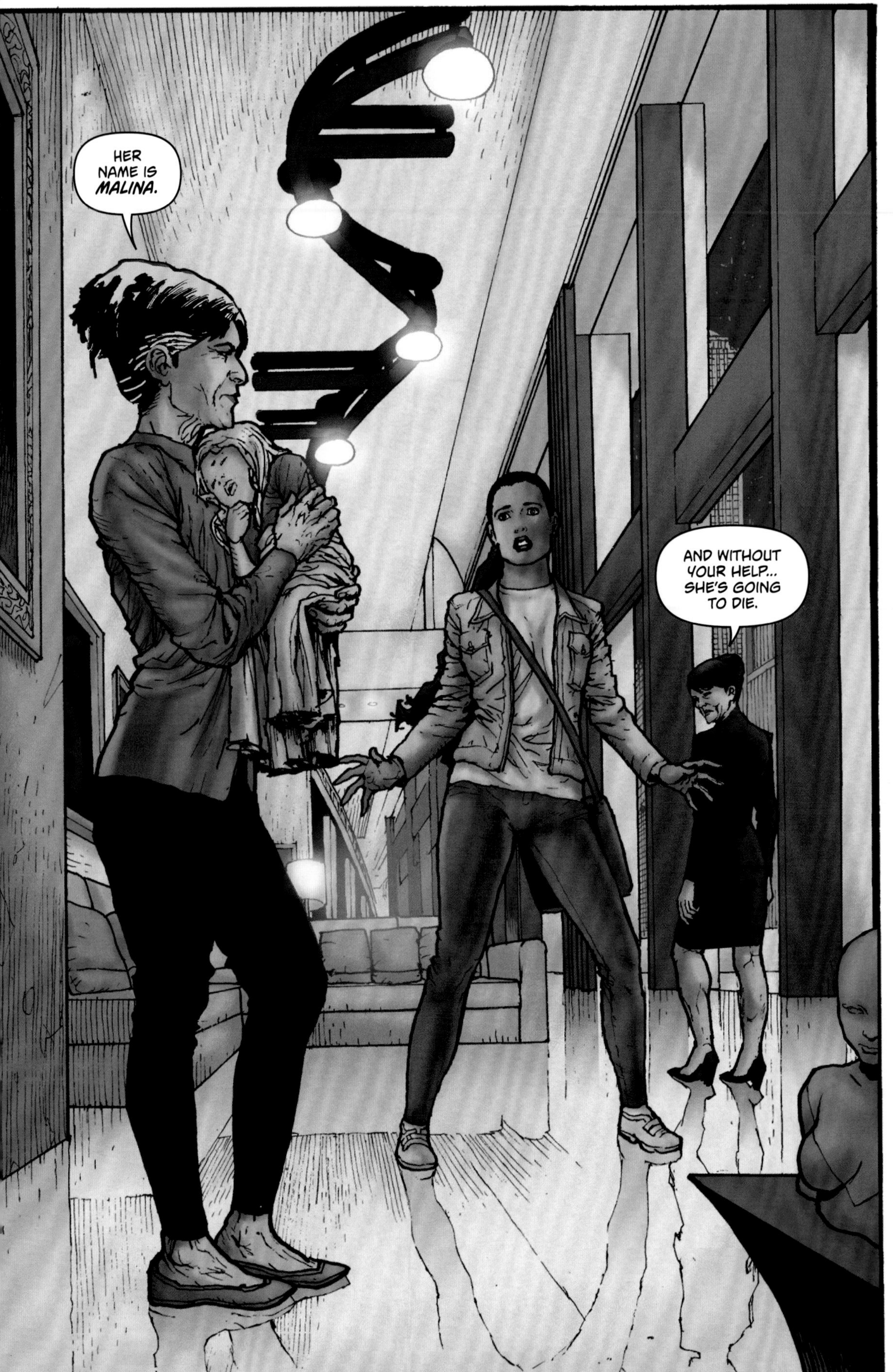
HER NAME IS *MALINA*.
AND WITHOUT YOUR HELP... SHE'S GOING TO DIE.

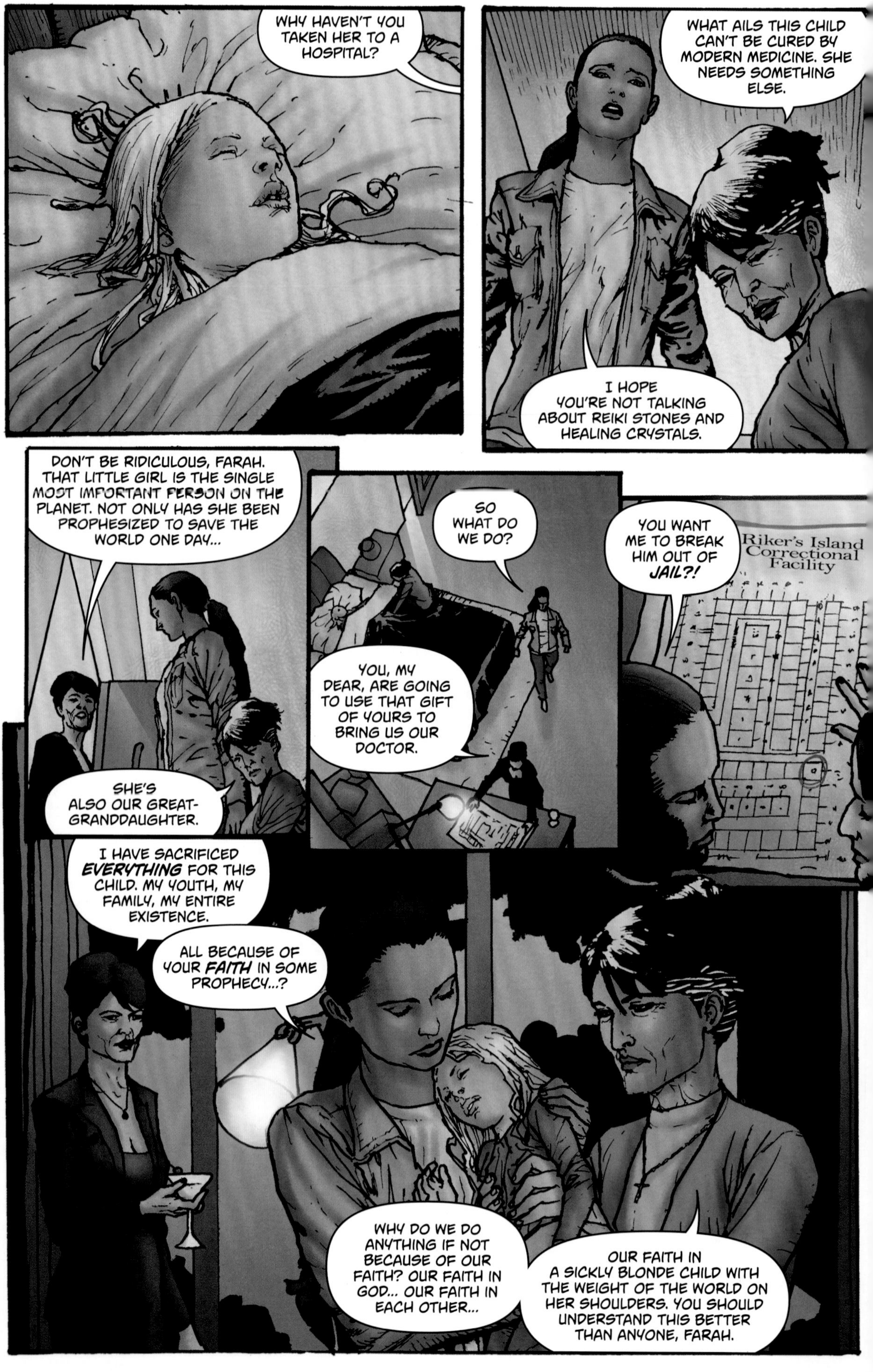

WHY HAVEN'T YOU TAKEN HER TO A HOSPITAL?
WHAT AILS THIS CHILD CAN'T BE CURED BY MODERN MEDICINE. SHE NEEDS SOMETHING ELSE.
I HOPE YOU'RE NOT TALKING ABOUT REIKI STONES AND HEALING CRYSTALS.
DON'T BE RIDICULOUS, FARAH. THAT LITTLE GIRL IS THE SINGLE MOST IMPORTANT PERSON ON THE PLANET. NOT ONLY HAS SHE BEEN PROPHESIZED TO SAVE THE WORLD ONE DAY...
SHE'S ALSO OUR GREAT-GRANDDAUGHTER.
SO WHAT DO WE DO?
YOU, MY DEAR, ARE GOING TO USE THAT GIFT OF YOURS TO BRING US OUR DOCTOR.
YOU WANT ME TO BREAK HIM OUT OF ***JAIL?!***
Riker's Island Correctional Facility
I HAVE SACRIFICED ***EVERYTHING*** FOR THIS CHILD. MY YOUTH, MY FAMILY, MY ENTIRE EXISTENCE.
ALL BECAUSE OF YOUR ***FAITH*** IN SOME PROPHECY...?
WHY DO WE DO ANYTHING IF NOT BECAUSE OF OUR FAITH? OUR FAITH IN GOD... OUR FAITH IN EACH OTHER...
OUR FAITH IN A SICKLY BLONDE CHILD WITH THE WEIGHT OF THE WORLD ON HER SHOULDERS. YOU SHOULD UNDERSTAND THIS BETTER THAN ANYONE, FARAH.

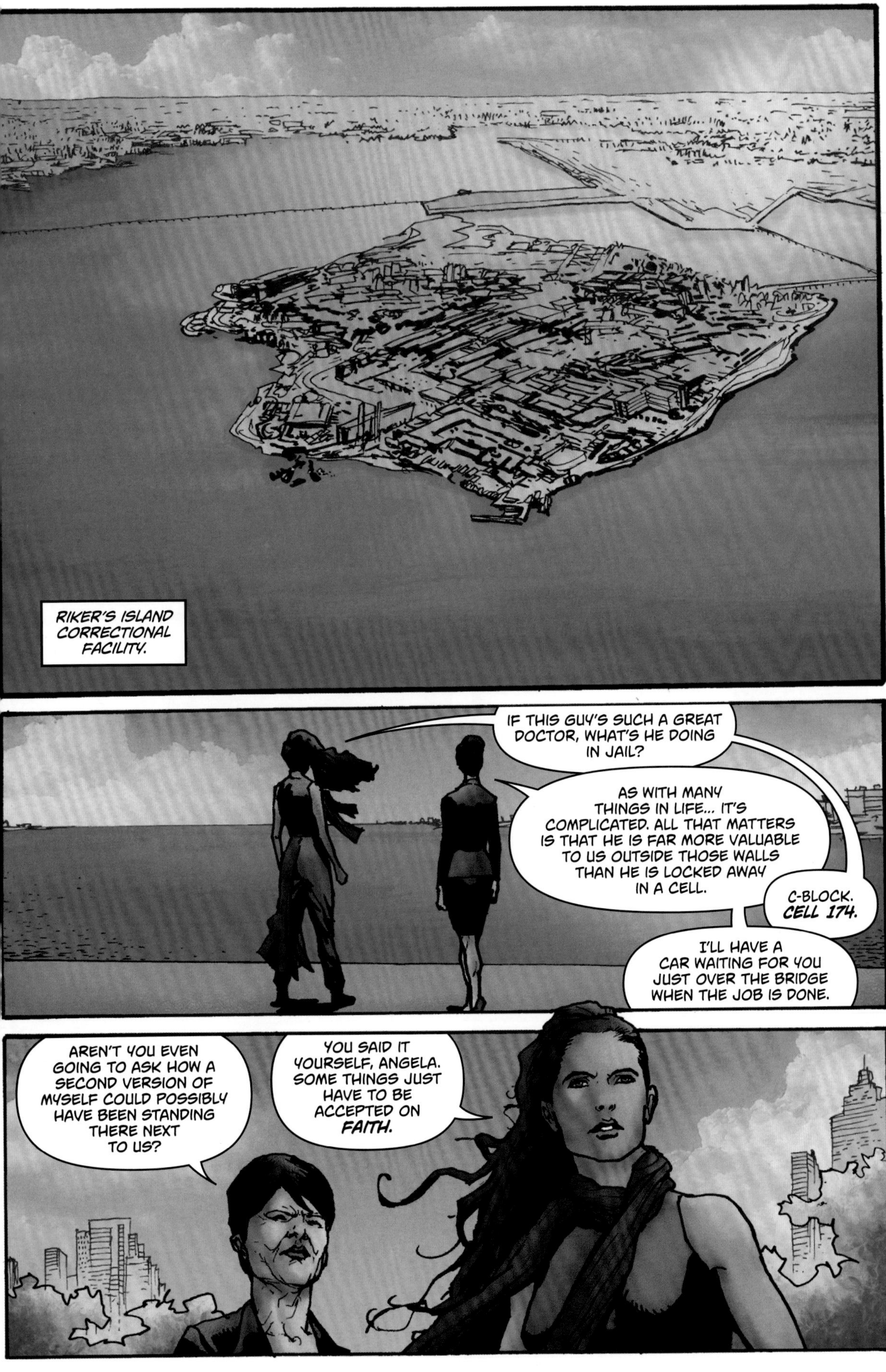
RIKER'S ISLAND CORRECTIONAL FACILITY.
IF THIS GUY'S SUCH A GREAT DOCTOR, WHAT'S HE DOING IN JAIL?
AS WITH MANY THINGS IN LIFE... IT'S COMPLICATED. ALL THAT MATTERS IS THAT HE IS FAR MORE VALUABLE TO US OUTSIDE THOSE WALLS THAN HE IS LOCKED AWAY IN A CELL.
C-BLOCK. CELL 174.
I'LL HAVE A CAR WAITING FOR YOU JUST OVER THE BRIDGE WHEN THE JOB IS DONE.
AREN'T YOU EVEN GOING TO ASK HOW A SECOND VERSION OF MYSELF COULD POSSIBLY HAVE BEEN STANDING THERE NEXT TO US?
YOU SAID IT YOURSELF, ANGELA. SOME THINGS JUST HAVE TO BE ACCEPTED ON FAITH.

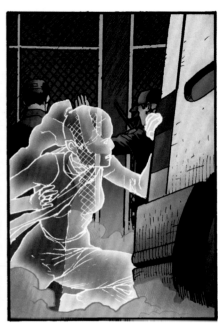

ill txt u mine if u txt me urs.

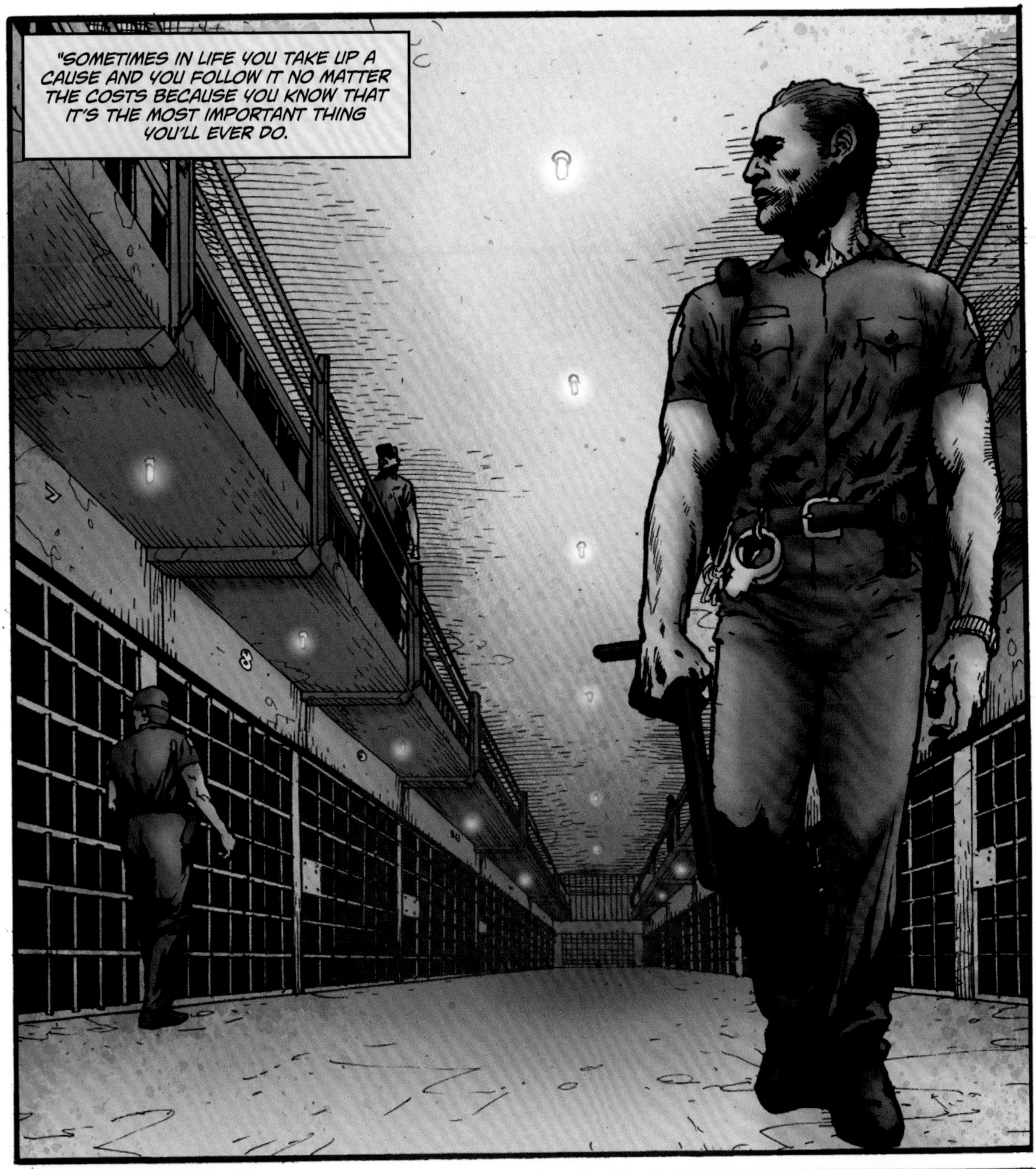
"SOMETIMES IN LIFE YOU TAKE UP A CAUSE AND YOU FOLLOW IT NO MATTER THE COSTS BECAUSE YOU KNOW THAT IT'S THE MOST IMPORTANT THING YOU'LL EVER DO.

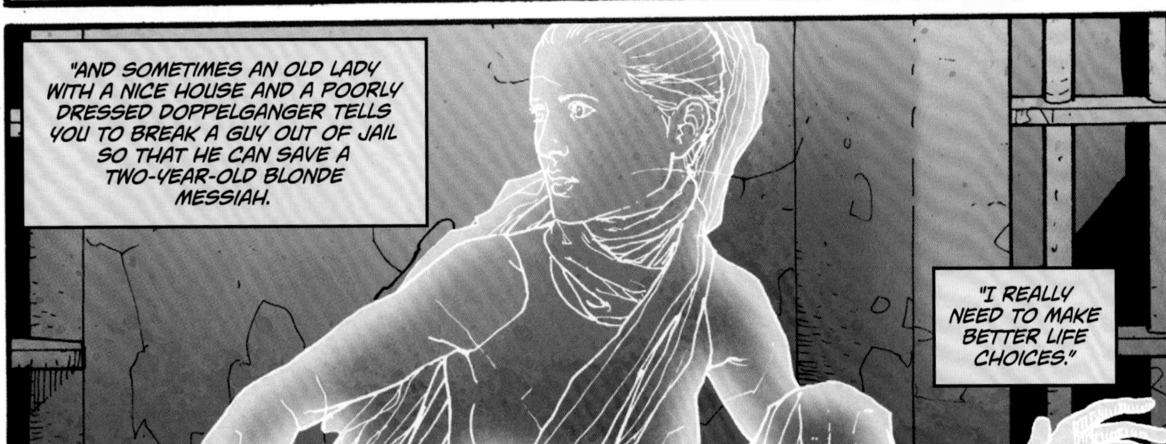
"AND SOMETIMES AN OLD LADY WITH A NICE HOUSE AND A POORLY DRESSED DOPPELGANGER TELLS YOU TO BREAK A GUY OUT OF JAIL SO THAT HE CAN SAVE A TWO-YEAR-OLD BLONDE MESSIAH.
"I REALLY NEED TO MAKE BETTER LIFE CHOICES."

QUIET NIGHT.

WHAT DO YOU EXPECT? NO ONE WOULD DARE KEEP *HIS HIGHNESS* AWAKE...

YEAH... SAY, DO YOU SMELL SOMETHIN'?

IT'S *JAIL.* I SMELL A LOTTA THINGS.

KINDA SMELLS LIKE... LADY'S PERFUME.

NAH, THIS IS *DIFFERENT.*

"SHIT."

THE CHEAP KIND MY DAUGHTER WEARS.

"OH, NO HE DIDN'T."

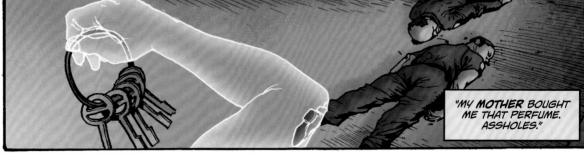

"MY *MOTHER* BOUGHT ME THAT PERFUME. ASSHOLES."

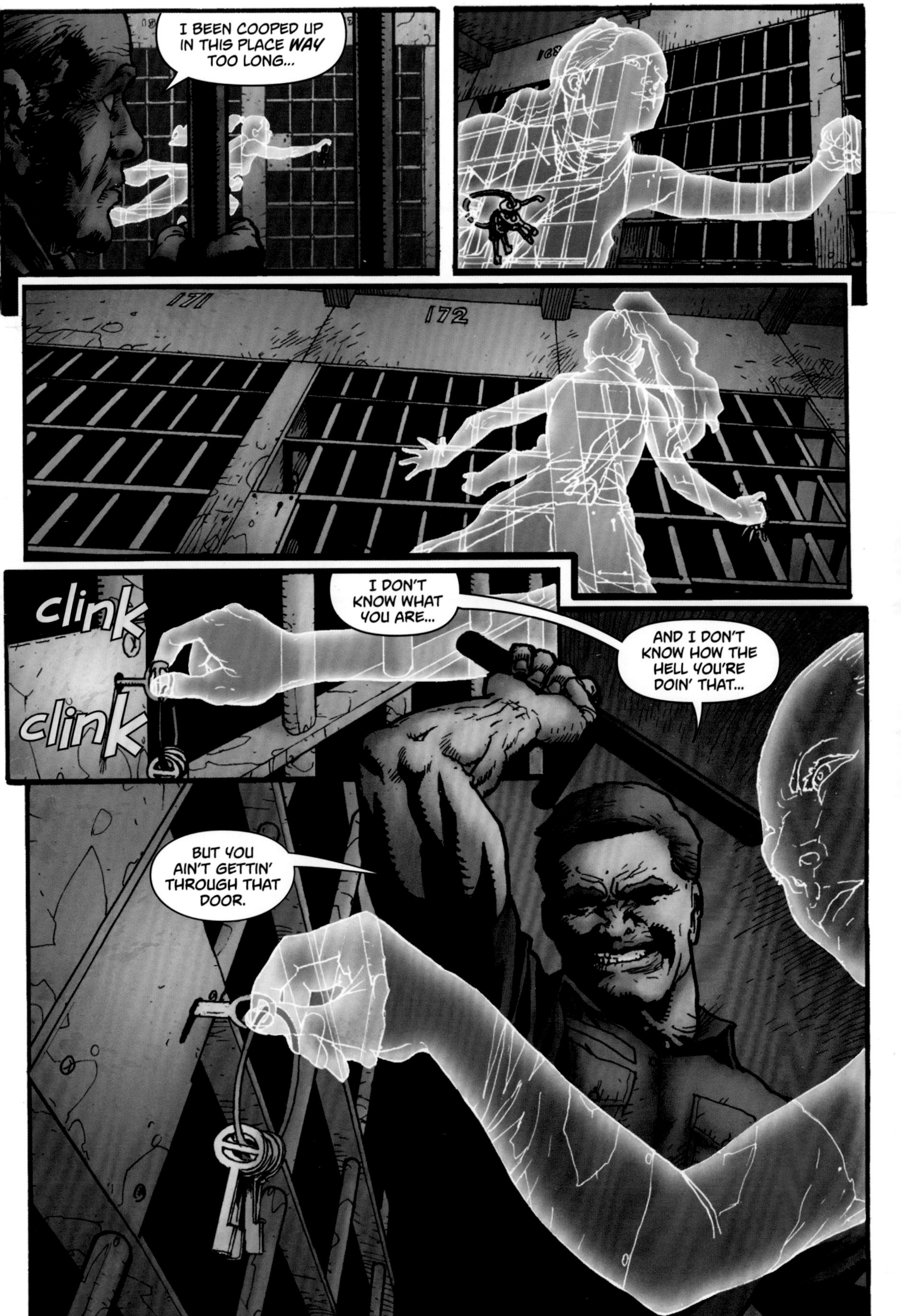
I BEEN COOPED UP IN THIS PLACE **WAY** TOO LONG...
171
172
clink
clink
I DON'T KNOW WHAT YOU ARE...
AND I DON'T KNOW HOW THE HELL YOU'RE DOIN' THAT...
BUT YOU AIN'T GETTIN' THROUGH THAT DOOR.

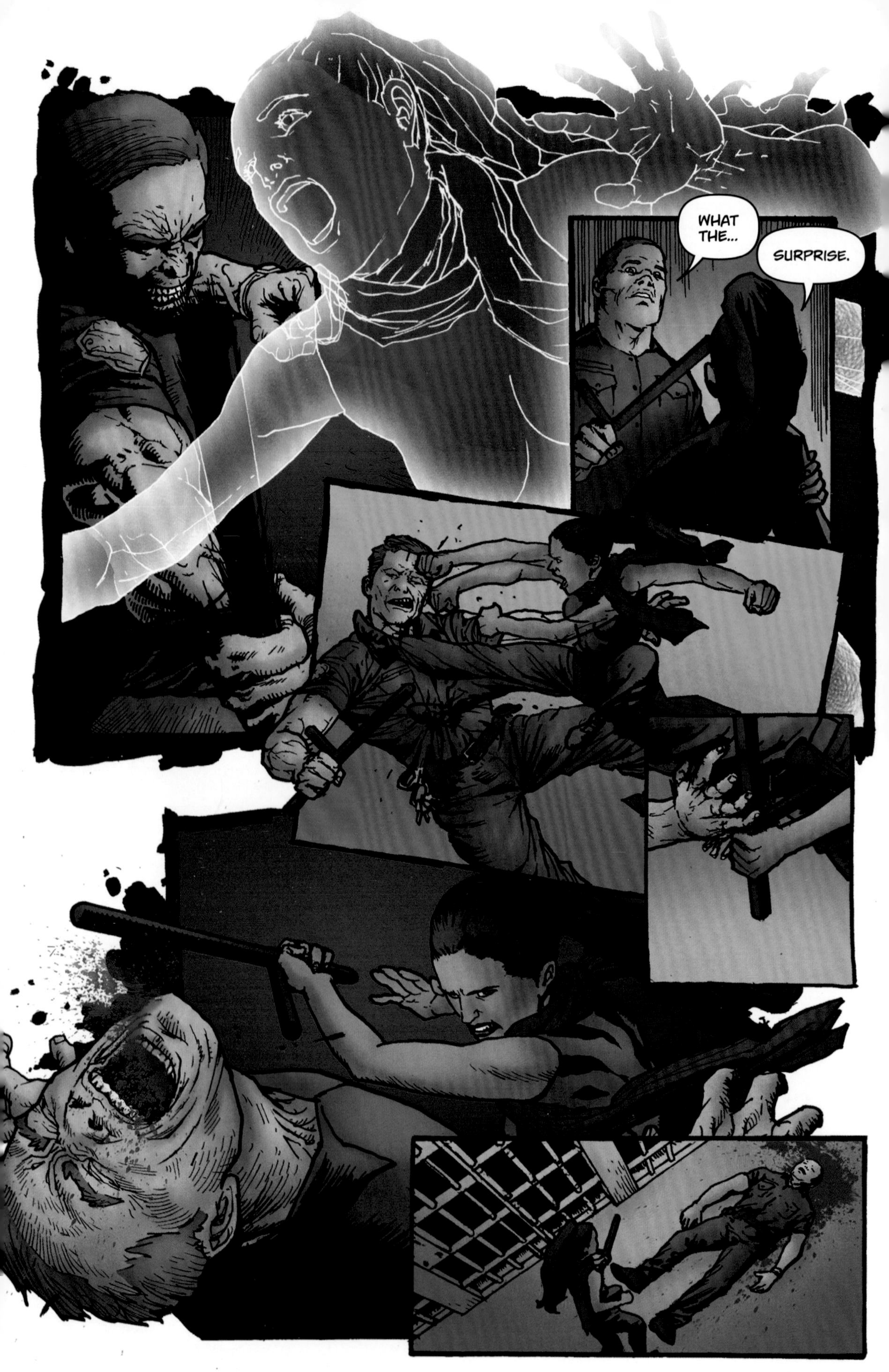
WHAT THE...
SURPRISE.

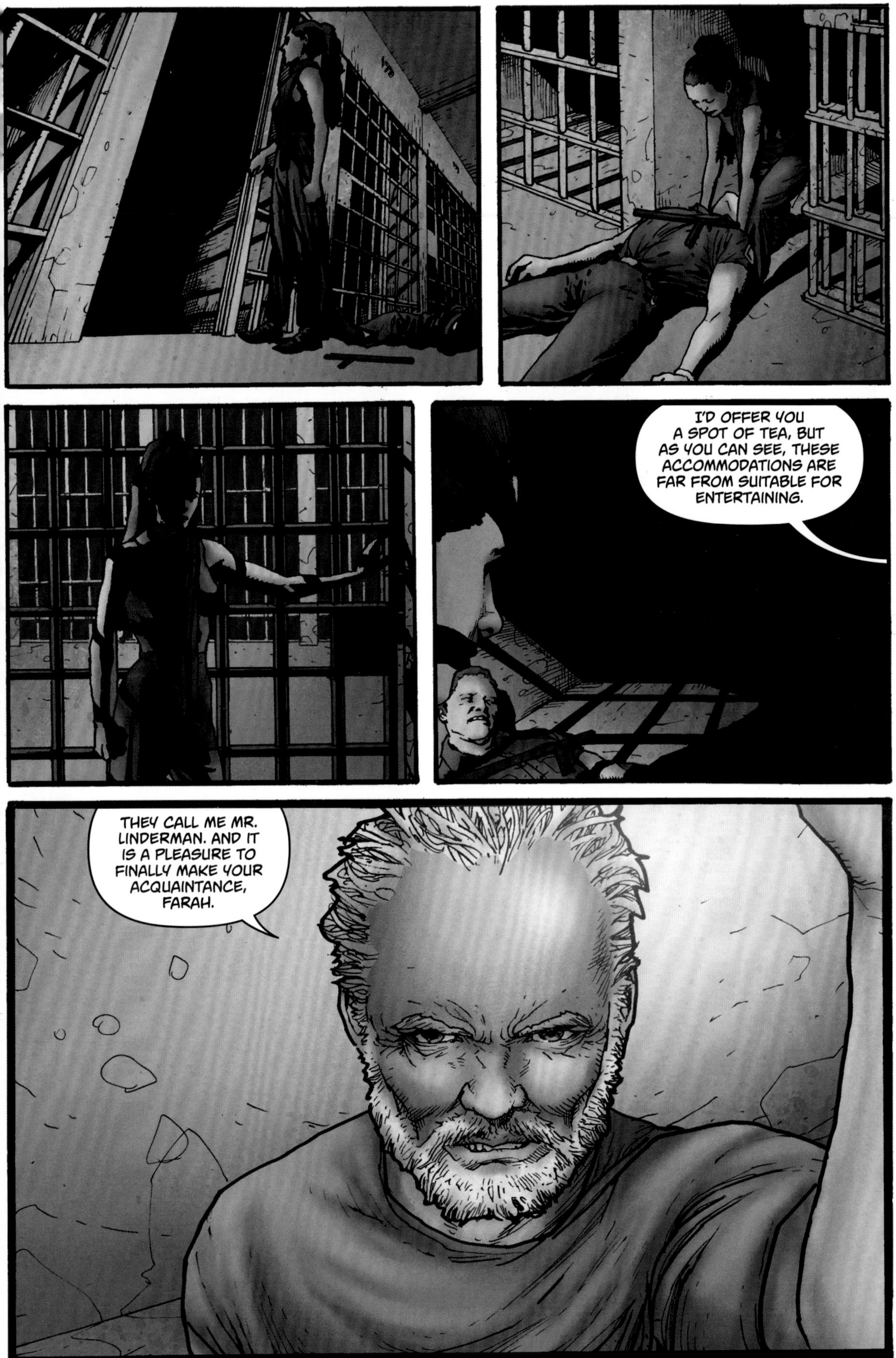
I'D OFFER YOU A SPOT OF TEA, BUT AS YOU CAN SEE, THESE ACCOMMODATIONS ARE FAR FROM SUITABLE FOR ENTERTAINING.
THEY CALL ME MR. LINDERMAN. AND IT IS A PLEASURE TO FINALLY MAKE YOUR ACQUAINTANCE, FARAH.
TO BE CONTINUED...

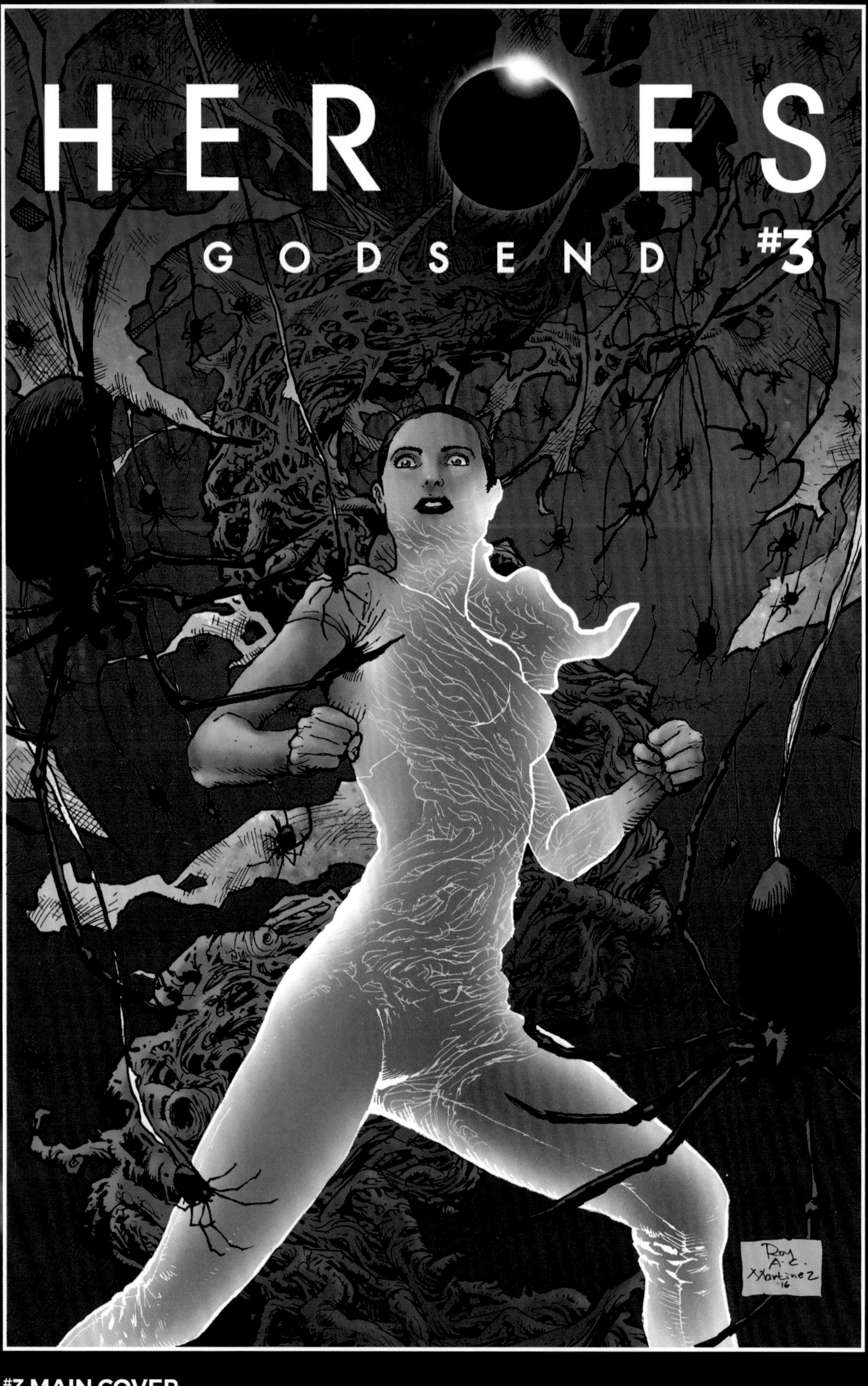
HEROES
GODSEND
#3
ROY A.C. XMartinez '16

#3 MAIN COVER
ARTWORK BY ROY ALLAN MARTINEZ

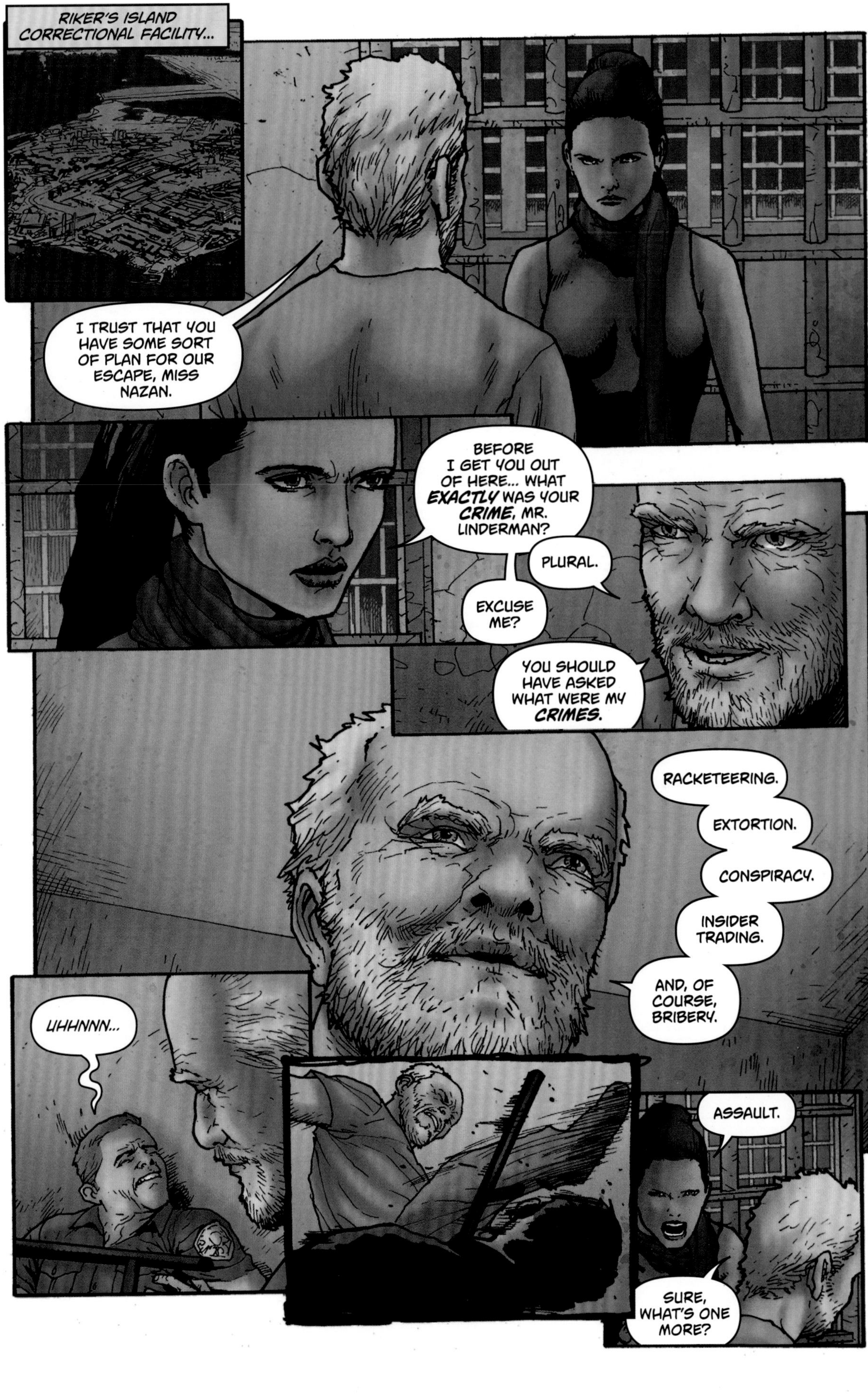
RIKER'S ISLAND CORRECTIONAL FACILITY...
I TRUST THAT YOU HAVE SOME SORT OF PLAN FOR OUR ESCAPE, MISS NAZAN.
BEFORE I GET YOU OUT OF HERE... WHAT EXACTLY WAS YOUR CRIME, MR. LINDERMAN?
PLURAL.
EXCUSE ME?
YOU SHOULD HAVE ASKED WHAT WERE MY CRIMES.
RACKETEERING.
EXTORTION.
CONSPIRACY.
INSIDER TRADING.
AND, OF COURSE, BRIBERY.
UHHNNN...
ASSAULT.
SURE, WHAT'S ONE MORE?

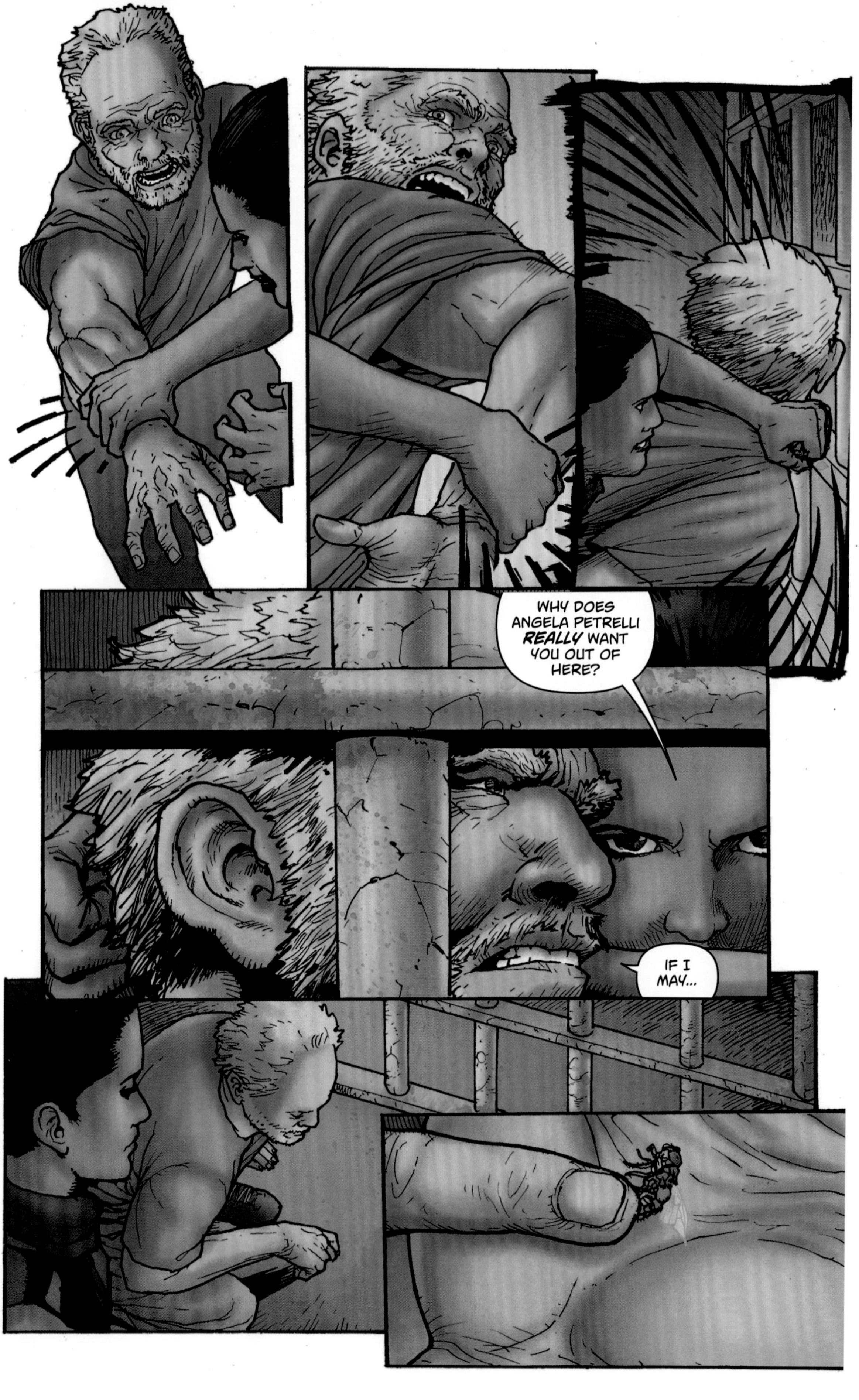
WHY DOES ANGELA PETRELLI REALLY WANT YOU OUT OF HERE?
IF I MAY...

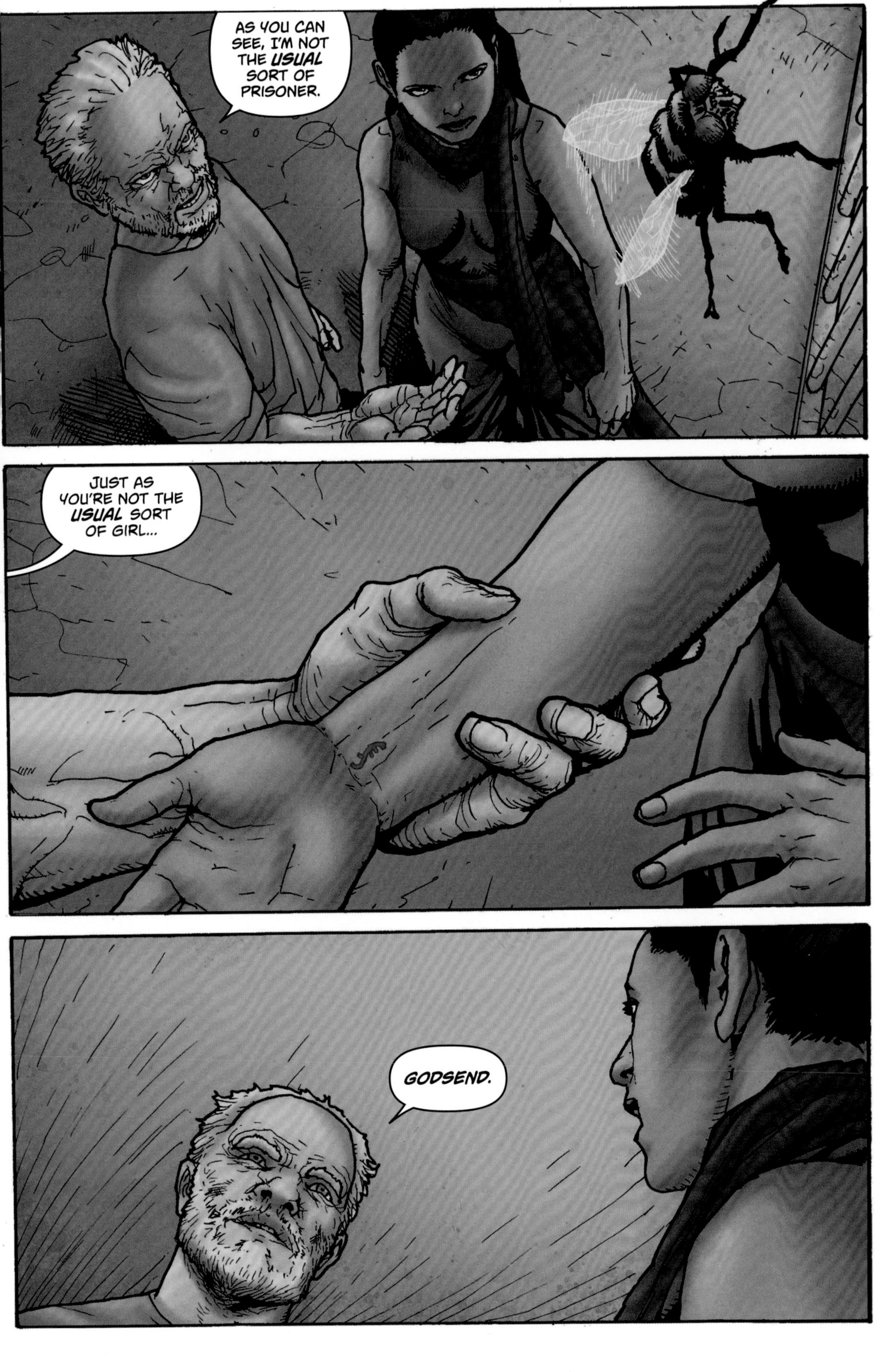
AS YOU CAN SEE, I'M NOT THE *USUAL* SORT OF PRISONER.
JUST AS YOU'RE NOT THE *USUAL* SORT OF GIRL...
GODSEND.

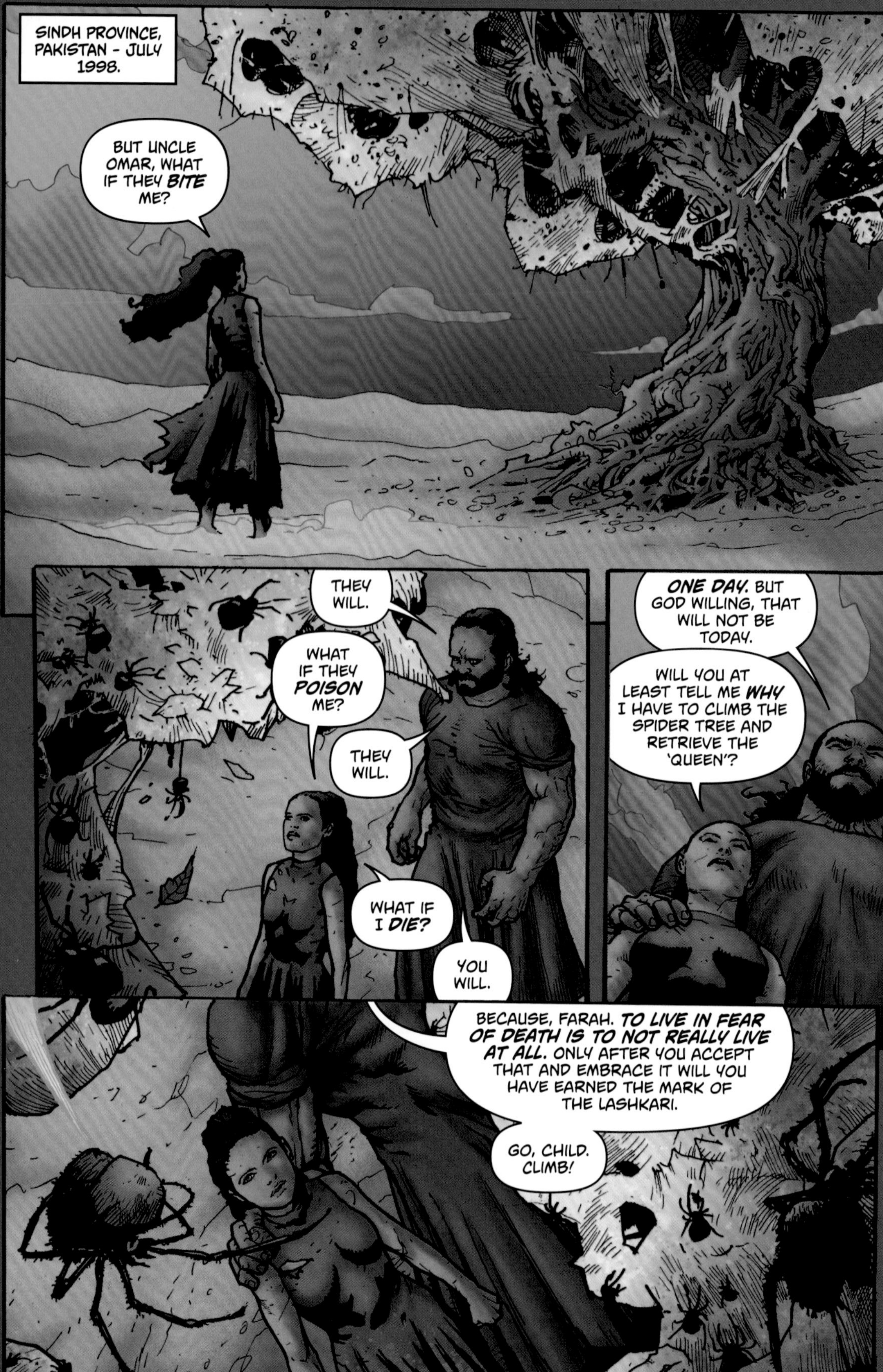
SINDH PROVINCE, PAKISTAN - JULY 1998.
BUT UNCLE OMAR, WHAT IF THEY BITE ME?
THEY WILL.
WHAT IF THEY POISON ME?
THEY WILL.
WHAT IF I DIE?
YOU WILL.
ONE DAY. BUT GOD WILLING, THAT WILL NOT BE TODAY.
WILL YOU AT LEAST TELL ME WHY I HAVE TO CLIMB THE SPIDER TREE AND RETRIEVE THE 'QUEEN'?
BECAUSE, FARAH. TO LIVE IN FEAR OF DEATH IS TO NOT REALLY LIVE AT ALL. ONLY AFTER YOU ACCEPT THAT AND EMBRACE IT WILL YOU HAVE EARNED THE MARK OF THE LASHKARI.
GO, CHILD. CLIMB!

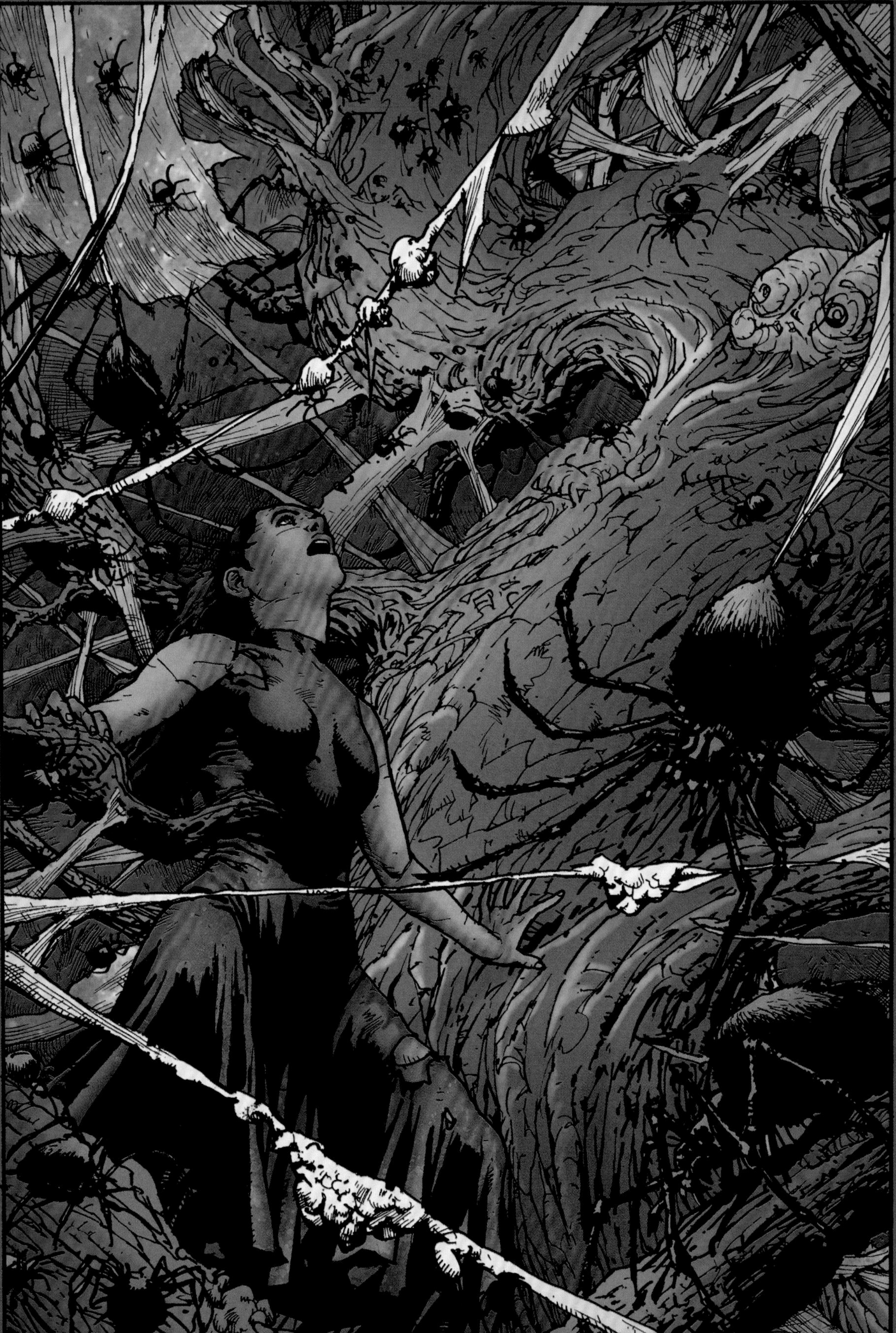

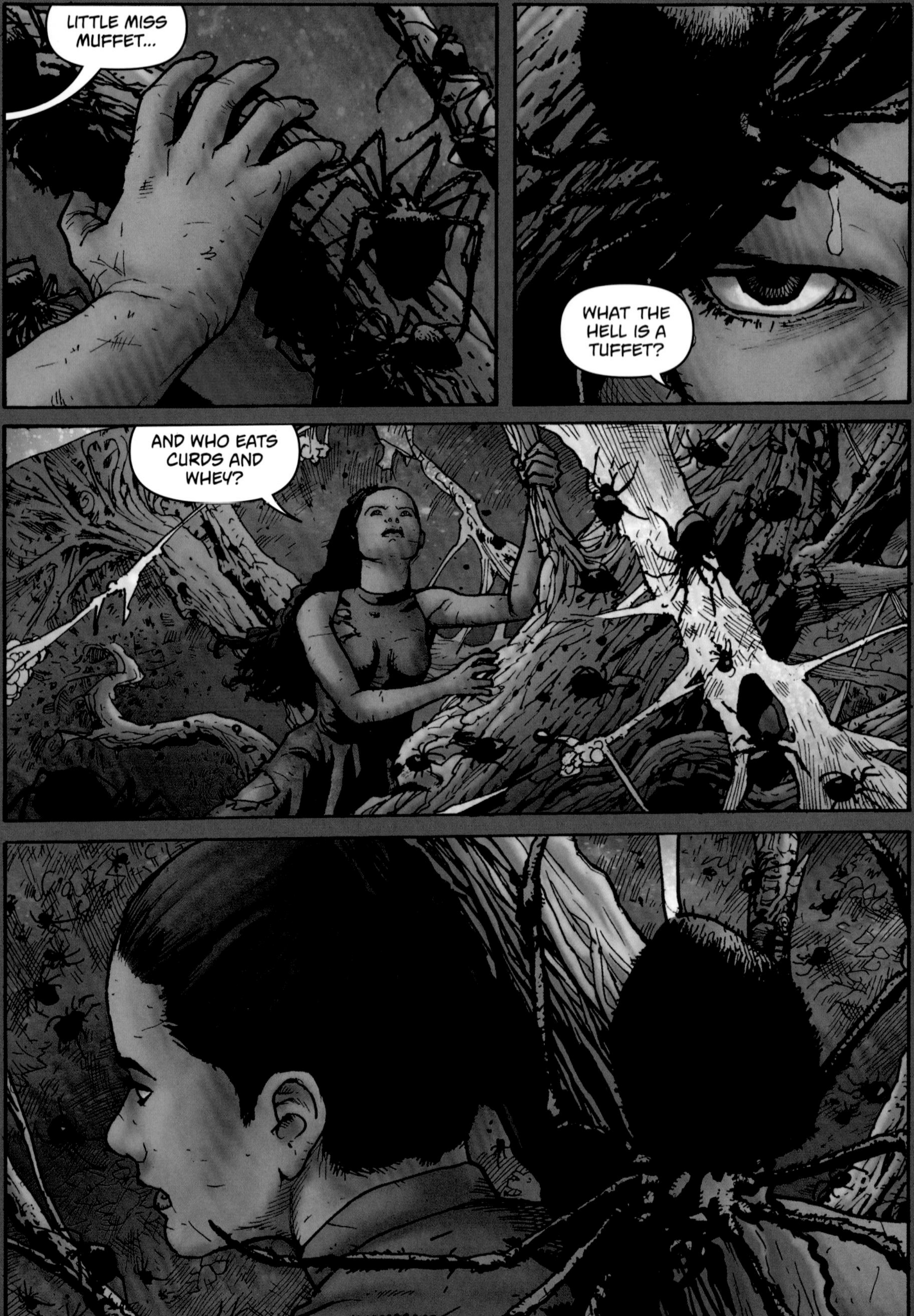
LITTLE MISS MUFFET...
WHAT THE HELL IS A TUFFET?
AND WHO EATS CURDS AND WHEY?

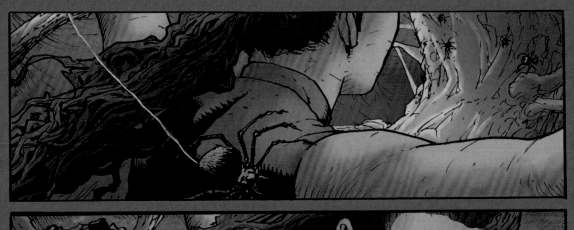

ALONG CAME A SPIDER...

WHO SAT DOWN BESIDE HER...

THAT'S WHAT HAPPENS WHEN YOU FUCK WITH MISS MUFFET.

SPLAT!

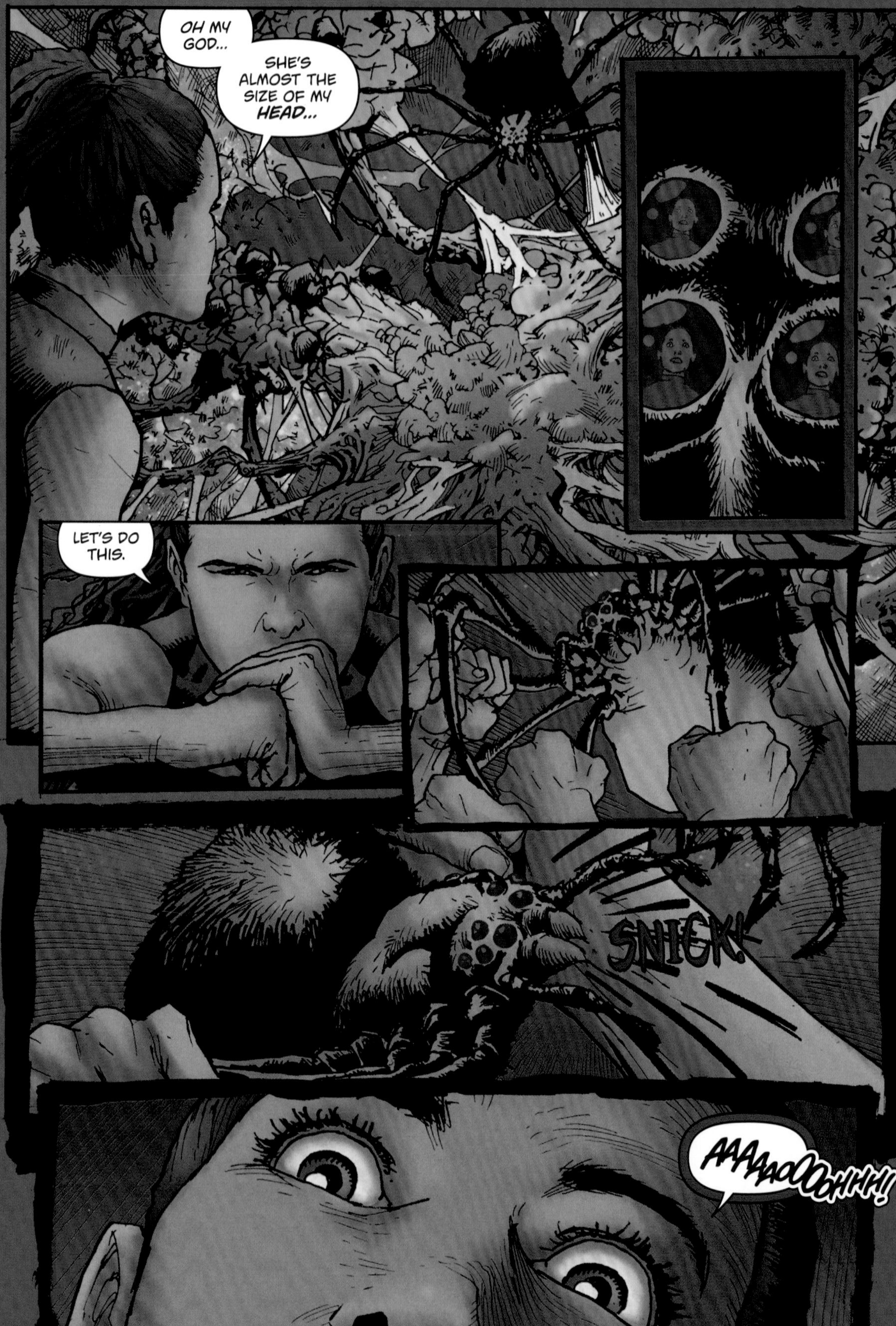
OH MY GOD...
SHE'S ALMOST THE SIZE OF MY HEAD...
LET'S DO THIS.
SNICK!
AAAAAOOOOHHH!!

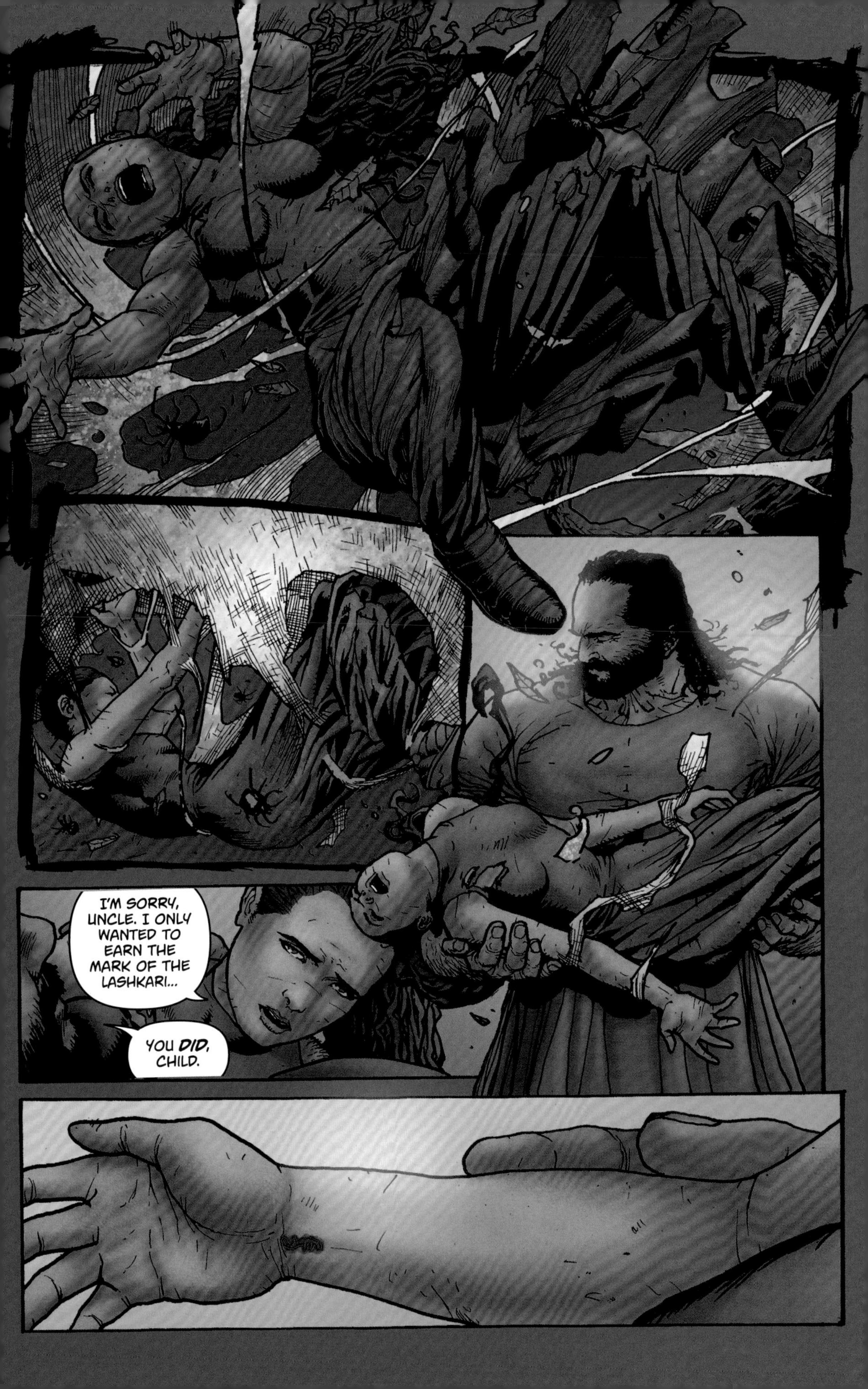
I'M SORRY, UNCLE. I ONLY WANTED TO EARN THE MARK OF THE LASHKARI...
YOU DID, CHILD.

MARCH 2002...

TO LIVE IN FEAR OF DEATH IS TO NOT REALLY LIVE AT ALL, MR. LINDERMAN.

SUPPOSE I'LL HAVE TO TAKE YOUR WORD FOR IT. NOW SHALL WE BE GOING?

JUST STAY BEHIND ME. I'LL CLEAR A PATH.

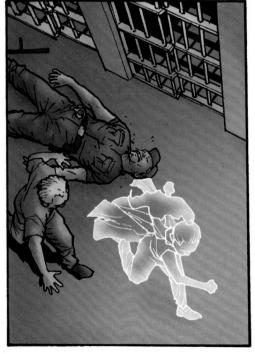

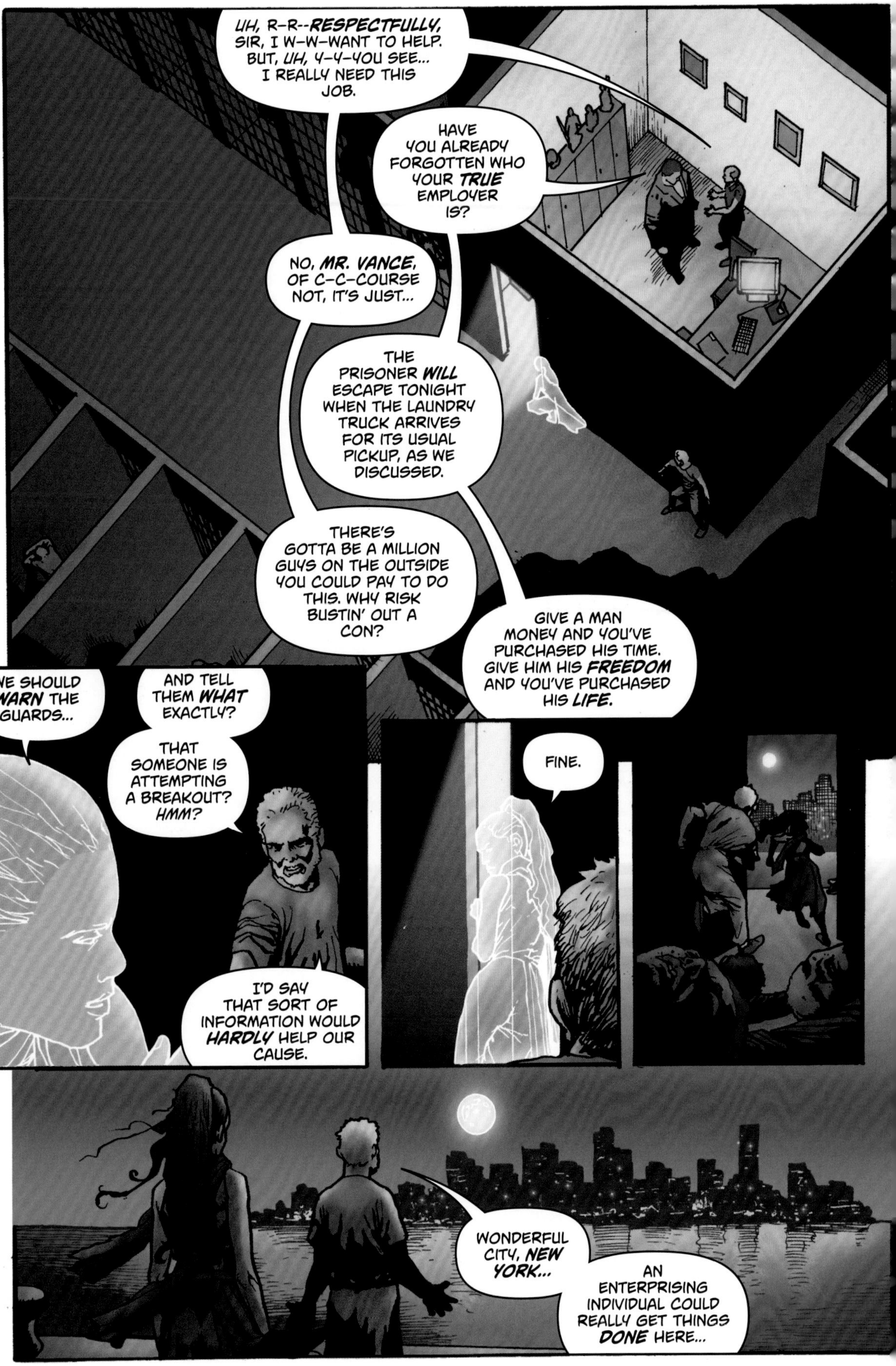
UH, R-R--RESPECTFULLY, SIR, I W-W-WANT TO HELP. BUT, UH, Y-Y-YOU SEE... I REALLY NEED THIS JOB.
HAVE YOU ALREADY FORGOTTEN WHO YOUR TRUE EMPLOYER IS?
NO, MR. VANCE, OF C-C-COURSE NOT, IT'S JUST...
THE PRISONER WILL ESCAPE TONIGHT WHEN THE LAUNDRY TRUCK ARRIVES FOR ITS USUAL PICKUP, AS WE DISCUSSED.
THERE'S GOTTA BE A MILLION GUYS ON THE OUTSIDE YOU COULD PAY TO DO THIS. WHY RISK BUSTIN' OUT A CON?
GIVE A MAN MONEY AND YOU'VE PURCHASED HIS TIME. GIVE HIM HIS FREEDOM AND YOU'VE PURCHASED HIS LIFE.
WE SHOULD WARN THE GUARDS...
AND TELL THEM WHAT EXACTLY?
THAT SOMEONE IS ATTEMPTING A BREAKOUT? HMM?
I'D SAY THAT SORT OF INFORMATION WOULD HARDLY HELP OUR CAUSE.
FINE.
WONDERFUL CITY, NEW YORK...
AN ENTERPRISING INDIVIDUAL COULD REALLY GET THINGS DONE HERE...

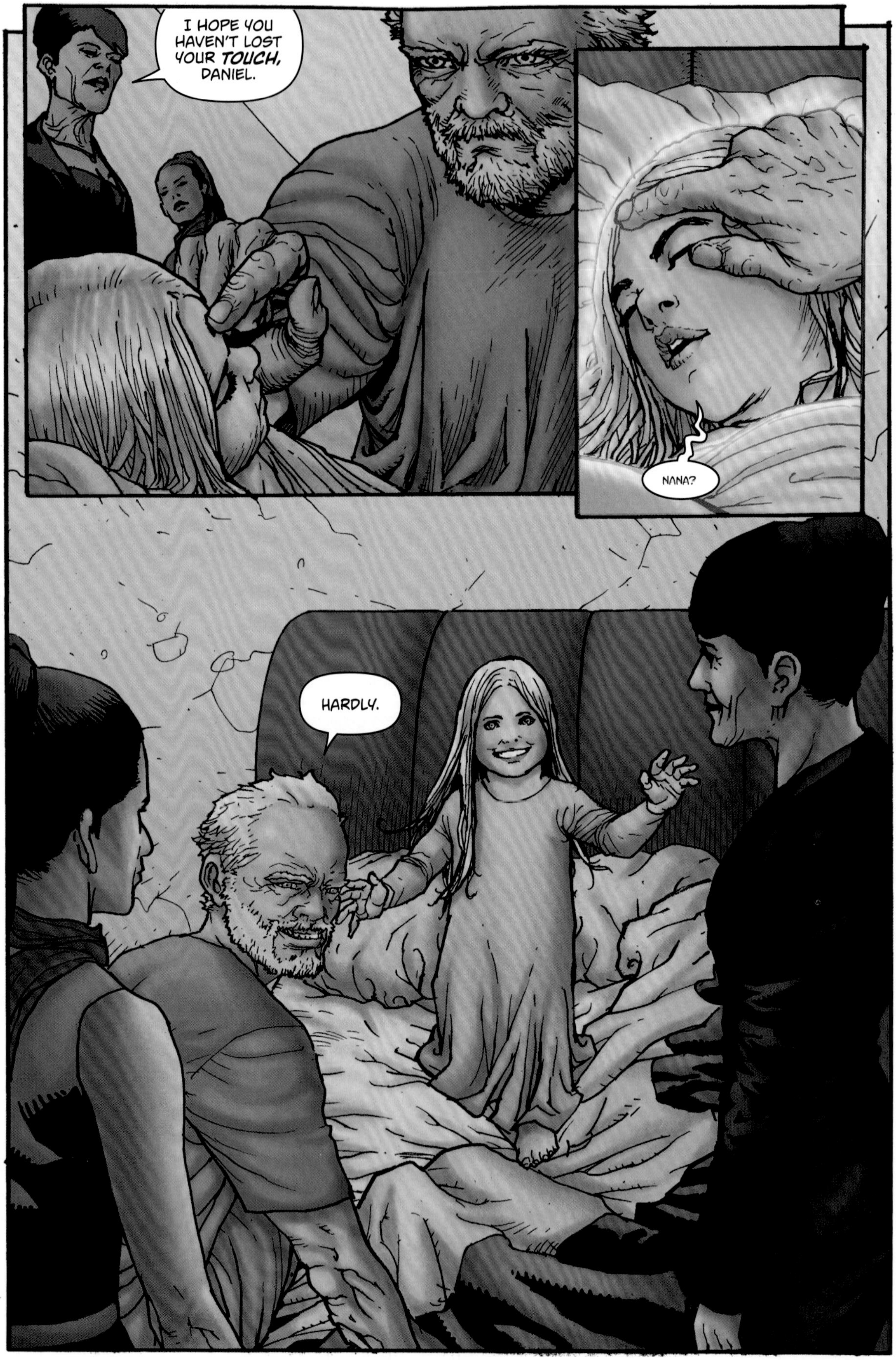
I HOPE YOU HAVEN'T LOST YOUR TOUCH, DANIEL.
NANA?
HARDLY.

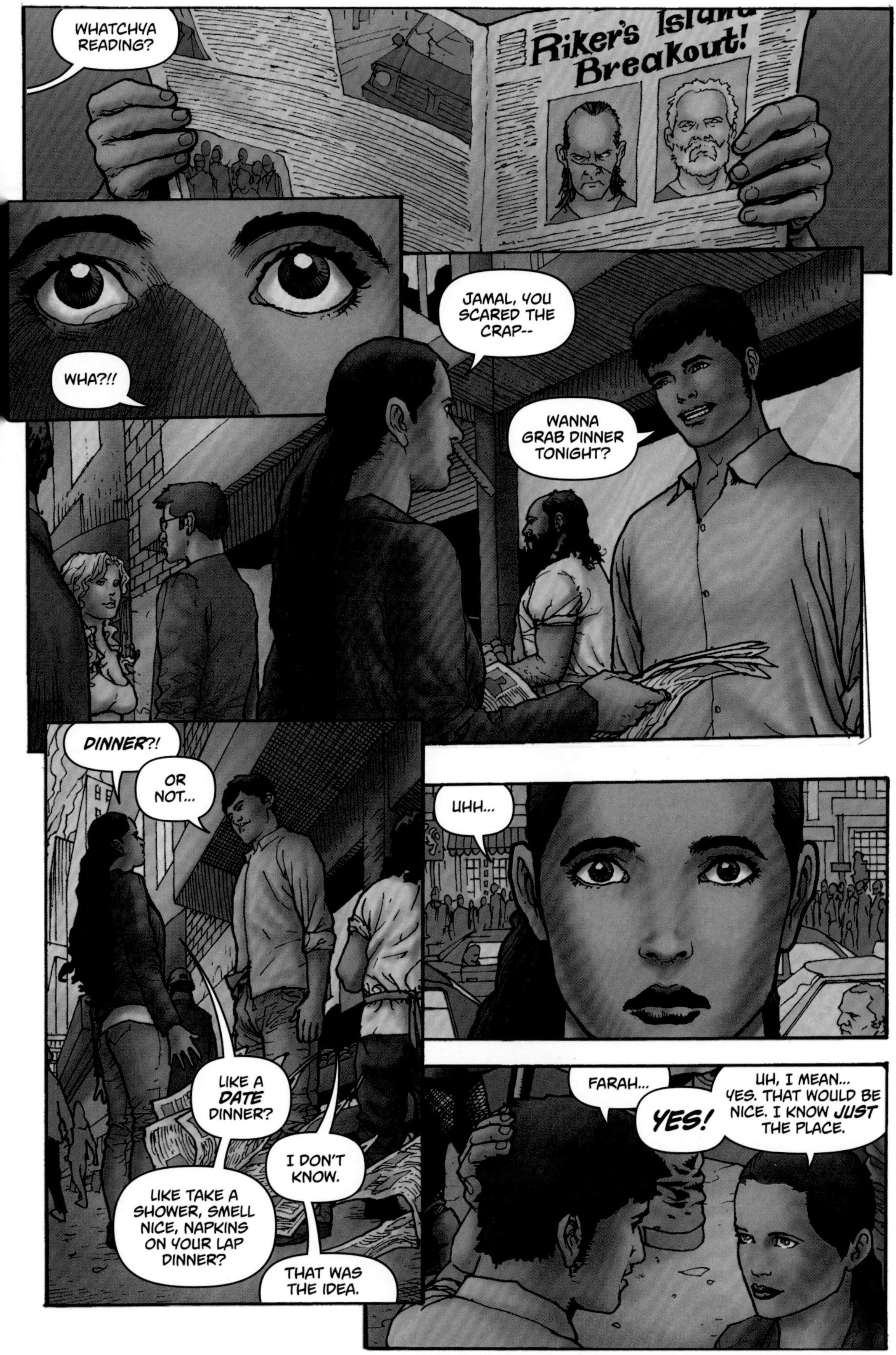
WHATCHYA READING?
Riker's Island Breakout!
WHA?!!
JAMAL, YOU SCARED THE CRAP--
WANNA GRAB DINNER TONIGHT?
DINNER?!
OR NOT...
LIKE A DATE DINNER?
LIKE TAKE A SHOWER, SMELL NICE, NAPKINS ON YOUR LAP DINNER?
I DON'T KNOW.
THAT WAS THE IDEA.
UHH...
FARAH...
YES!
UH, I MEAN... YES. THAT WOULD BE NICE. I KNOW JUST THE PLACE.

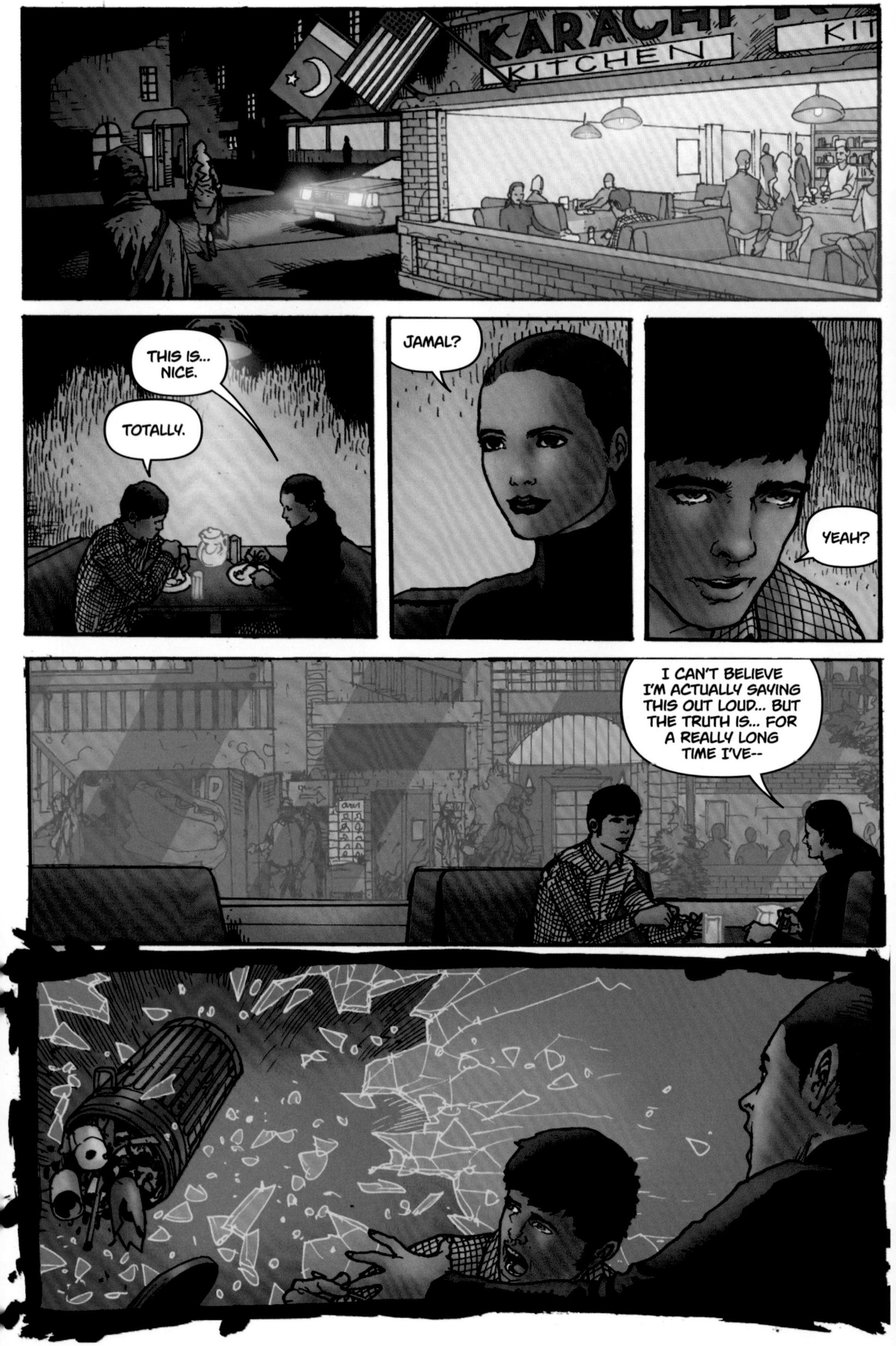
KARACHI
KITCHEN
THIS IS... NICE.
TOTALLY.
JAMAL?
YEAH?
I CAN'T BELIEVE I'M ACTUALLY SAYING THIS OUT LOUD... BUT THE TRUTH IS... FOR A REALLY LONG TIME I'VE--

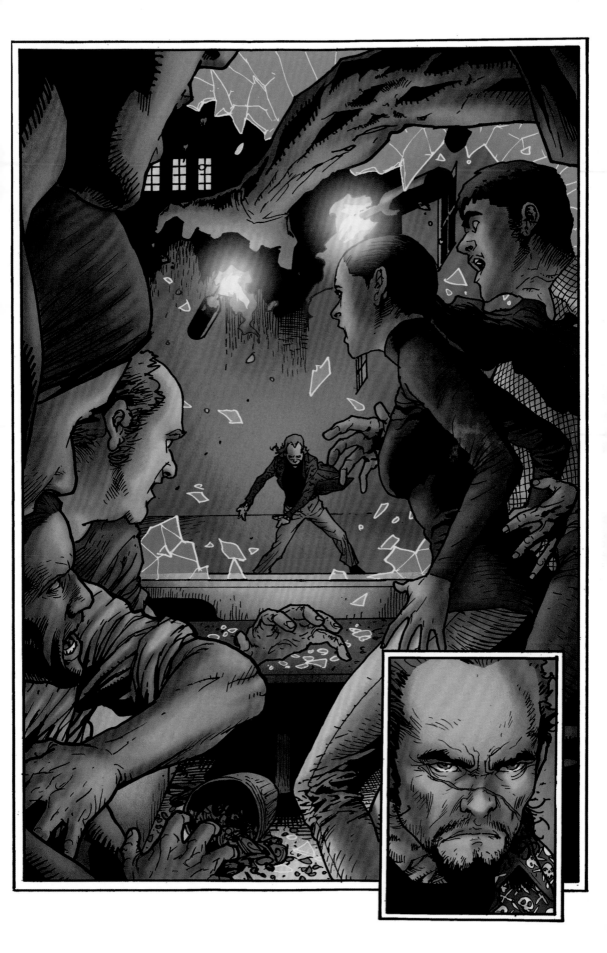

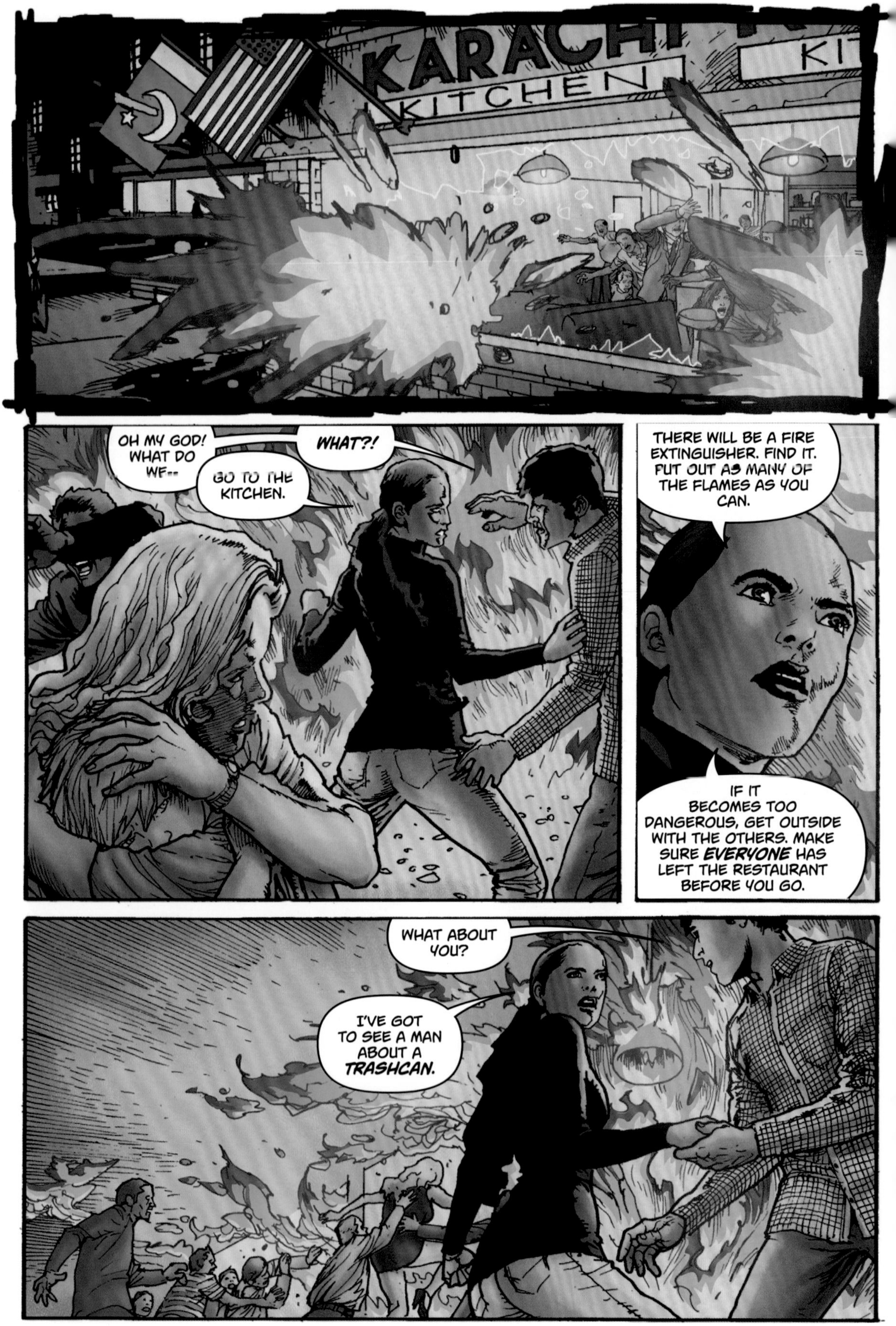
KARACHI
KITCHEN
OH MY GOD! WHAT DO WE--
WHAT?!
GO TO THE KITCHEN.
THERE WILL BE A FIRE EXTINGUISHER. FIND IT. PUT OUT AS MANY OF THE FLAMES AS YOU CAN.
IF IT BECOMES TOO DANGEROUS, GET OUTSIDE WITH THE OTHERS. MAKE SURE *EVERYONE* HAS LEFT THE RESTAURANT BEFORE YOU GO.
WHAT ABOUT YOU?
I'VE GOT TO SEE A MAN ABOUT A *TRASHCAN.*

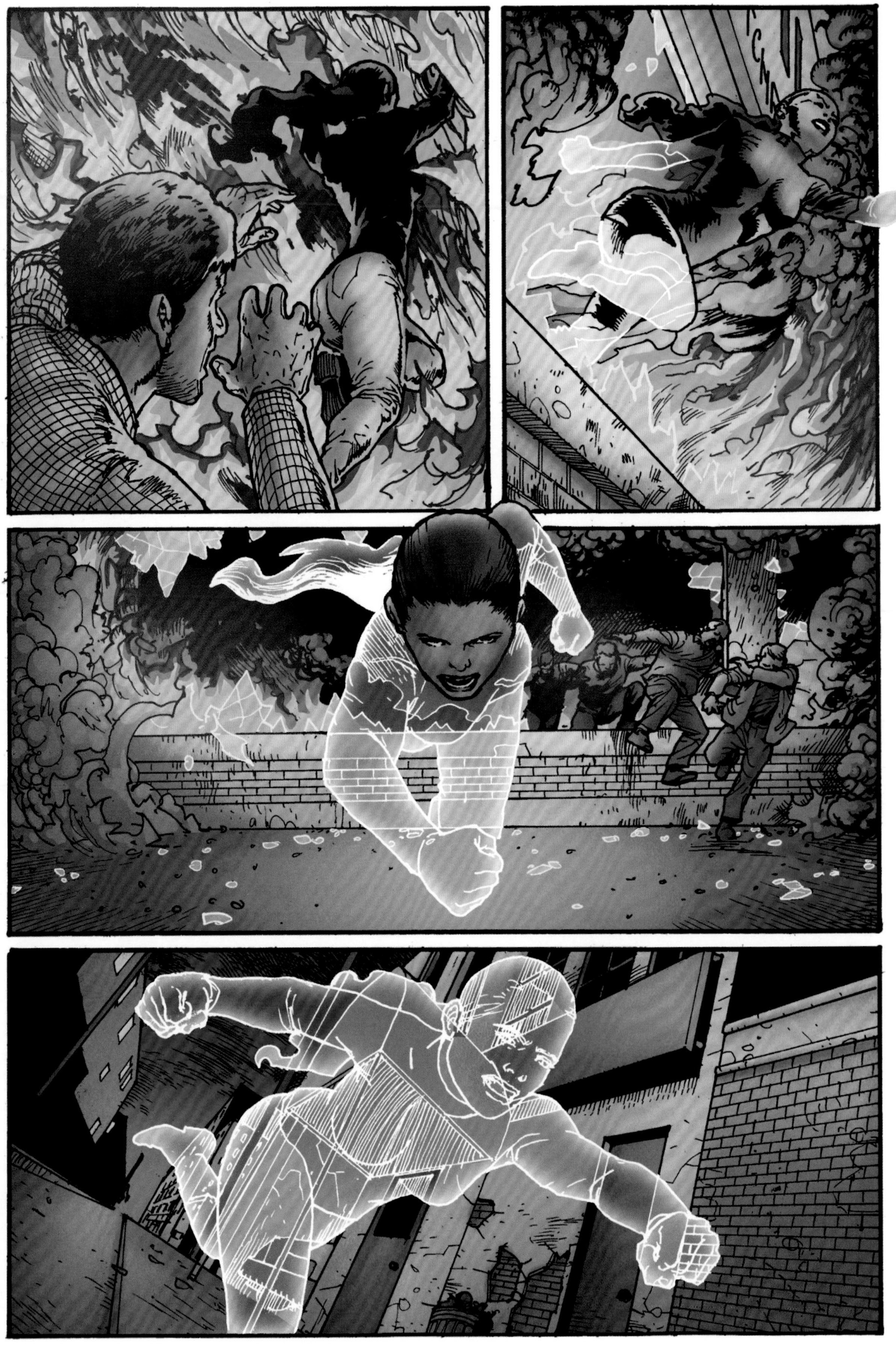

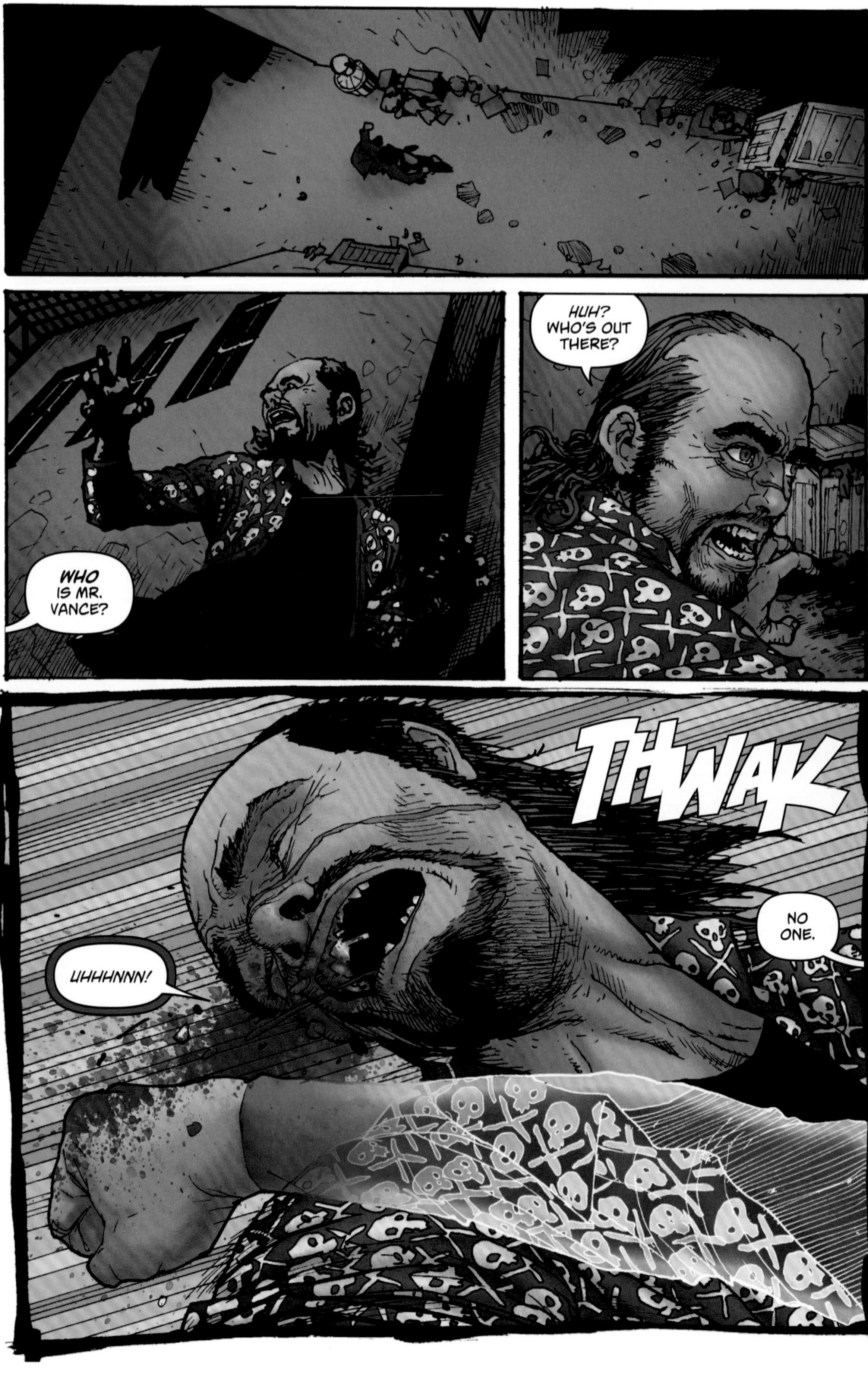
WHO IS MR. VANCE?
HUH? WHO'S OUT THERE?
THWAK
NO ONE.
UHHHNNN!

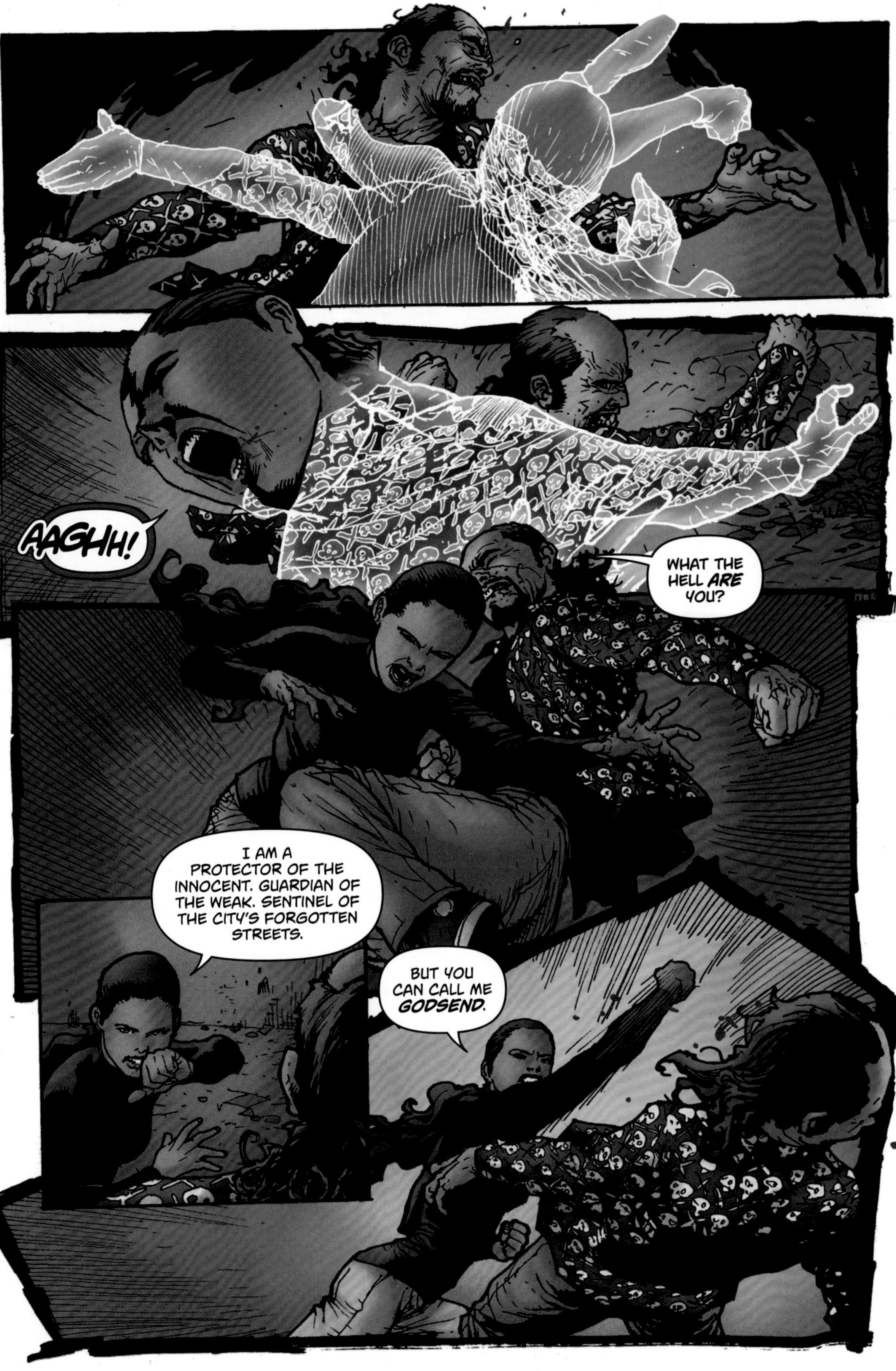
AAGHH!
WHAT THE HELL ARE YOU?
I AM A PROTECTOR OF THE INNOCENT. GUARDIAN OF THE WEAK. SENTINEL OF THE CITY'S FORGOTTEN STREETS.
BUT YOU CAN CALL ME GODSEND.

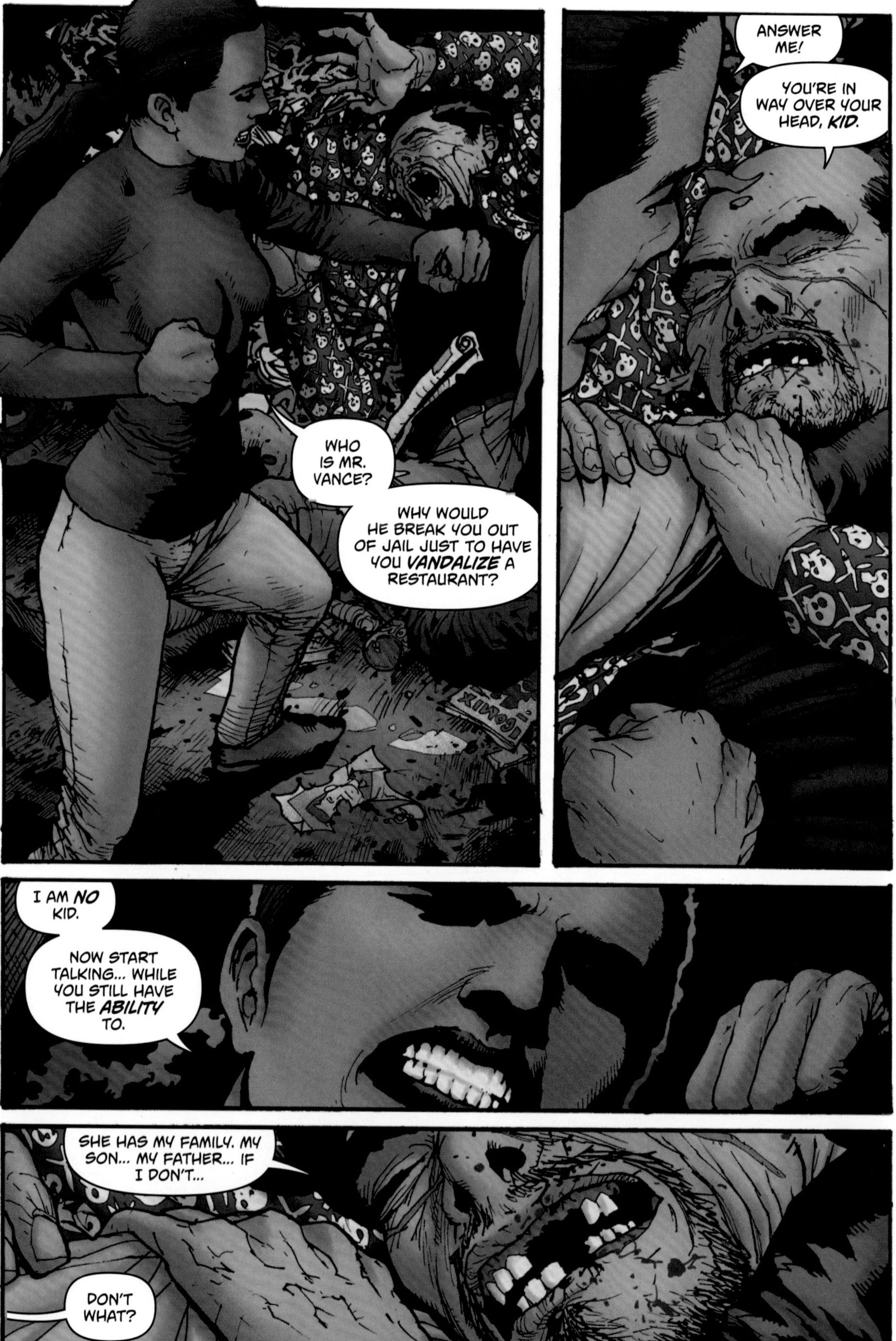
WHO IS MR. VANCE?
WHY WOULD HE BREAK YOU OUT OF JAIL JUST TO HAVE YOU VANDALIZE A RESTAURANT?
ANSWER ME!
YOU'RE IN WAY OVER YOUR HEAD, KID.
I AM NO KID.
NOW START TALKING... WHILE YOU STILL HAVE THE ABILITY TO.
SHE HAS MY FAMILY. MY SON... MY FATHER... IF I DON'T...
DON'T WHAT?

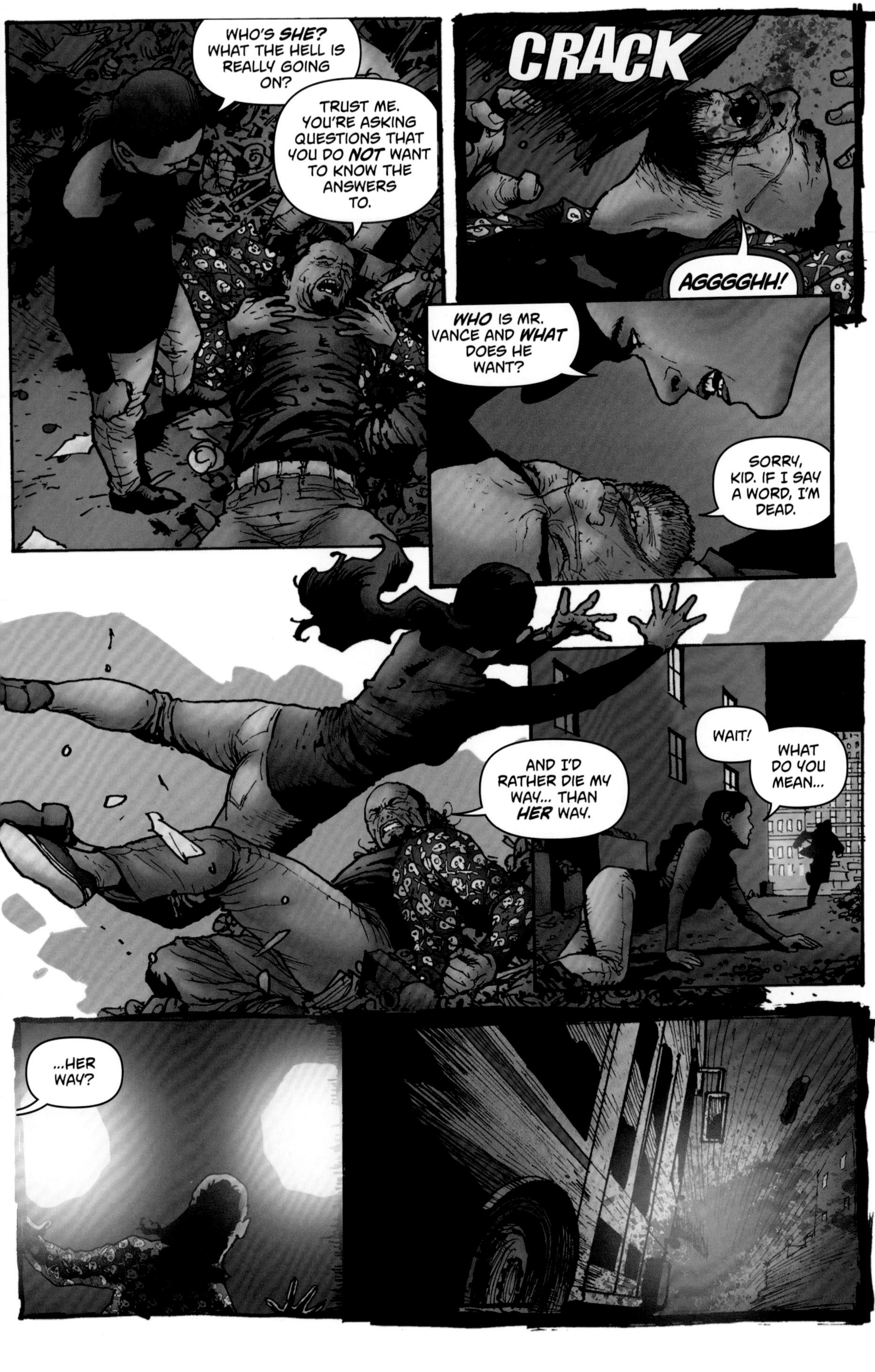
WHO'S SHE? WHAT THE HELL IS REALLY GOING ON?
TRUST ME. YOU'RE ASKING QUESTIONS THAT YOU DO NOT WANT TO KNOW THE ANSWERS TO.
CRACK
AGGGGHH!
WHO IS MR. VANCE AND WHAT DOES HE WANT?
SORRY, KID. IF I SAY A WORD, I'M DEAD.
AND I'D RATHER DIE MY WAY... THAN HER WAY.
WAIT!
WHAT DO YOU MEAN...
...HER WAY?

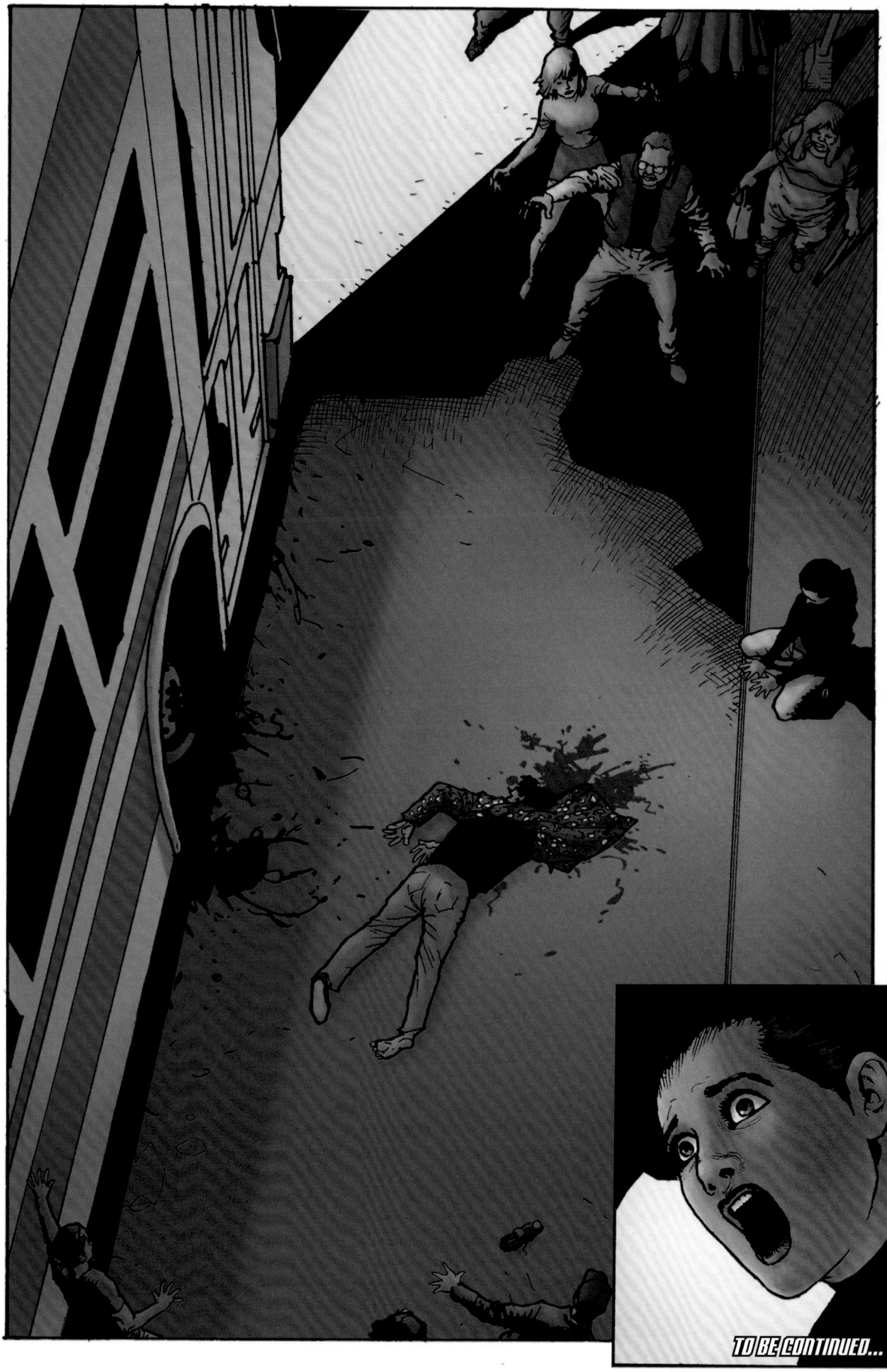
TO BE CONTINUED...

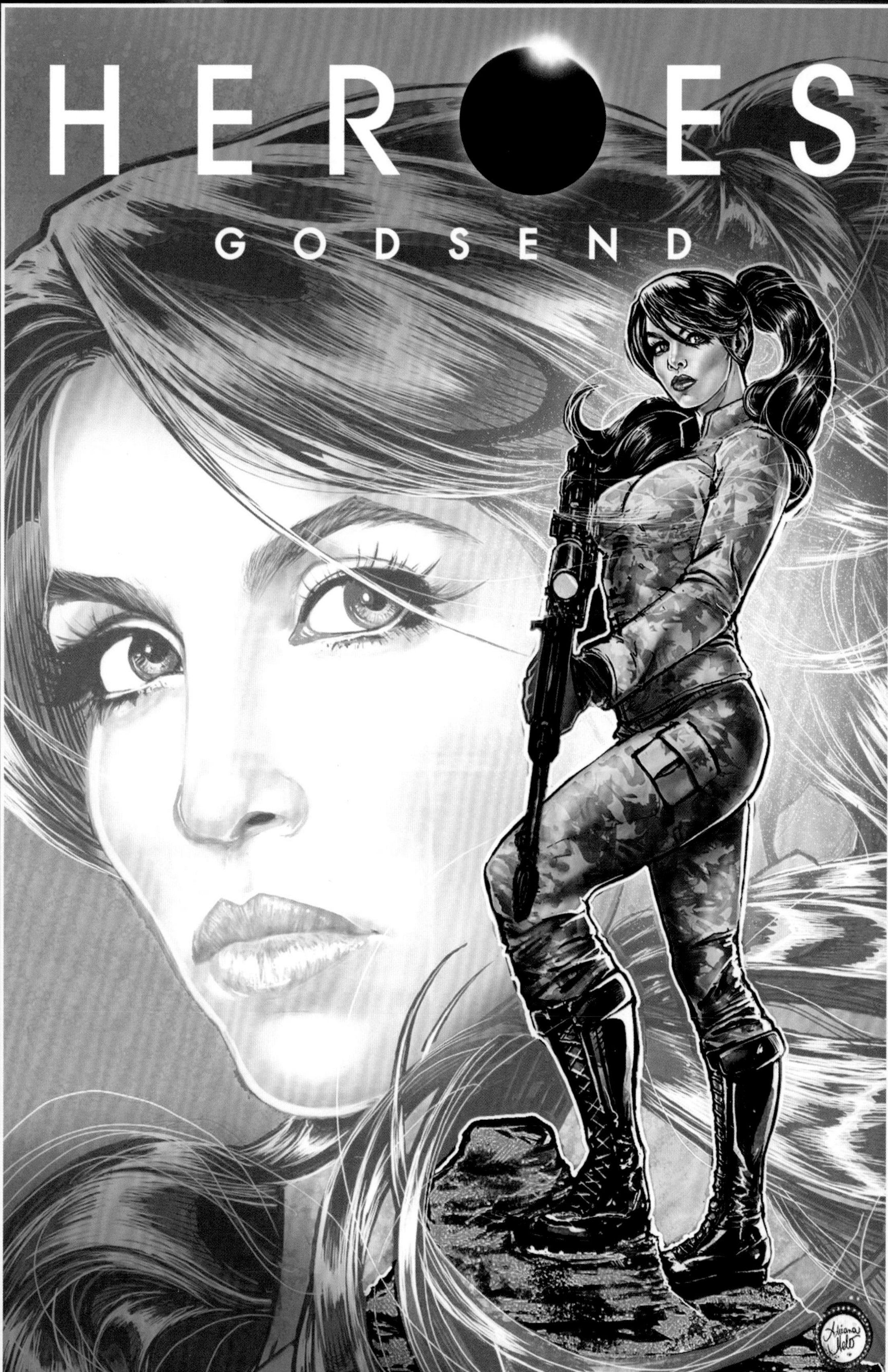
HEROES
GODSEND

#3 VARIANT COVER
ARTWORK BY ADRIANA MELO

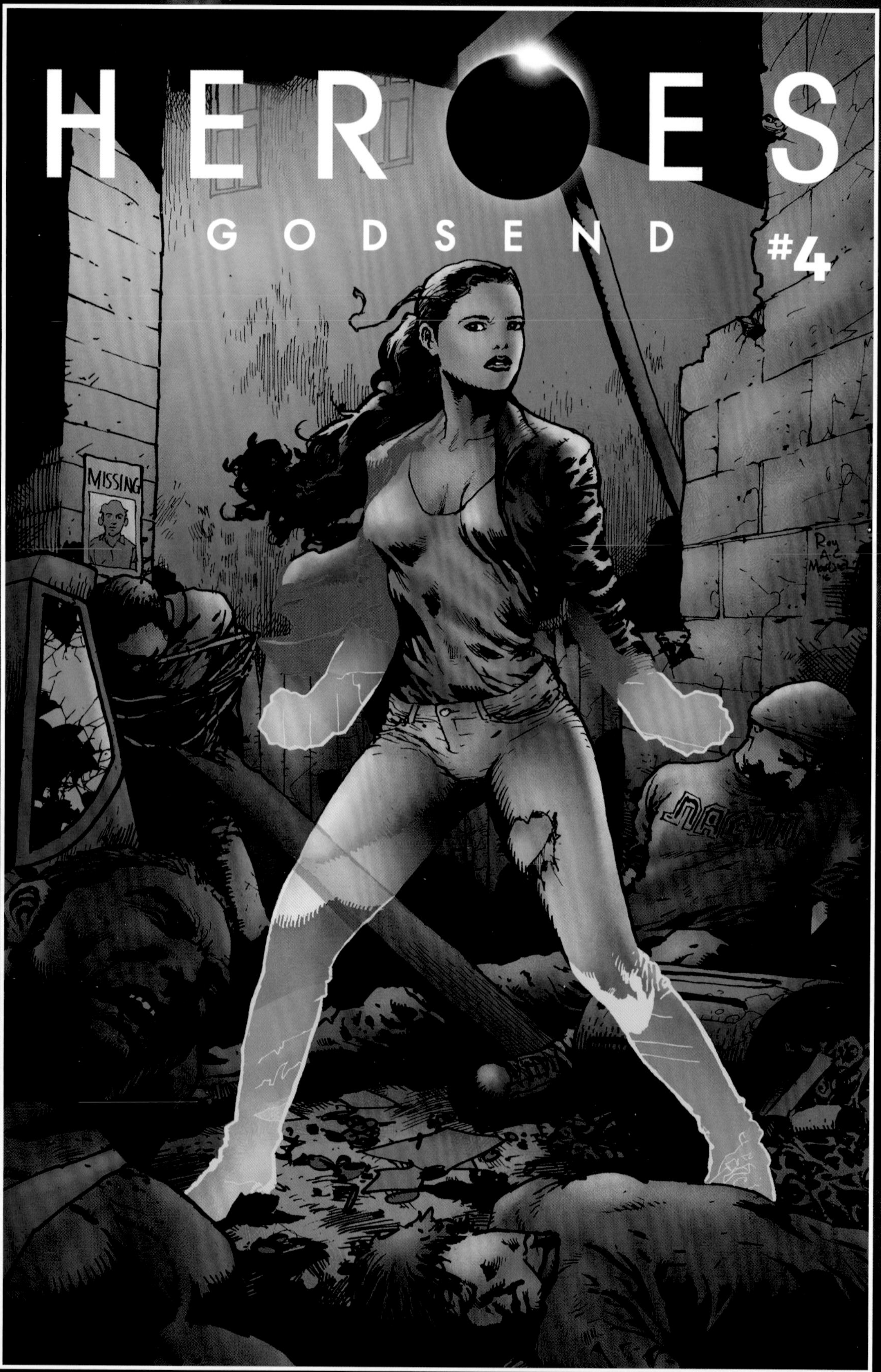
HEROES
GODSEND
#4
MISSING

#4 MAIN COVER

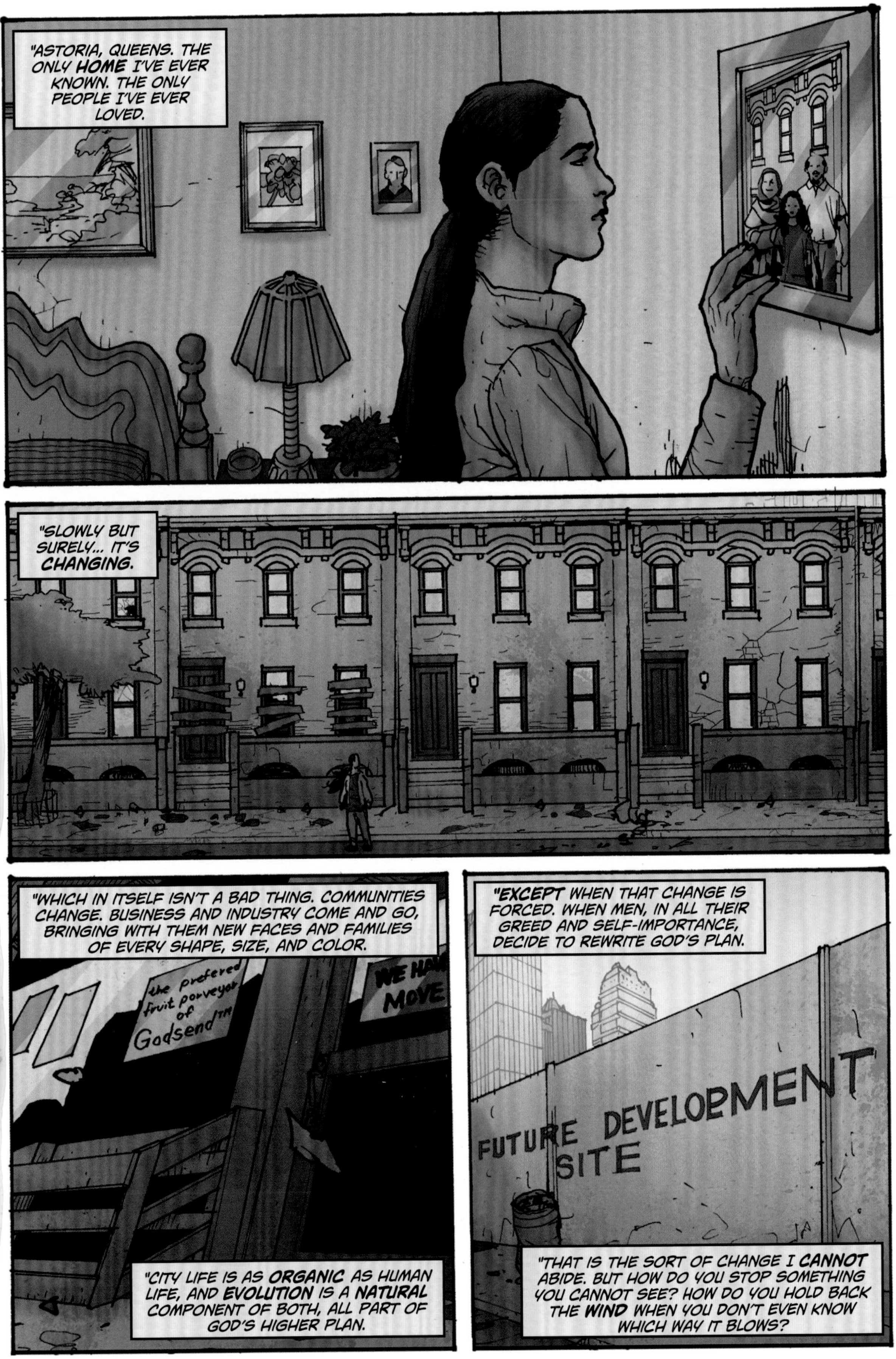
"ASTORIA, QUEENS. THE ONLY HOME I'VE EVER KNOWN. THE ONLY PEOPLE I'VE EVER LOVED.
"SLOWLY BUT SURELY... IT'S CHANGING.
"WHICH IN ITSELF ISN'T A BAD THING. COMMUNITIES CHANGE. BUSINESS AND INDUSTRY COME AND GO, BRINGING WITH THEM NEW FACES AND FAMILIES OF EVERY SHAPE, SIZE, AND COLOR.
the prefered fruit porveyor of Godsend™
WE HA MOVE
"CITY LIFE IS AS ORGANIC AS HUMAN LIFE, AND EVOLUTION IS A NATURAL COMPONENT OF BOTH, ALL PART OF GOD'S HIGHER PLAN.
"EXCEPT WHEN THAT CHANGE IS FORCED. WHEN MEN, IN ALL THEIR GREED AND SELF-IMPORTANCE, DECIDE TO REWRITE GOD'S PLAN.
FUTURE DEVELOPMENT SITE
"THAT IS THE SORT OF CHANGE I CANNOT ABIDE. BUT HOW DO YOU STOP SOMETHING YOU CANNOT SEE? HOW DO YOU HOLD BACK THE WIND WHEN YOU DON'T EVEN KNOW WHICH WAY IT BLOWS?

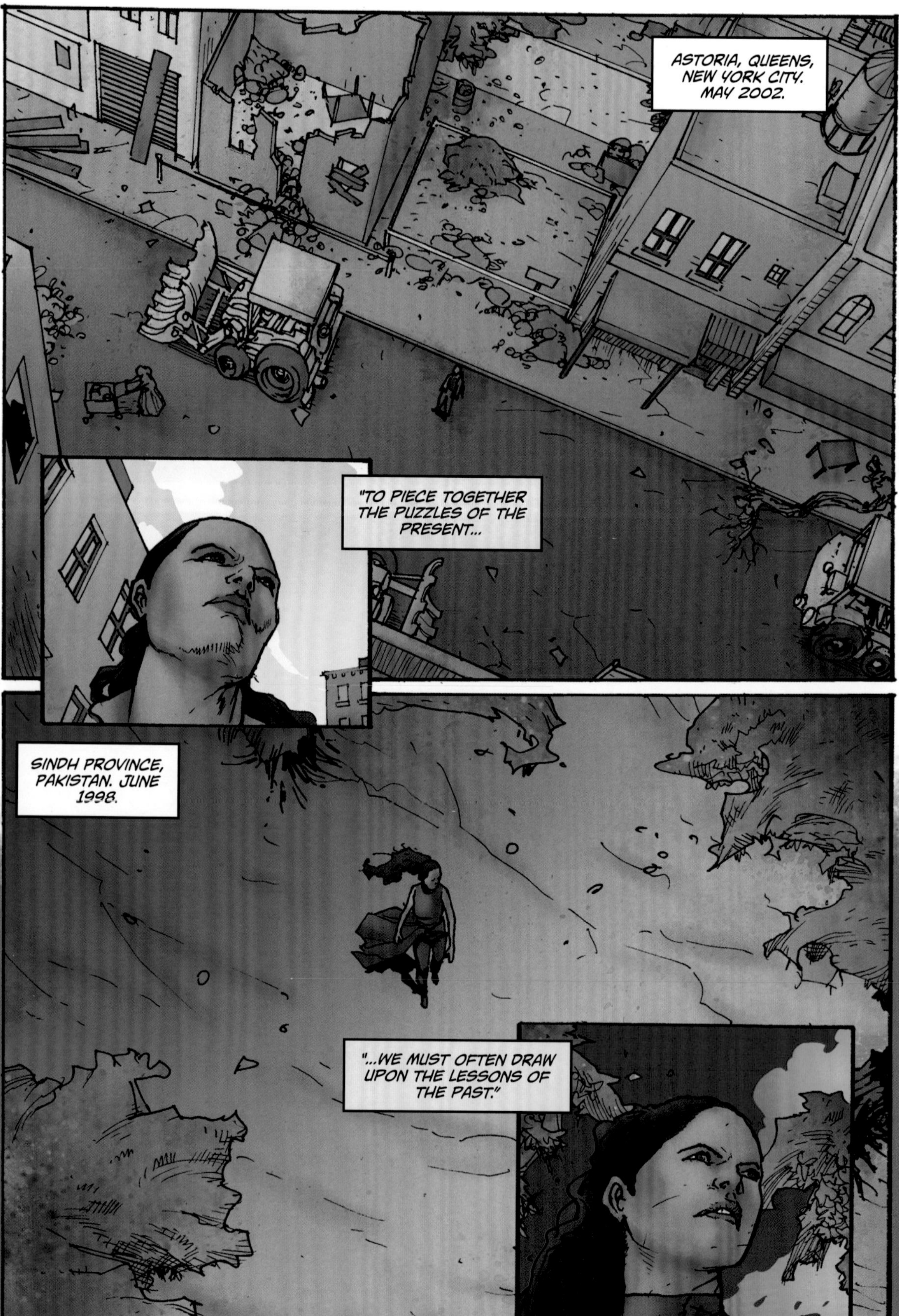
ASTORIA, QUEENS, NEW YORK CITY. MAY 2002.
"TO PIECE TOGETHER THE PUZZLES OF THE PRESENT...
SINDH PROVINCE, PAKISTAN. JUNE 1998.
"...WE MUST OFTEN DRAW UPON THE LESSONS OF THE PAST."

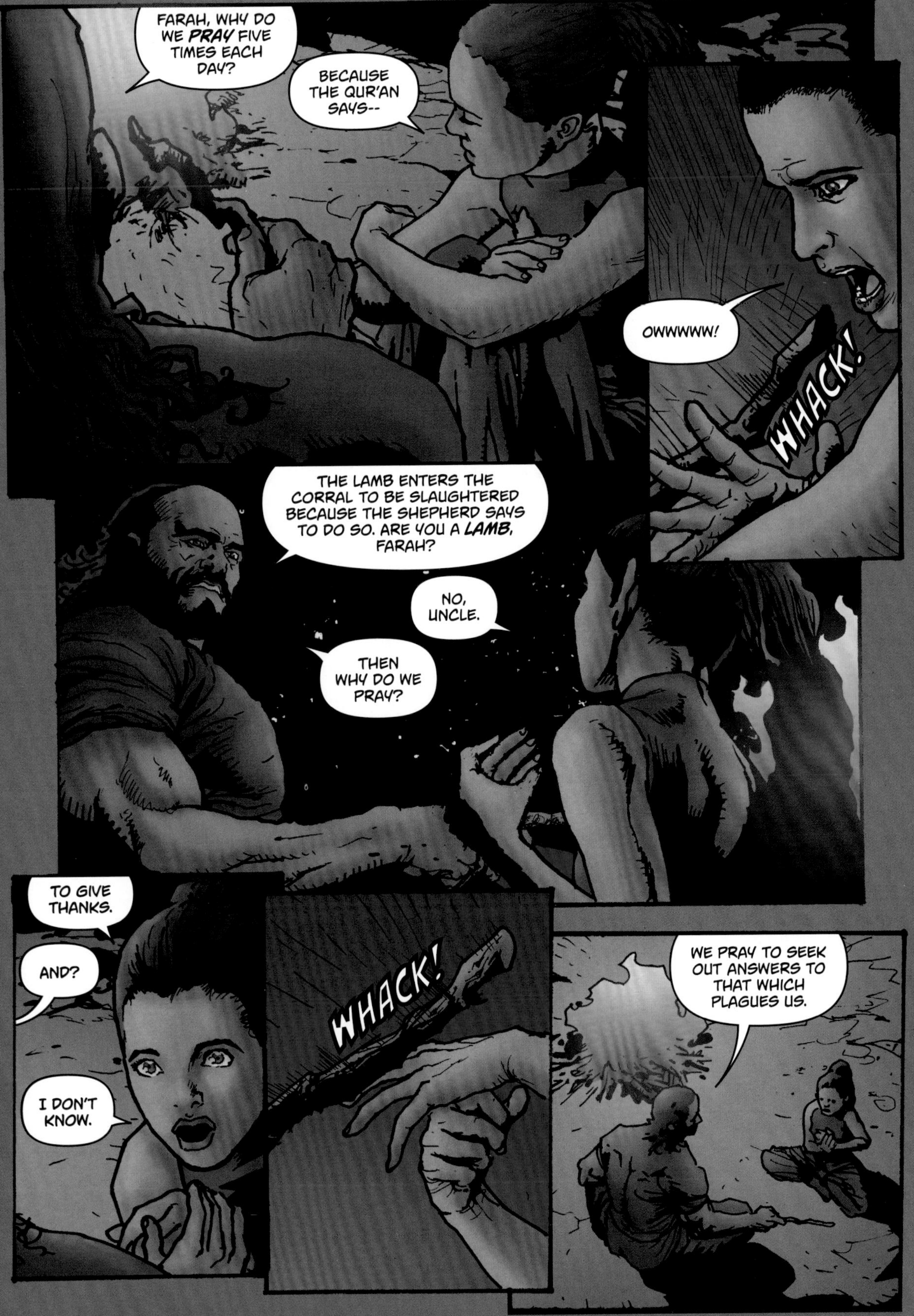
FARAH, WHY DO WE PRAY FIVE TIMES EACH DAY?
BECAUSE THE QUR'AN SAYS--
OWWWWW!
WHACK!
THE LAMB ENTERS THE CORRAL TO BE SLAUGHTERED BECAUSE THE SHEPHERD SAYS TO DO SO. ARE YOU A LAMB, FARAH?
NO, UNCLE.
THEN WHY DO WE PRAY?
TO GIVE THANKS.
AND?
I DON'T KNOW.
WHACK!
WE PRAY TO SEEK OUT ANSWERS TO THAT WHICH PLAGUES US.

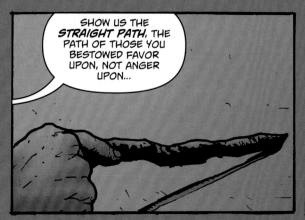

SHOW US THE **STRAIGHT PATH**, THE PATH OF THOSE YOU BESTOWED FAVOR UPON, NOT ANGER UPON...

...AND NOT OF THOSE WHO GO ASTRAY.

DO NOT BE THE LAMB, CHILD. BE THE **SHEPHERD**. BUT REMEMBER THAT EVEN THE SHEPHERD MUST OFTEN LOOK UP AND ASK FOR DIRECTION.

YES, UNCLE OMAR.

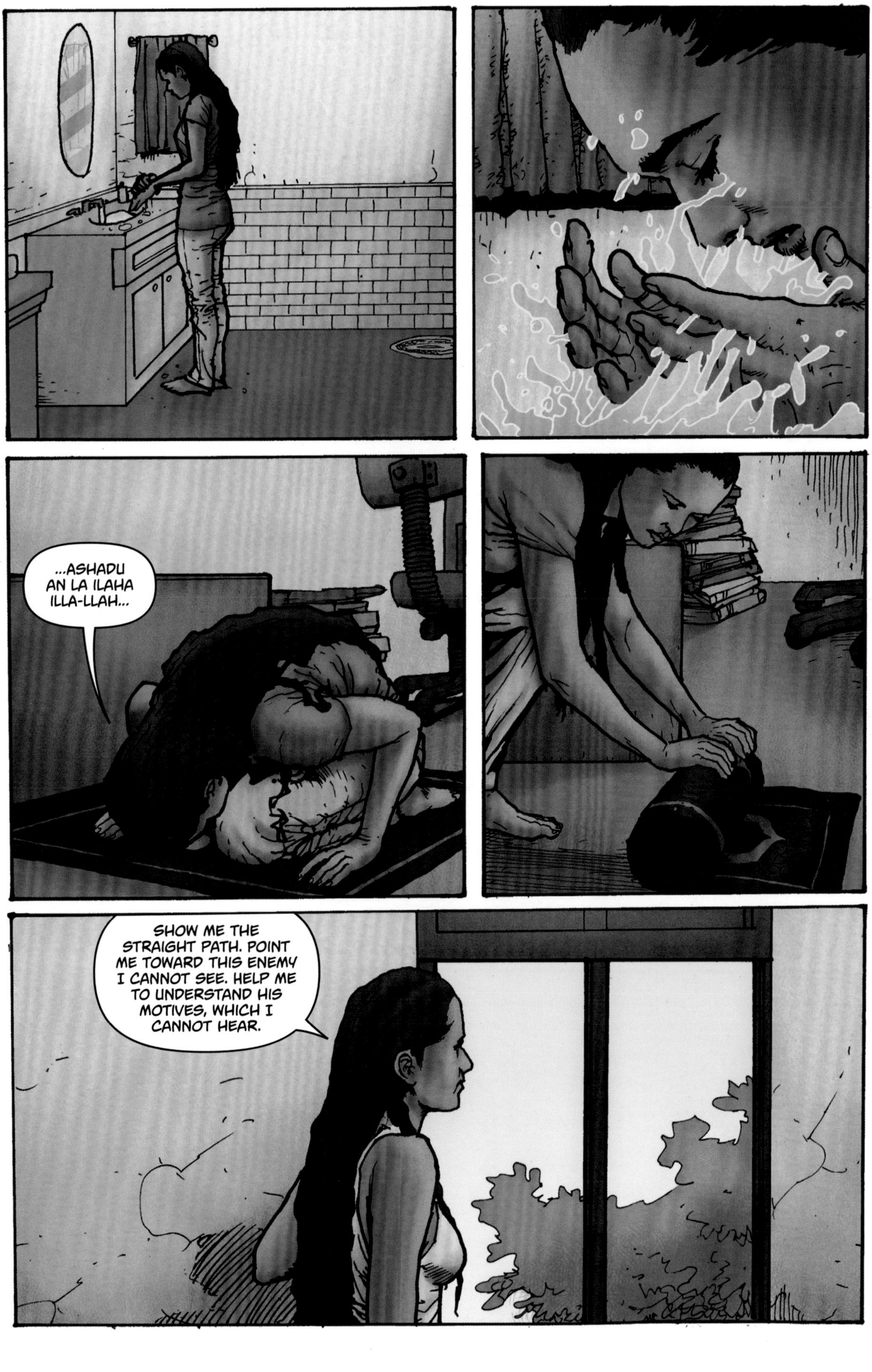
...ASHADU AN LA ILAHA ILLA-LLAH...
SHOW ME THE STRAIGHT PATH. POINT ME TOWARD THIS ENEMY I CANNOT SEE. HELP ME TO UNDERSTAND HIS MOTIVES, WHICH I CANNOT HEAR.

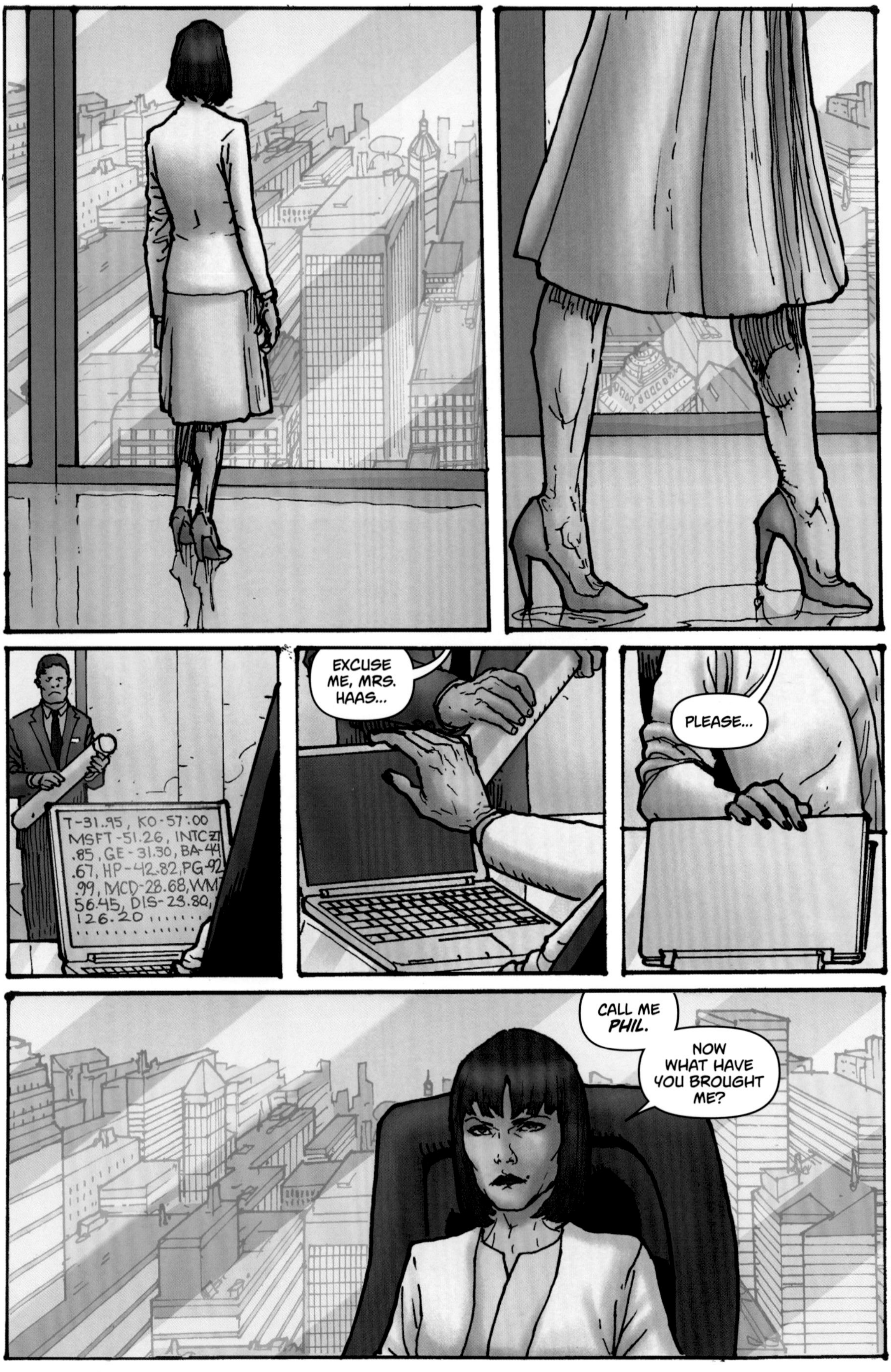
T-31.95, KO-57.00
MSFT-51.26, INTC
.85, GE-31.30, BA-44
.67, HP-42.82, PG-92
.99, MCD-28.68, WM
56.45, DIS-23.80,
126.20
EXCUSE ME, MRS. HAAS...
PLEASE...
CALL ME *PHIL.*
NOW WHAT HAVE YOU BROUGHT ME?

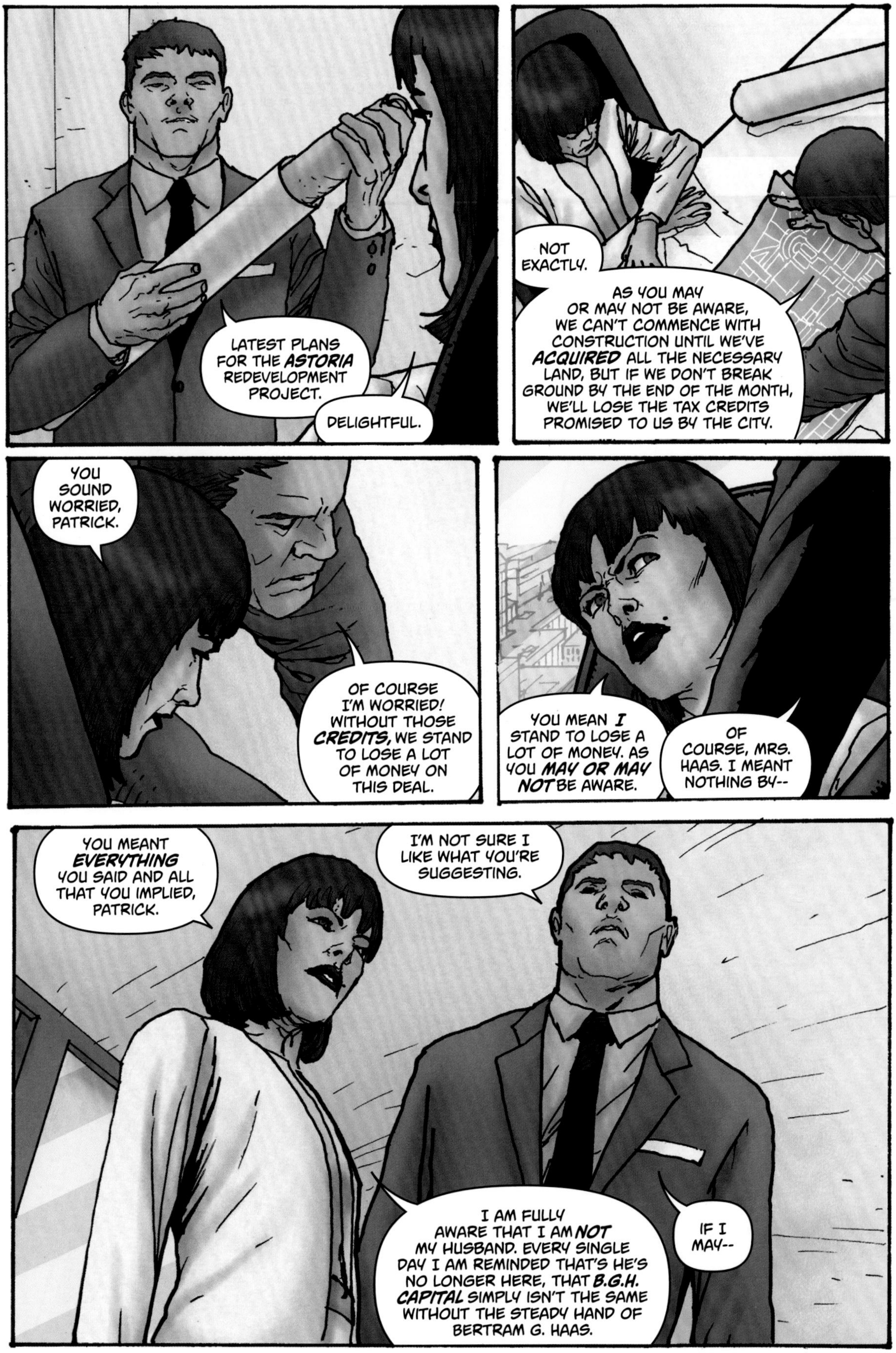
LATEST PLANS FOR THE ASTORIA REDEVELOPMENT PROJECT.
DELIGHTFUL.
NOT EXACTLY.
AS YOU MAY OR MAY NOT BE AWARE, WE CAN'T COMMENCE WITH CONSTRUCTION UNTIL WE'VE ACQUIRED ALL THE NECESSARY LAND, BUT IF WE DON'T BREAK GROUND BY THE END OF THE MONTH, WE'LL LOSE THE TAX CREDITS PROMISED TO US BY THE CITY.
YOU SOUND WORRIED, PATRICK.
OF COURSE I'M WORRIED! WITHOUT THOSE CREDITS, WE STAND TO LOSE A LOT OF MONEY ON THIS DEAL.
YOU MEAN I STAND TO LOSE A LOT OF MONEY. AS YOU MAY OR MAY NOT BE AWARE.
OF COURSE, MRS. HAAS. I MEANT NOTHING BY--
YOU MEANT EVERYTHING YOU SAID AND ALL THAT YOU IMPLIED, PATRICK.
I'M NOT SURE I LIKE WHAT YOU'RE SUGGESTING.
I AM FULLY AWARE THAT I AM NOT MY HUSBAND. EVERY SINGLE DAY I AM REMINDED THAT'S HE'S NO LONGER HERE, THAT B.G.H. CAPITAL SIMPLY ISN'T THE SAME WITHOUT THE STEADY HAND OF BERTRAM G. HAAS.
IF I MAY--

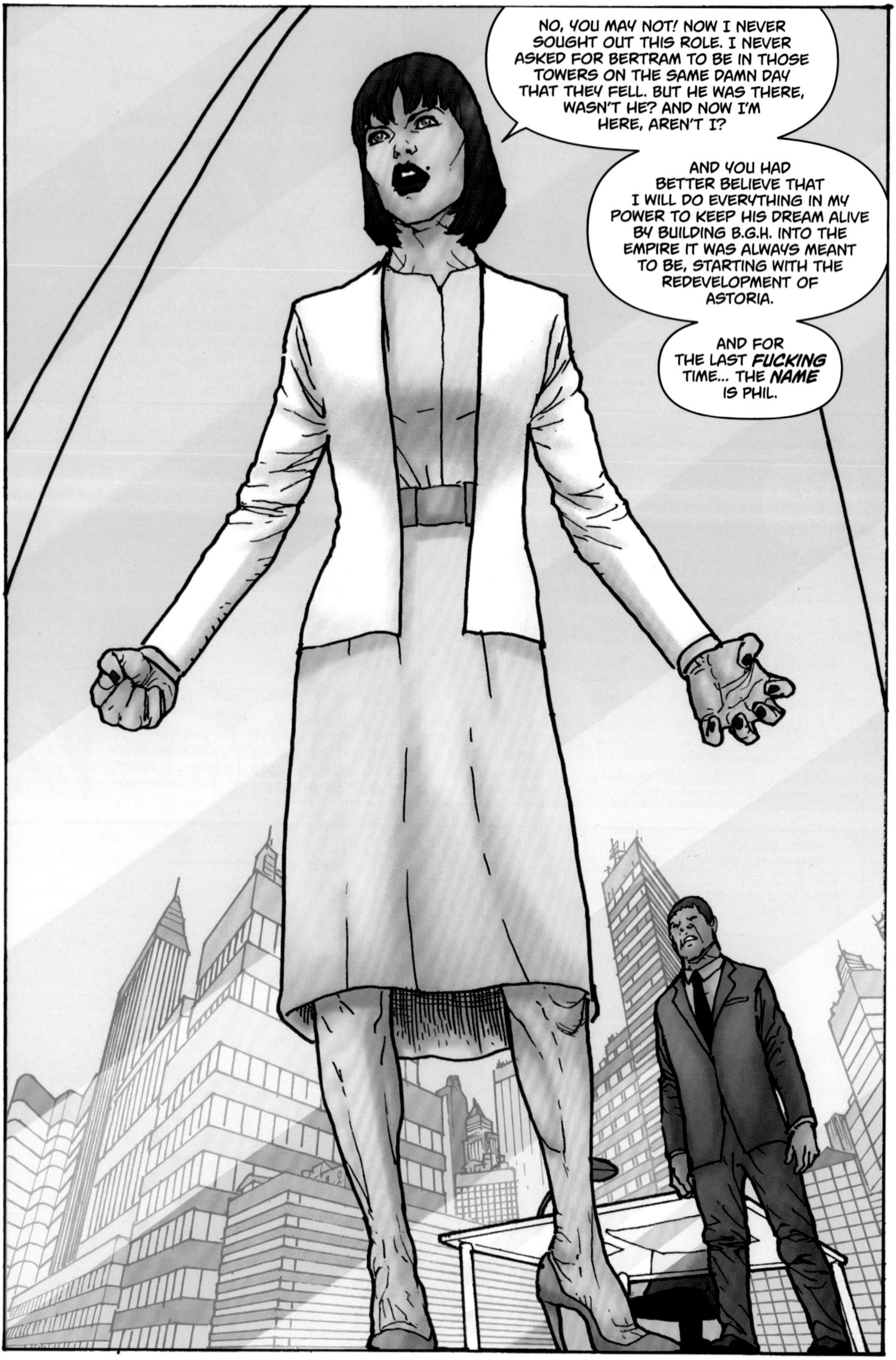
NO, YOU MAY NOT! NOW I NEVER SOUGHT OUT THIS ROLE. I NEVER ASKED FOR BERTRAM TO BE IN THOSE TOWERS ON THE SAME DAMN DAY THAT THEY FELL. BUT HE WAS THERE, WASN'T HE? AND NOW I'M HERE, AREN'T I?
AND YOU HAD BETTER BELIEVE THAT I WILL DO EVERYTHING IN MY POWER TO KEEP HIS DREAM ALIVE BY BUILDING B.G.H. INTO THE EMPIRE IT WAS ALWAYS MEANT TO BE, STARTING WITH THE REDEVELOPMENT OF ASTORIA.
AND FOR THE LAST ***FUCKING*** TIME... THE ***NAME*** IS PHIL.

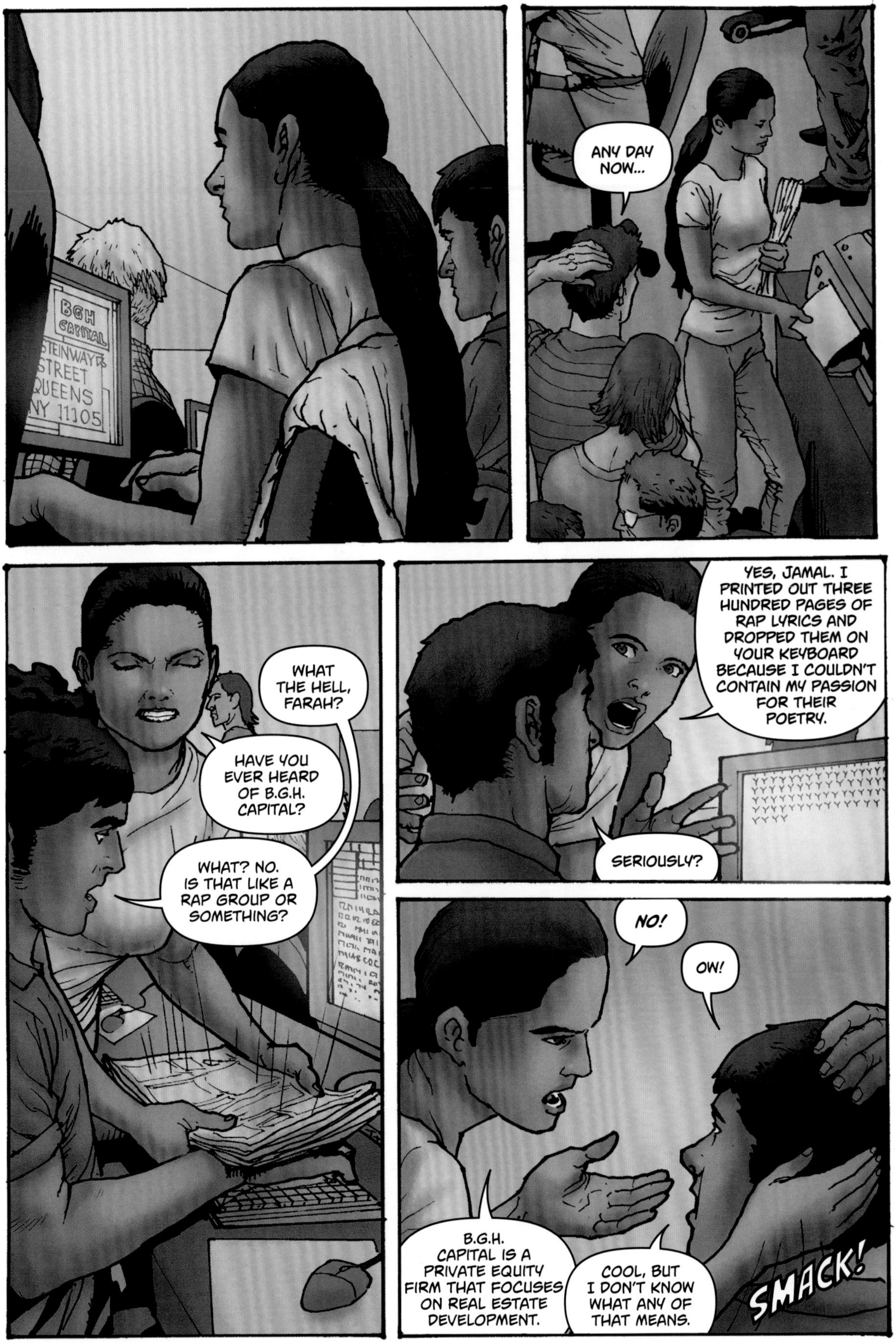
BGH CAPITAL
STEINWAY STREET QUEENS NY 11105
ANY DAY NOW...
WHAT THE HELL, FARAH?
HAVE YOU EVER HEARD OF B.G.H. CAPITAL?
WHAT? NO. IS THAT LIKE A RAP GROUP OR SOMETHING?
YES, JAMAL. I PRINTED OUT THREE HUNDRED PAGES OF RAP LYRICS AND DROPPED THEM ON YOUR KEYBOARD BECAUSE I COULDN'T CONTAIN MY PASSION FOR THEIR POETRY.
SERIOUSLY?
NO!
OW!
B.G.H. CAPITAL IS A PRIVATE EQUITY FIRM THAT FOCUSES ON REAL ESTATE DEVELOPMENT.
COOL, BUT I DON'T KNOW WHAT ANY OF THAT MEANS.
SMACK!

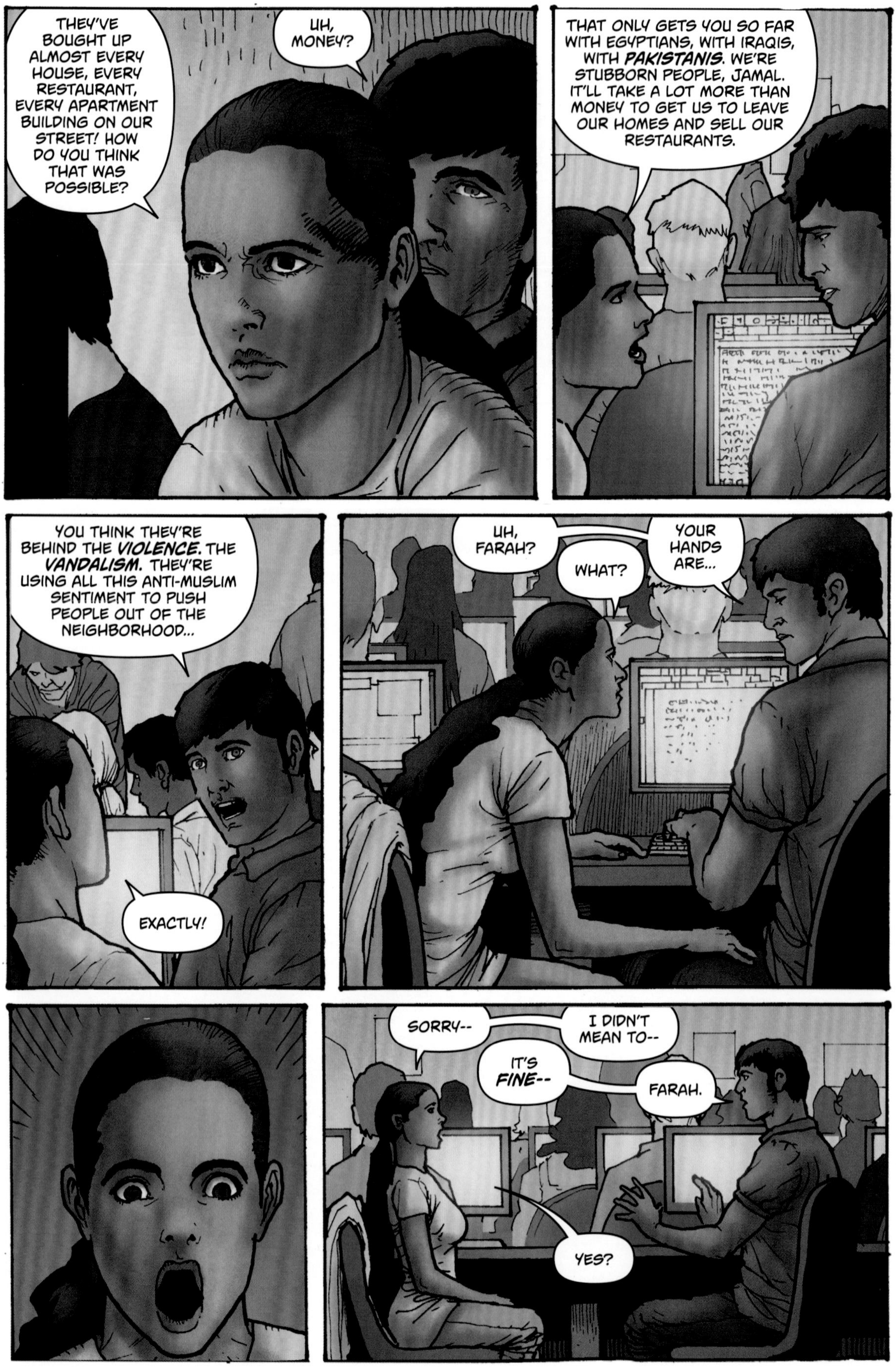
THEY'VE BOUGHT UP ALMOST EVERY HOUSE, EVERY RESTAURANT, EVERY APARTMENT BUILDING ON OUR STREET! HOW DO YOU THINK THAT WAS POSSIBLE?
UH, MONEY?
THAT ONLY GETS YOU SO FAR WITH EGYPTIANS, WITH IRAQIS, WITH PAKISTANIS. WE'RE STUBBORN PEOPLE, JAMAL. IT'LL TAKE A LOT MORE THAN MONEY TO GET US TO LEAVE OUR HOMES AND SELL OUR RESTAURANTS.
YOU THINK THEY'RE BEHIND THE VIOLENCE. THE VANDALISM. THEY'RE USING ALL THIS ANTI-MUSLIM SENTIMENT TO PUSH PEOPLE OUT OF THE NEIGHBORHOOD...
EXACTLY!
UH, FARAH?
WHAT?
YOUR HANDS ARE...
SORRY--
I DIDN'T MEAN TO--
IT'S FINE--
FARAH.
YES?

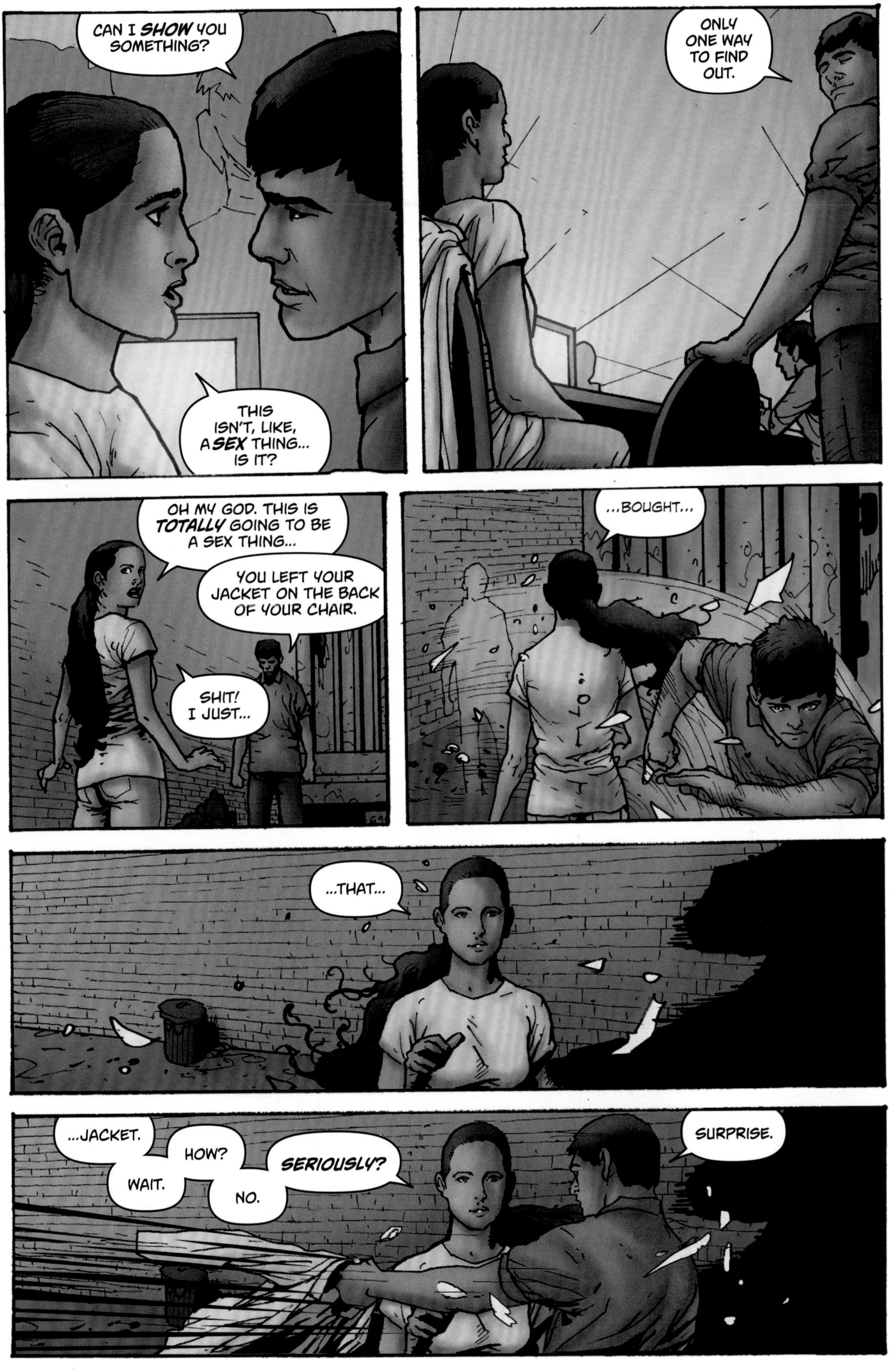

CAN I SHOW YOU SOMETHING?
THIS ISN'T, LIKE, A SEX THING... IS IT?
ONLY ONE WAY TO FIND OUT.
OH MY GOD. THIS IS TOTALLY GOING TO BE A SEX THING...
YOU LEFT YOUR JACKET ON THE BACK OF YOUR CHAIR.
SHIT! I JUST...
...BOUGHT...
...THAT...
...JACKET.
WAIT.
HOW?
NO.
SERIOUSLY?
SURPRISE.

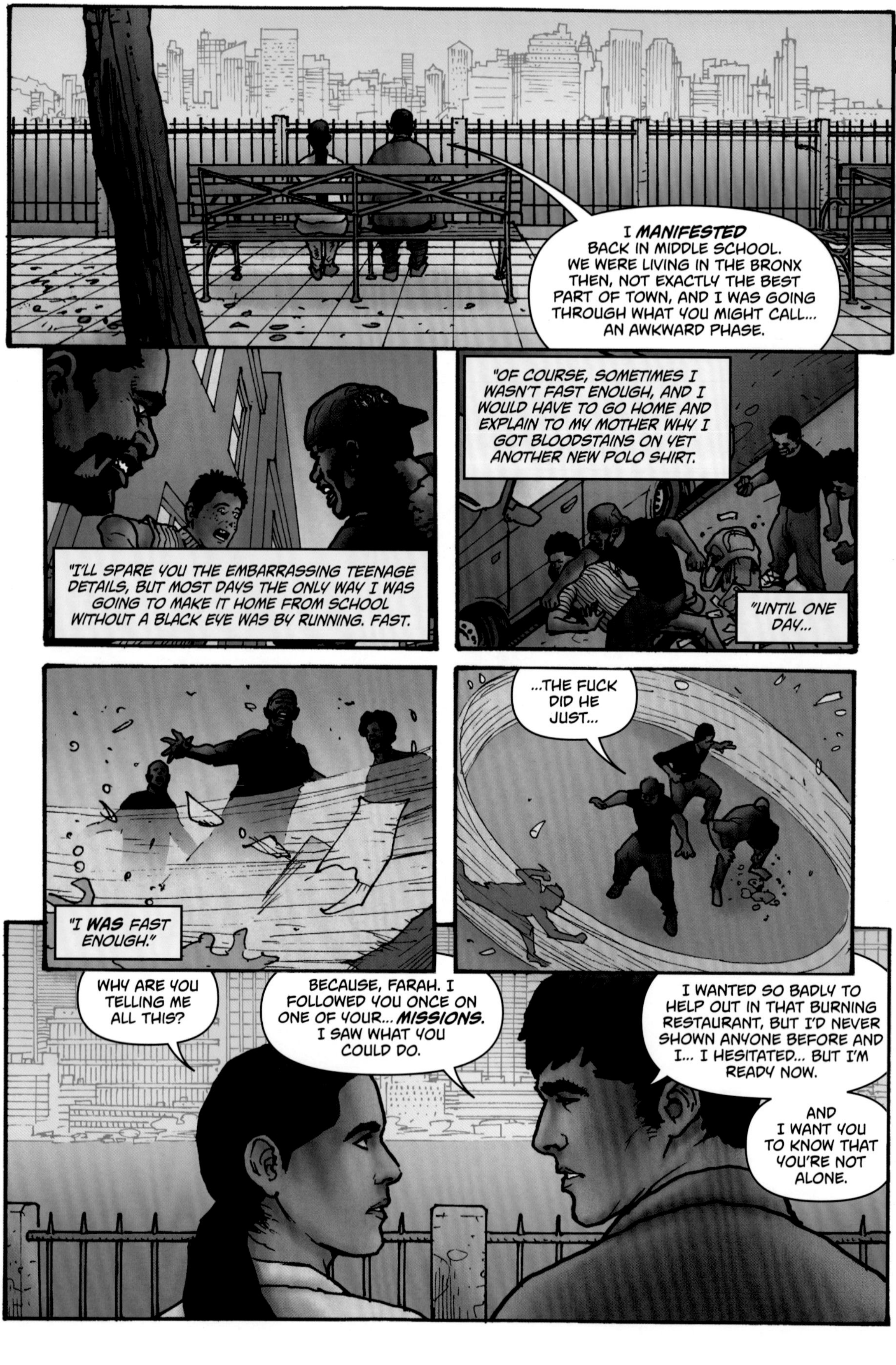
I MANIFESTED BACK IN MIDDLE SCHOOL. WE WERE LIVING IN THE BRONX THEN, NOT EXACTLY THE BEST PART OF TOWN, AND I WAS GOING THROUGH WHAT YOU MIGHT CALL... AN AWKWARD PHASE.
"I'LL SPARE YOU THE EMBARRASSING TEENAGE DETAILS, BUT MOST DAYS THE ONLY WAY I WAS GOING TO MAKE IT HOME FROM SCHOOL WITHOUT A BLACK EYE WAS BY RUNNING. FAST.
"OF COURSE, SOMETIMES I WASN'T FAST ENOUGH, AND I WOULD HAVE TO GO HOME AND EXPLAIN TO MY MOTHER WHY I GOT BLOODSTAINS ON YET ANOTHER NEW POLO SHIRT.
"UNTIL ONE DAY...
"I WAS FAST ENOUGH."
...THE FUCK DID HE JUST...
WHY ARE YOU TELLING ME ALL THIS?
BECAUSE, FARAH. I FOLLOWED YOU ONCE ON ONE OF YOUR... MISSIONS. I SAW WHAT YOU COULD DO.
I WANTED SO BADLY TO HELP OUT IN THAT BURNING RESTAURANT, BUT I'D NEVER SHOWN ANYONE BEFORE AND I... I HESITATED... BUT I'M READY NOW.
AND I WANT YOU TO KNOW THAT YOU'RE NOT ALONE.

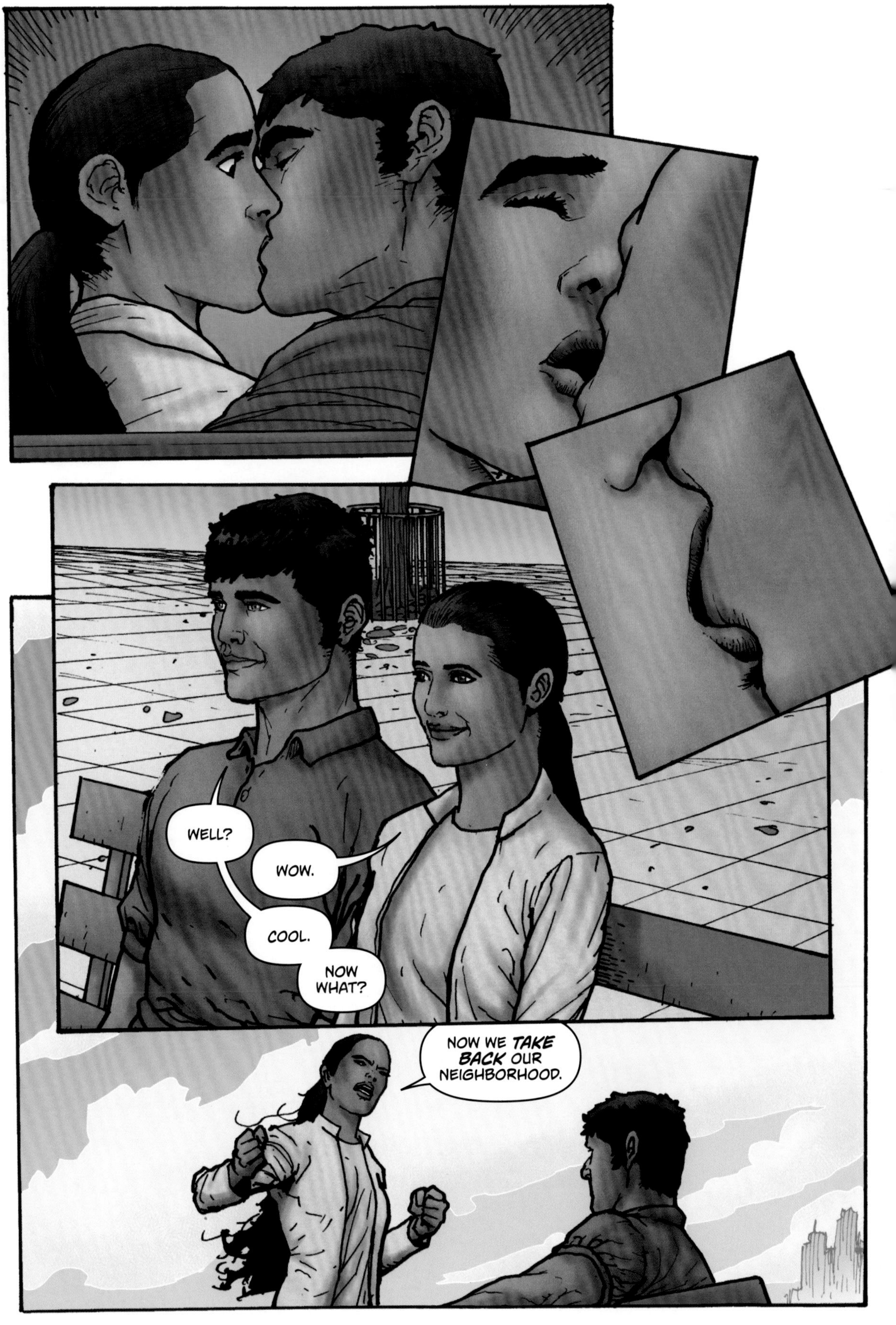
WELL?
WOW.
COOL.
NOW WHAT?
NOW WE *TAKE BACK* OUR NEIGHBORHOOD.

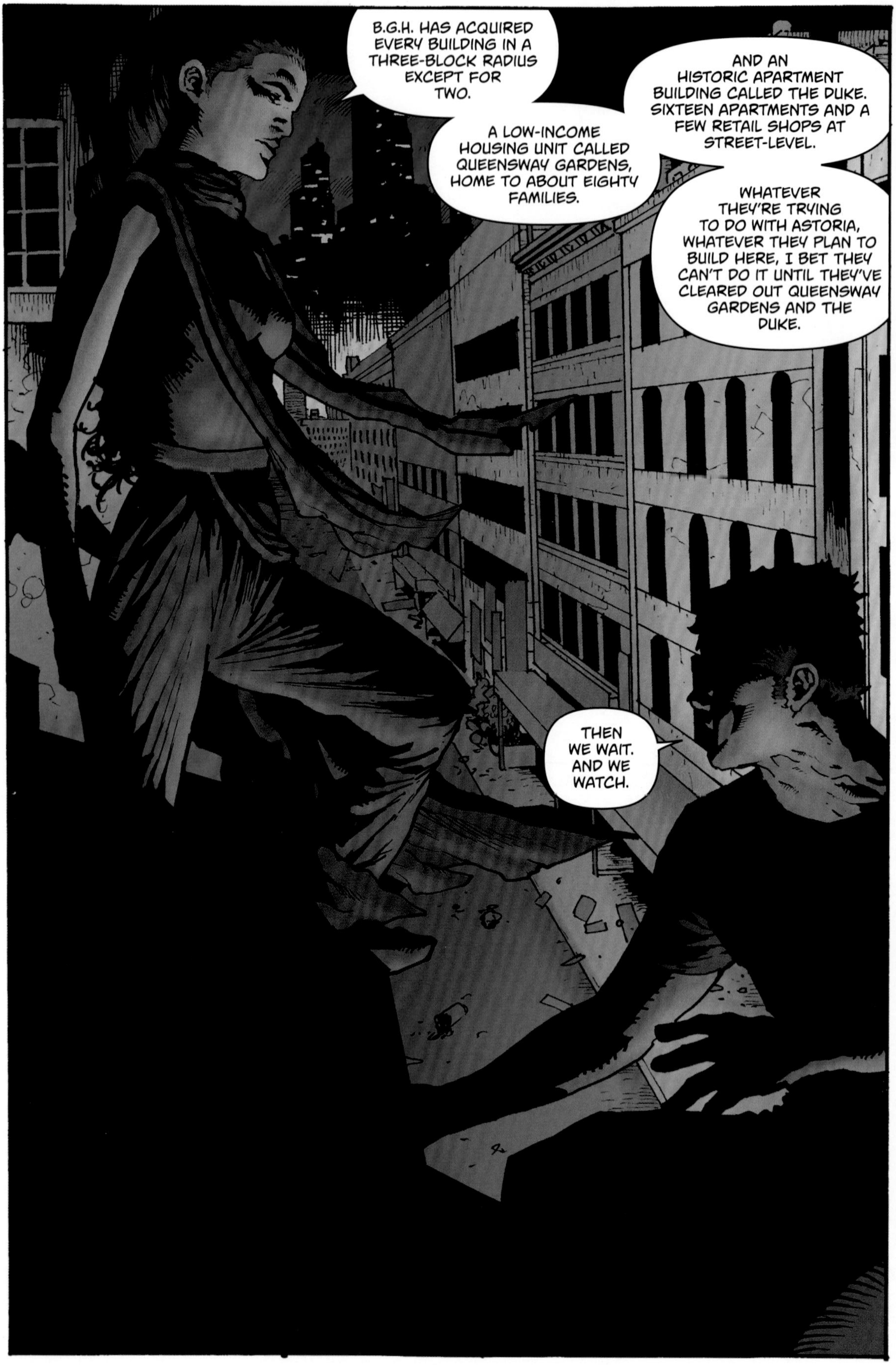
B.G.H. HAS ACQUIRED EVERY BUILDING IN A THREE-BLOCK RADIUS EXCEPT FOR TWO.
A LOW-INCOME HOUSING UNIT CALLED QUEENSWAY GARDENS, HOME TO ABOUT EIGHTY FAMILIES.
AND AN HISTORIC APARTMENT BUILDING CALLED THE DUKE. SIXTEEN APARTMENTS AND A FEW RETAIL SHOPS AT STREET-LEVEL.
WHATEVER THEY'RE TRYING TO DO WITH ASTORIA, WHATEVER THEY PLAN TO BUILD HERE, I BET THEY CAN'T DO IT UNTIL THEY'VE CLEARED OUT QUEENSWAY GARDENS AND THE DUKE.
THEN WE WAIT. AND WE WATCH.

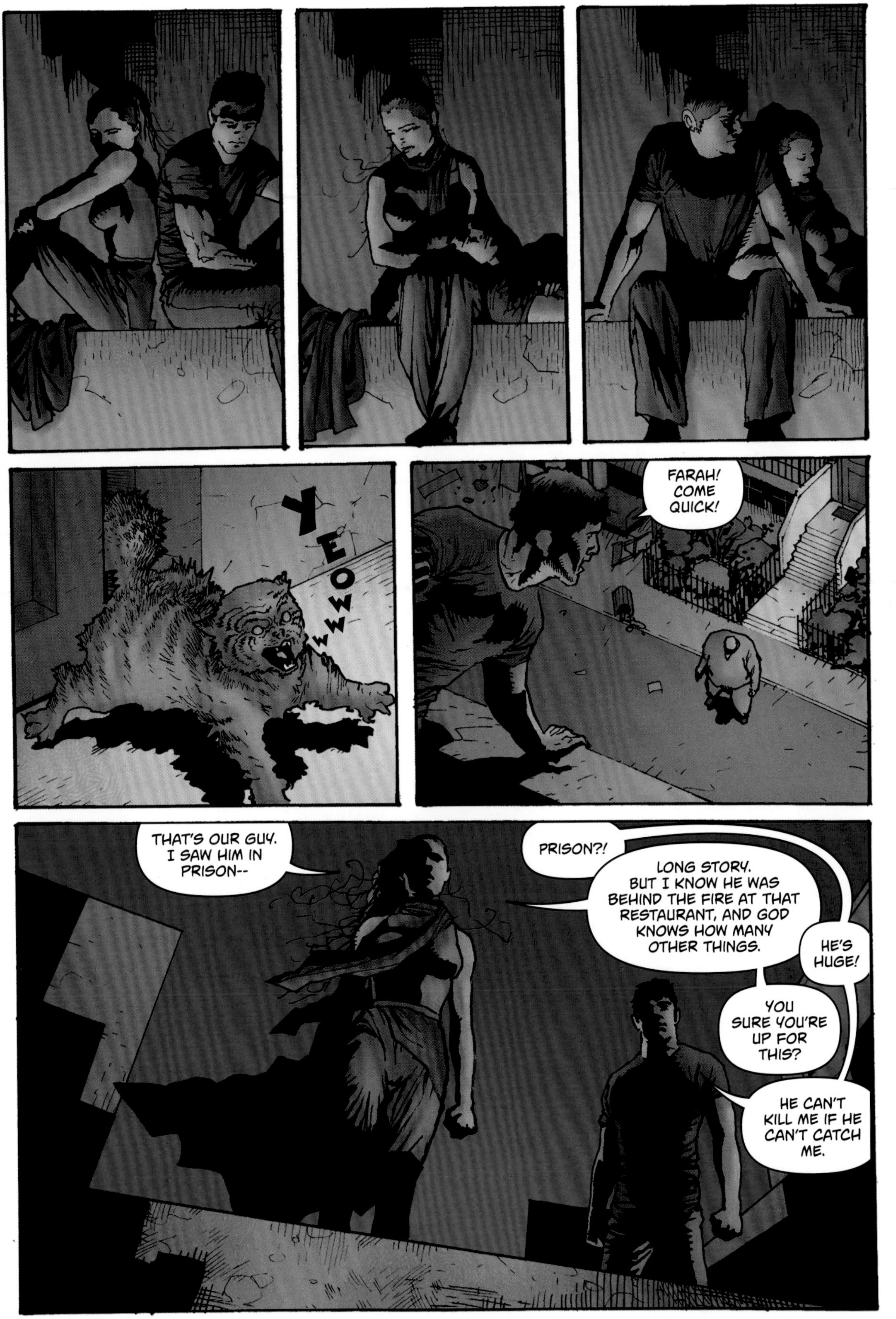
YEOWWW
FARAH! COME QUICK!
THAT'S OUR GUY. I SAW HIM IN PRISON--
PRISON?!
LONG STORY. BUT I KNOW HE WAS BEHIND THE FIRE AT THAT RESTAURANT, AND GOD KNOWS HOW MANY OTHER THINGS.
HE'S HUGE!
YOU SURE YOU'RE UP FOR THIS?
HE CAN'T KILL ME IF HE CAN'T CATCH ME.

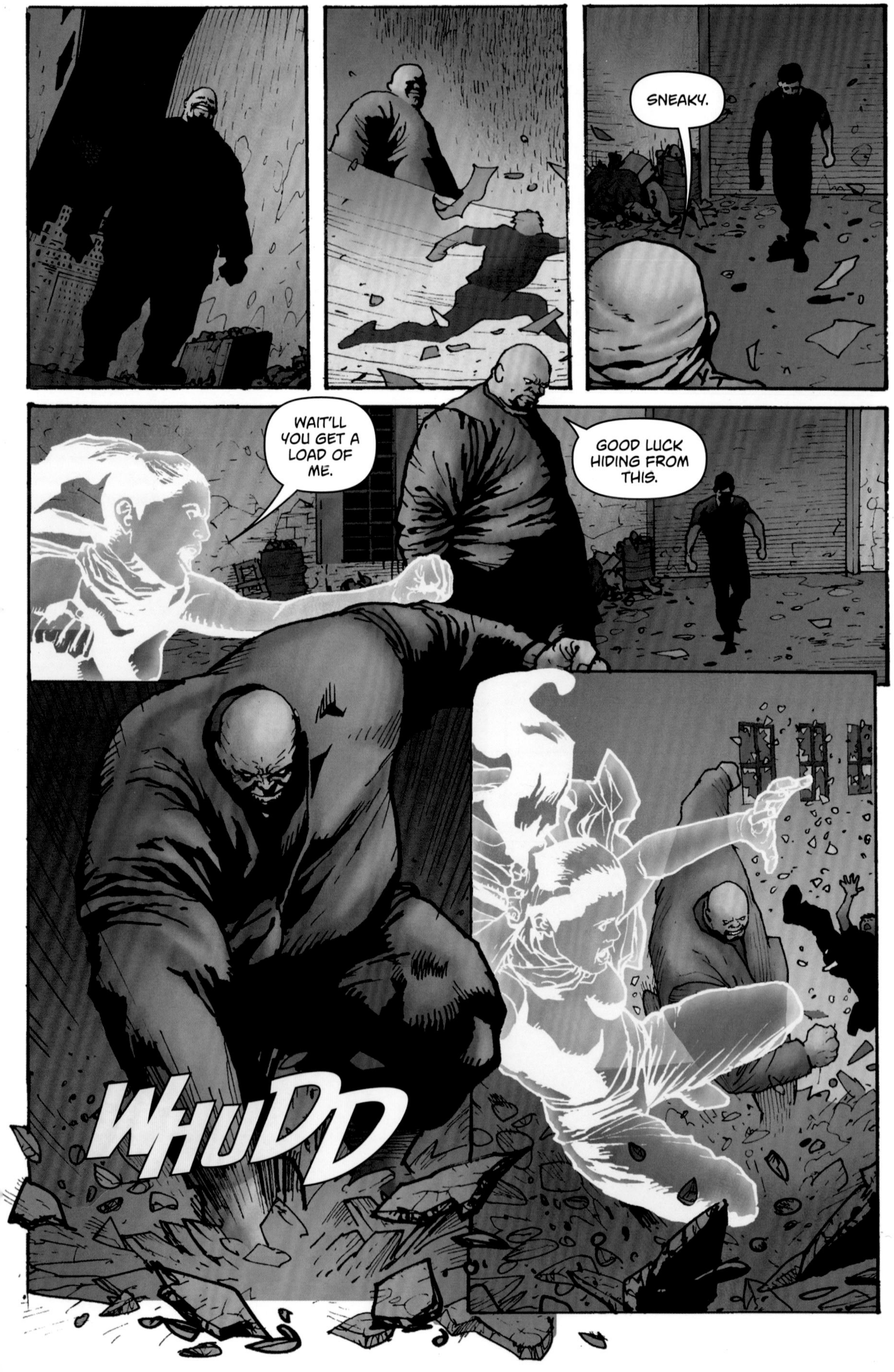
SNEAKY.
WAIT'LL YOU GET A LOAD OF ME.
GOOD LUCK HIDING FROM THIS.
WHUDD

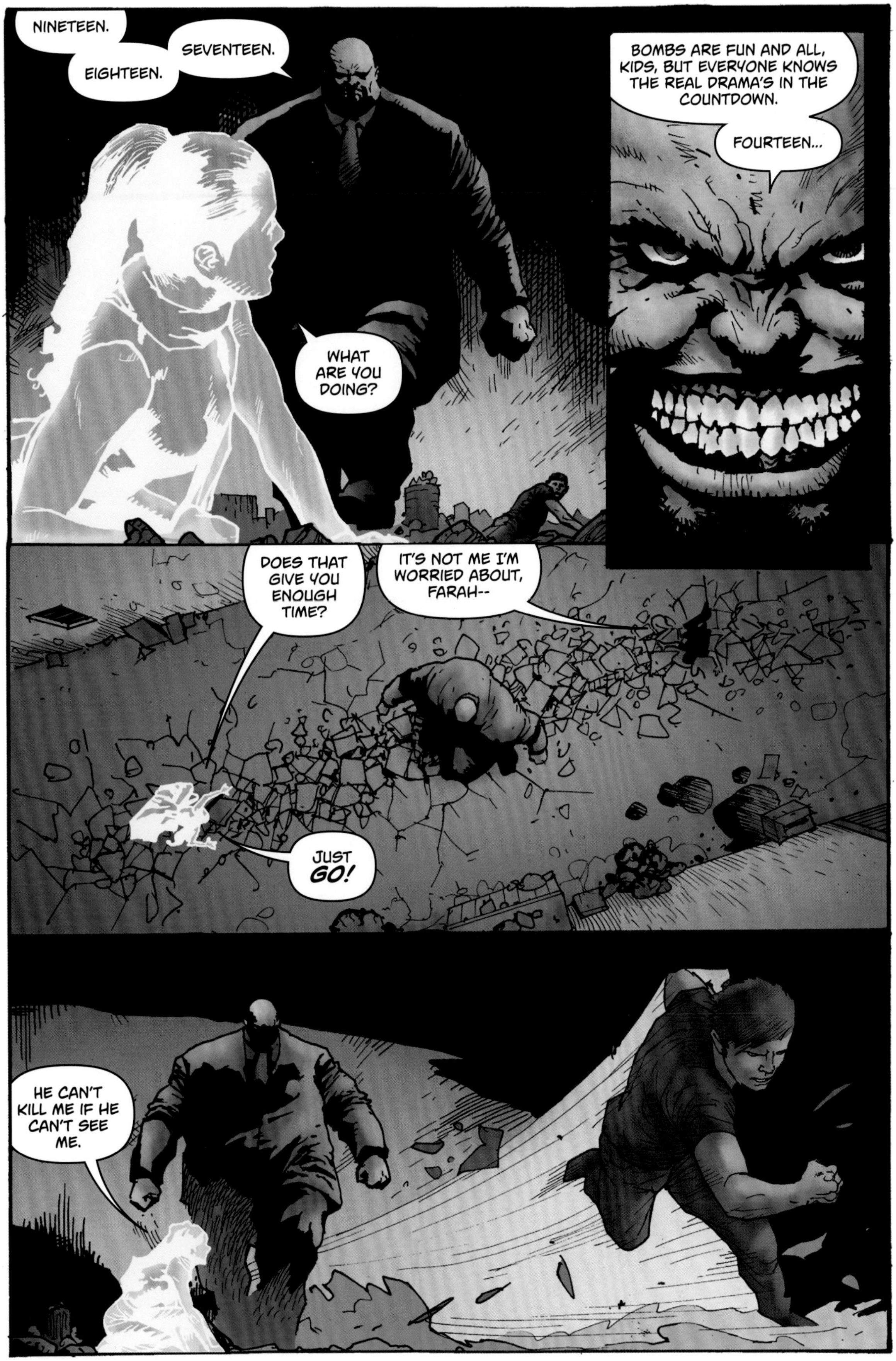
NINETEEN.
EIGHTEEN.
SEVENTEEN.
WHAT ARE YOU DOING?
BOMBS ARE FUN AND ALL, KIDS, BUT EVERYONE KNOWS THE REAL DRAMA'S IN THE COUNTDOWN.
FOURTEEN...
DOES THAT GIVE YOU ENOUGH TIME?
IT'S NOT ME I'M WORRIED ABOUT, FARAH--
JUST GO!
HE CAN'T KILL ME IF HE CAN'T SEE ME.

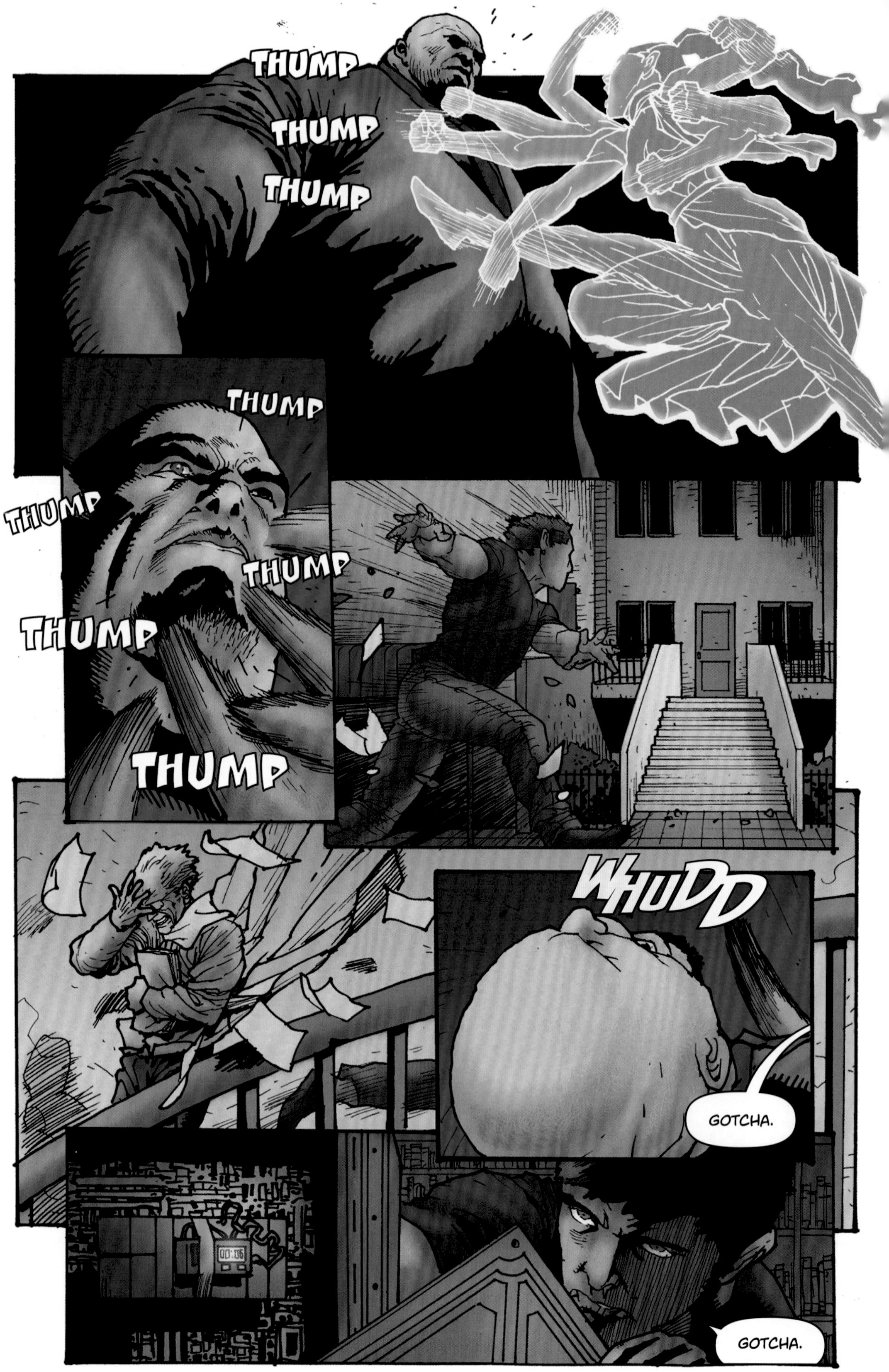
THUMP
THUMP
THUMP
THUMP
THUMP
THUMP
THUMP
THUMP
WHUDD
GOTCHA.
GOTCHA.

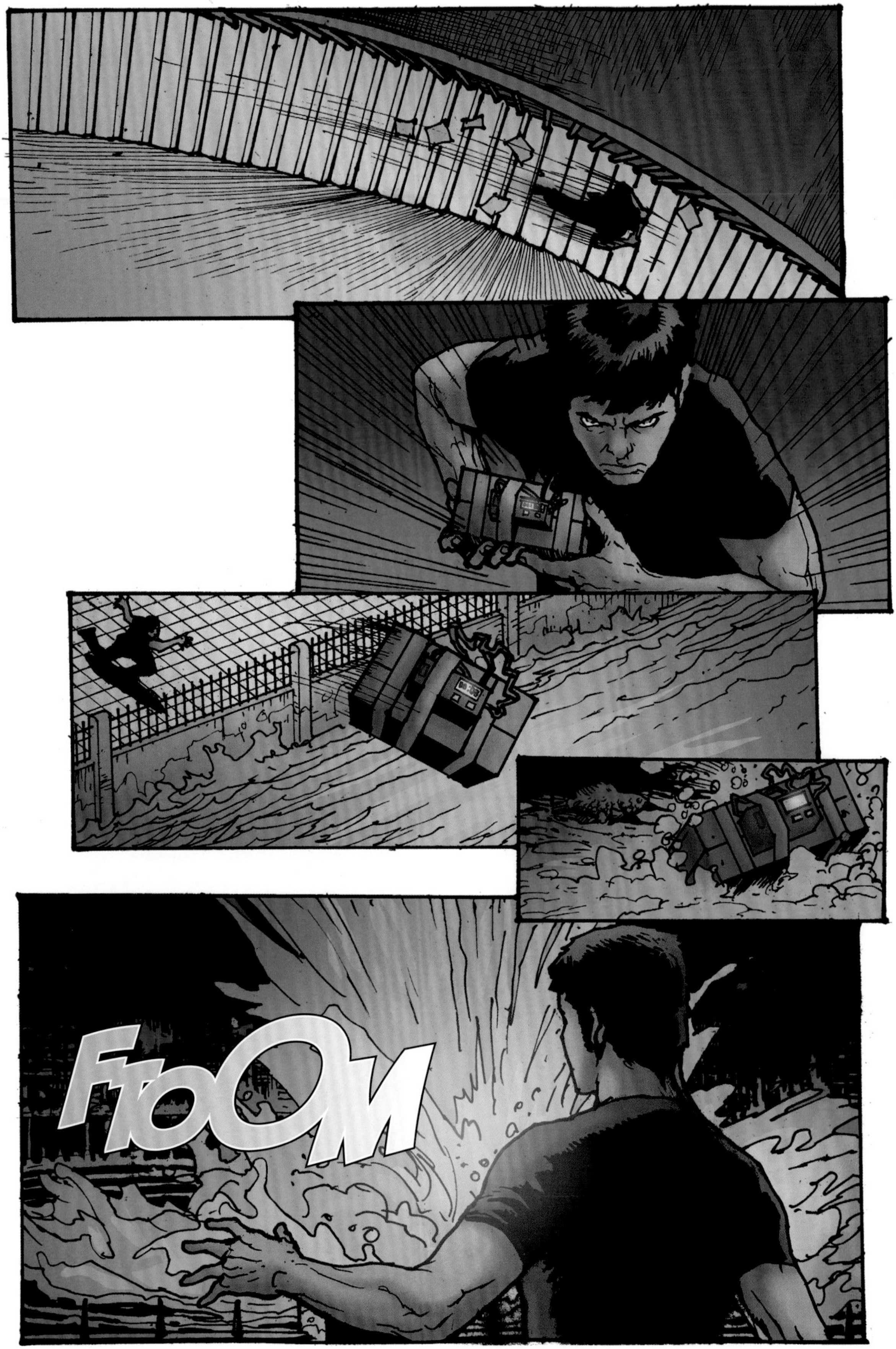
FtoOM

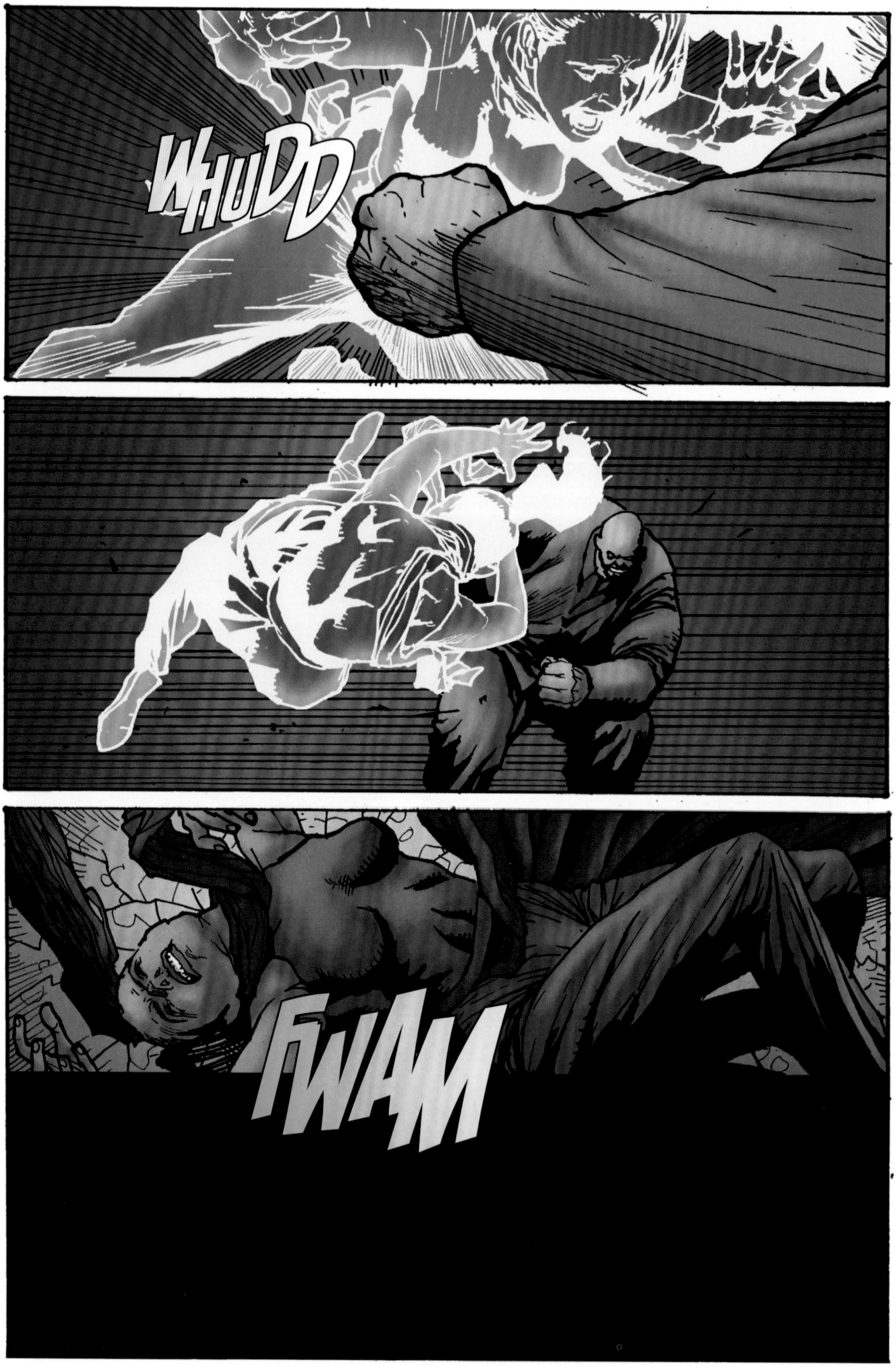
WHUDD
FWAM

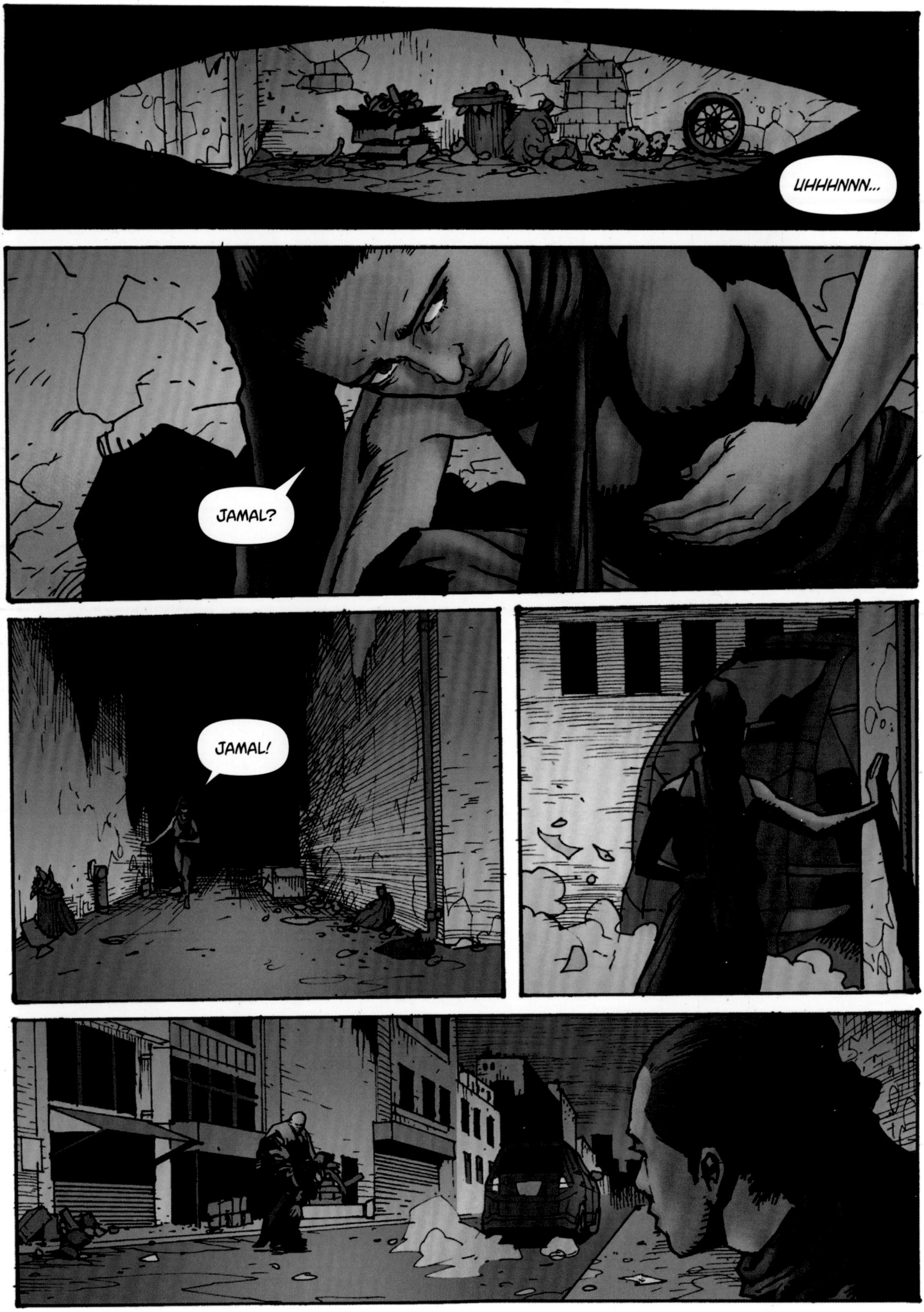
UHHHNNN...
JAMAL?
JAMAL!

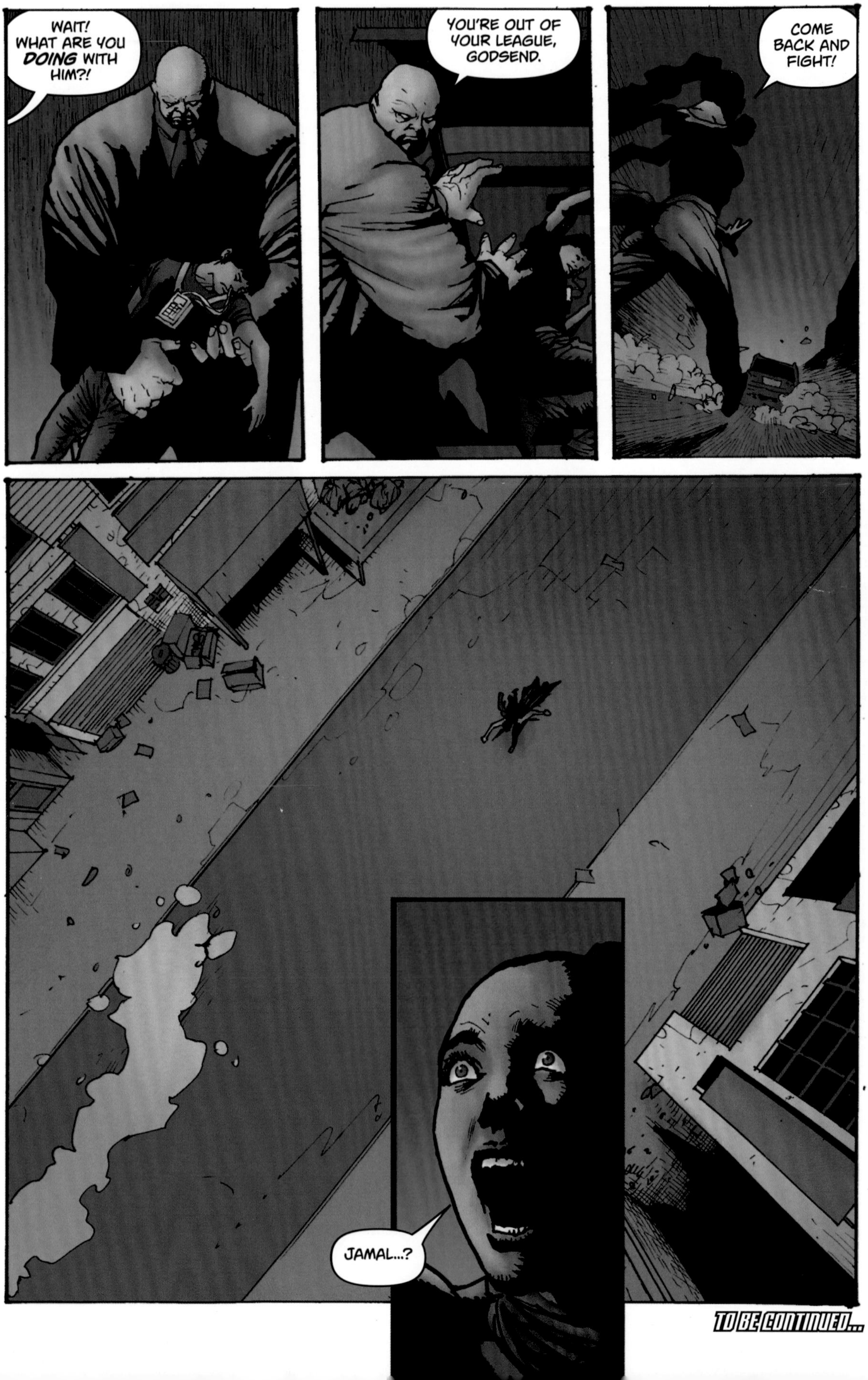
WAIT! WHAT ARE YOU DOING WITH HIM?!
YOU'RE OUT OF YOUR LEAGUE, GODSEND.
COME BACK AND FIGHT!
JAMAL...?

TO BE CONTINUED...

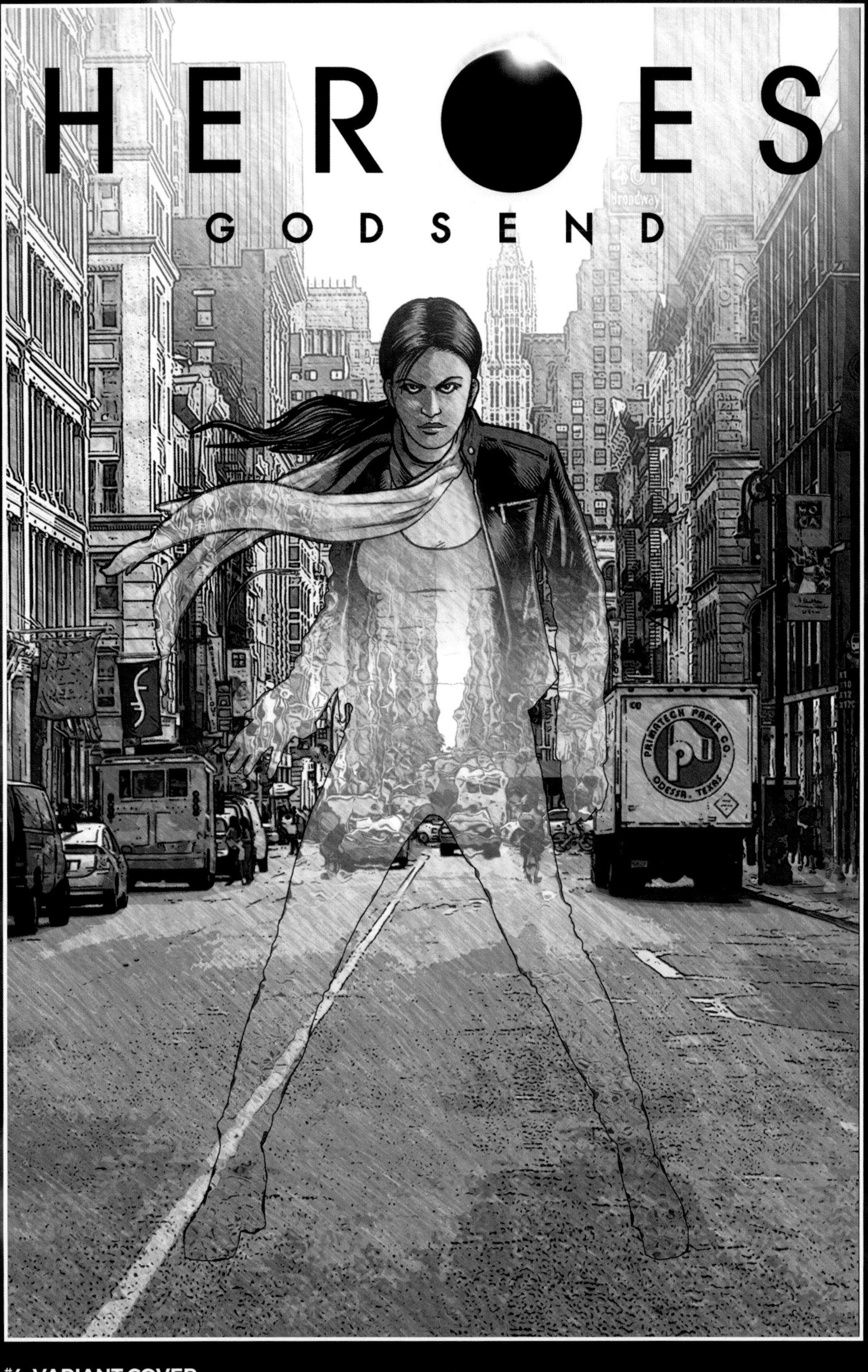
HEROES
GODSEND
401 Broadway
PRIMATECH PAPER CO.
ODESSA, TEXAS

#4 VARIANT COVER
ARTWORK BY GARY SPENCER MILLIDGE

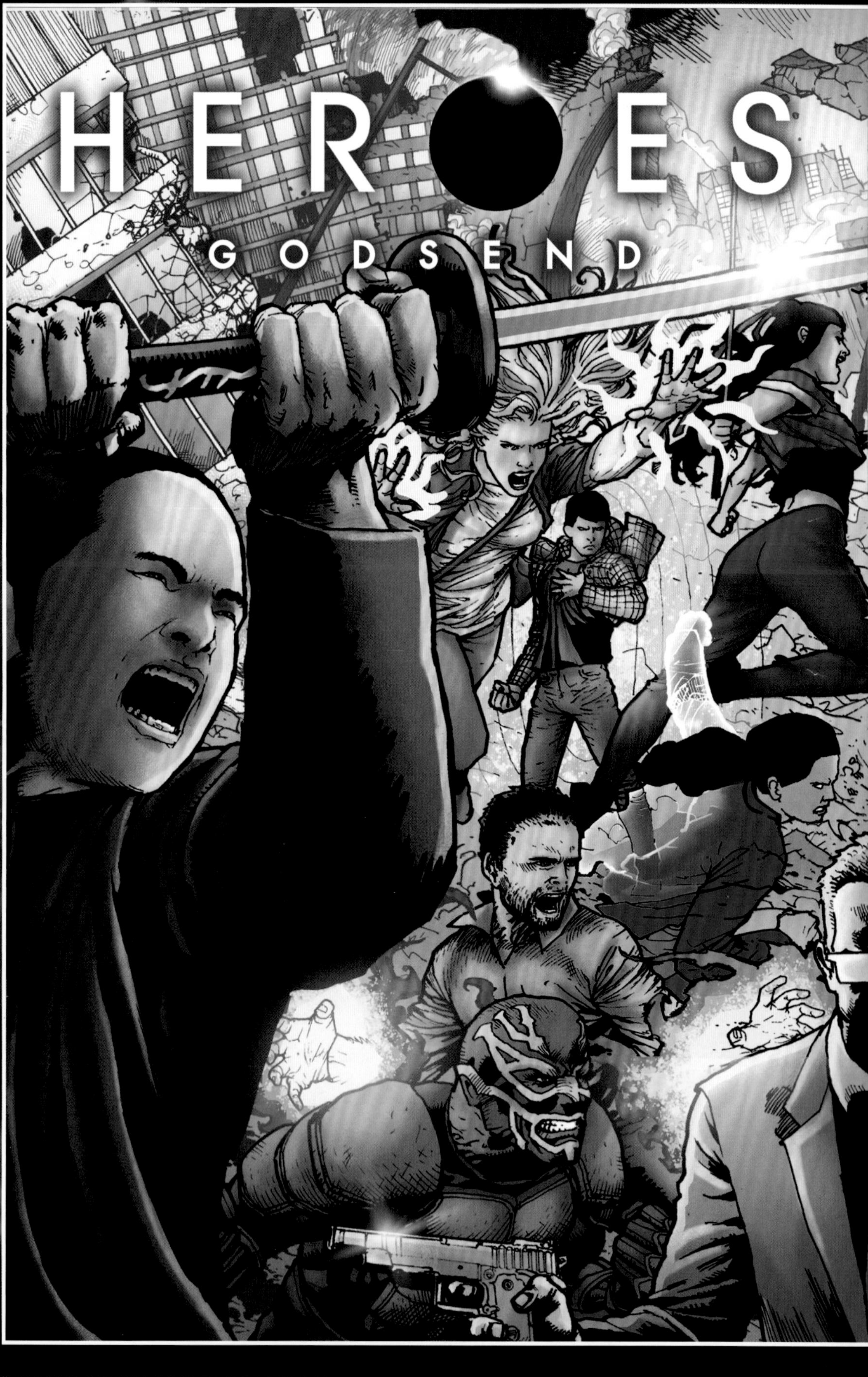
HEROES
GODSEND

#5 MAIN COVER & VARIANT COVER
ARTWORK BY ROY ALLAN MARTINEZ

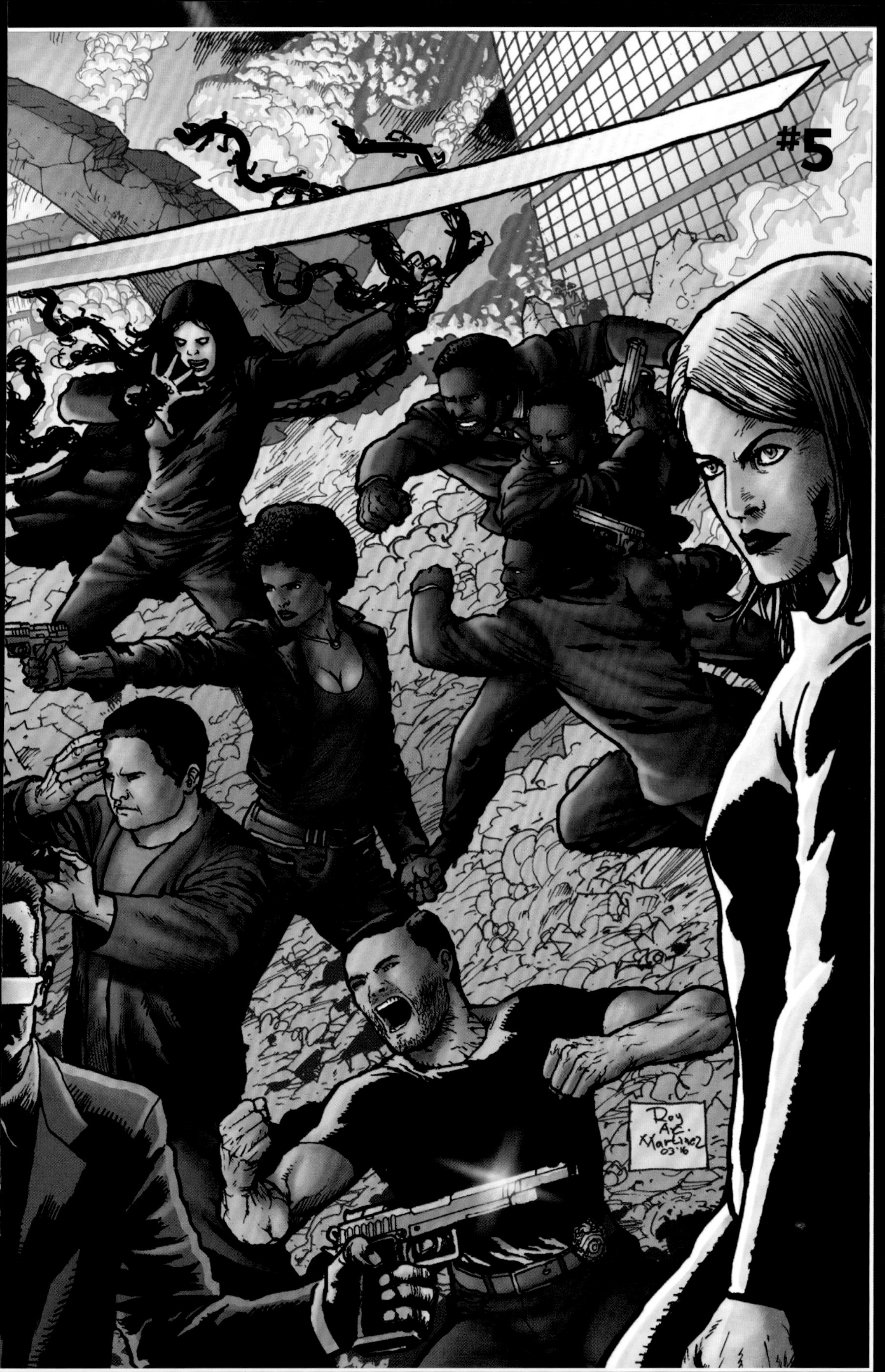#5
Roy A.C. Martinez 03'16

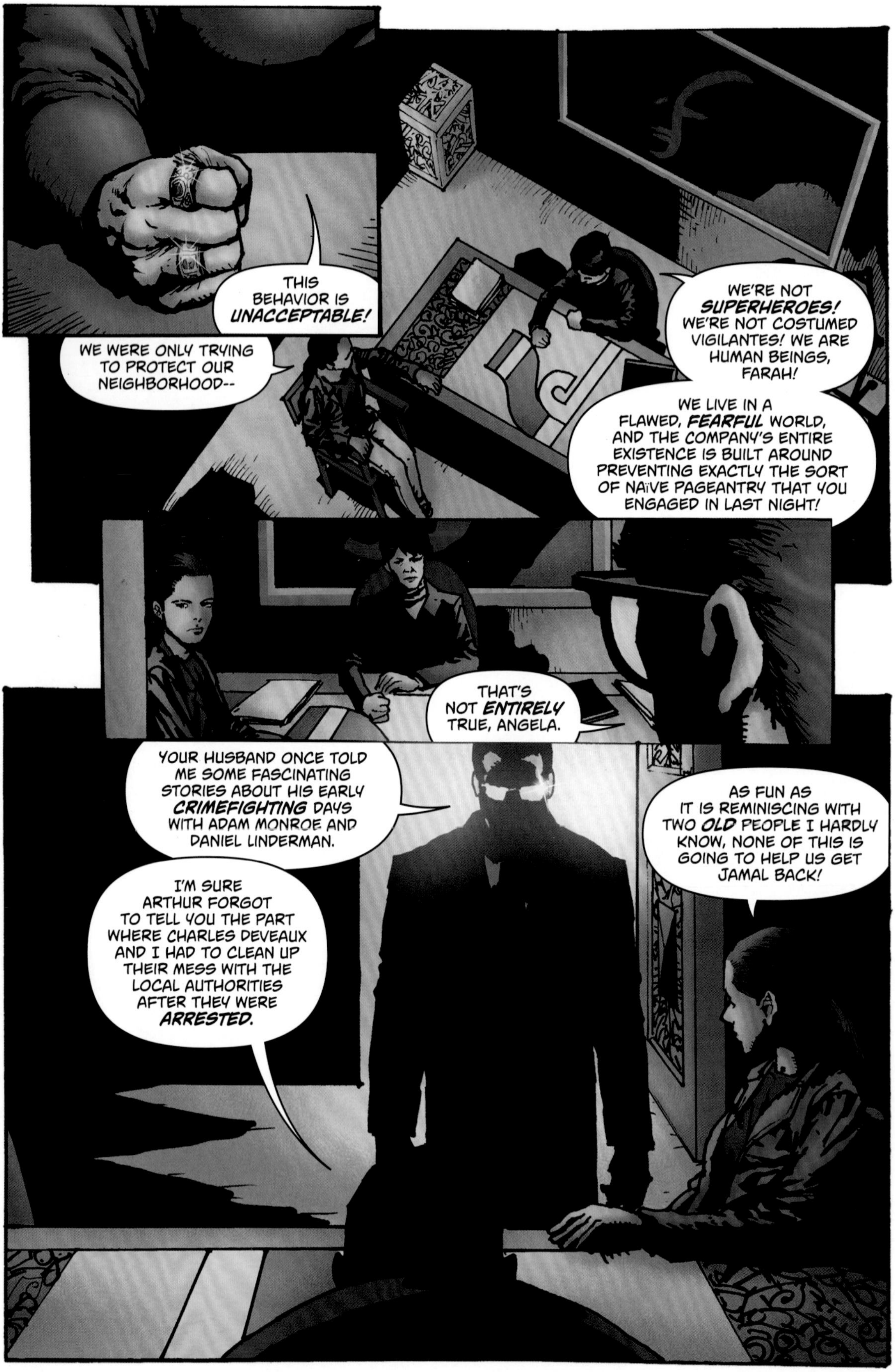
THIS BEHAVIOR IS UNACCEPTABLE!
WE WERE ONLY TRYING TO PROTECT OUR NEIGHBORHOOD--
WE'RE NOT SUPERHEROES! WE'RE NOT COSTUMED VIGILANTES! WE ARE HUMAN BEINGS, FARAH!
WE LIVE IN A FLAWED, FEARFUL WORLD, AND THE COMPANY'S ENTIRE EXISTENCE IS BUILT AROUND PREVENTING EXACTLY THE SORT OF NAÏVE PAGEANTRY THAT YOU ENGAGED IN LAST NIGHT!
THAT'S NOT ENTIRELY TRUE, ANGELA.
YOUR HUSBAND ONCE TOLD ME SOME FASCINATING STORIES ABOUT HIS EARLY CRIMEFIGHTING DAYS WITH ADAM MONROE AND DANIEL LINDERMAN.
I'M SURE ARTHUR FORGOT TO TELL YOU THE PART WHERE CHARLES DEVEAUX AND I HAD TO CLEAN UP THEIR MESS WITH THE LOCAL AUTHORITIES AFTER THEY WERE ARRESTED.
AS FUN AS IT IS REMINISCING WITH TWO OLD PEOPLE I HARDLY KNOW, NONE OF THIS IS GOING TO HELP US GET JAMAL BACK!

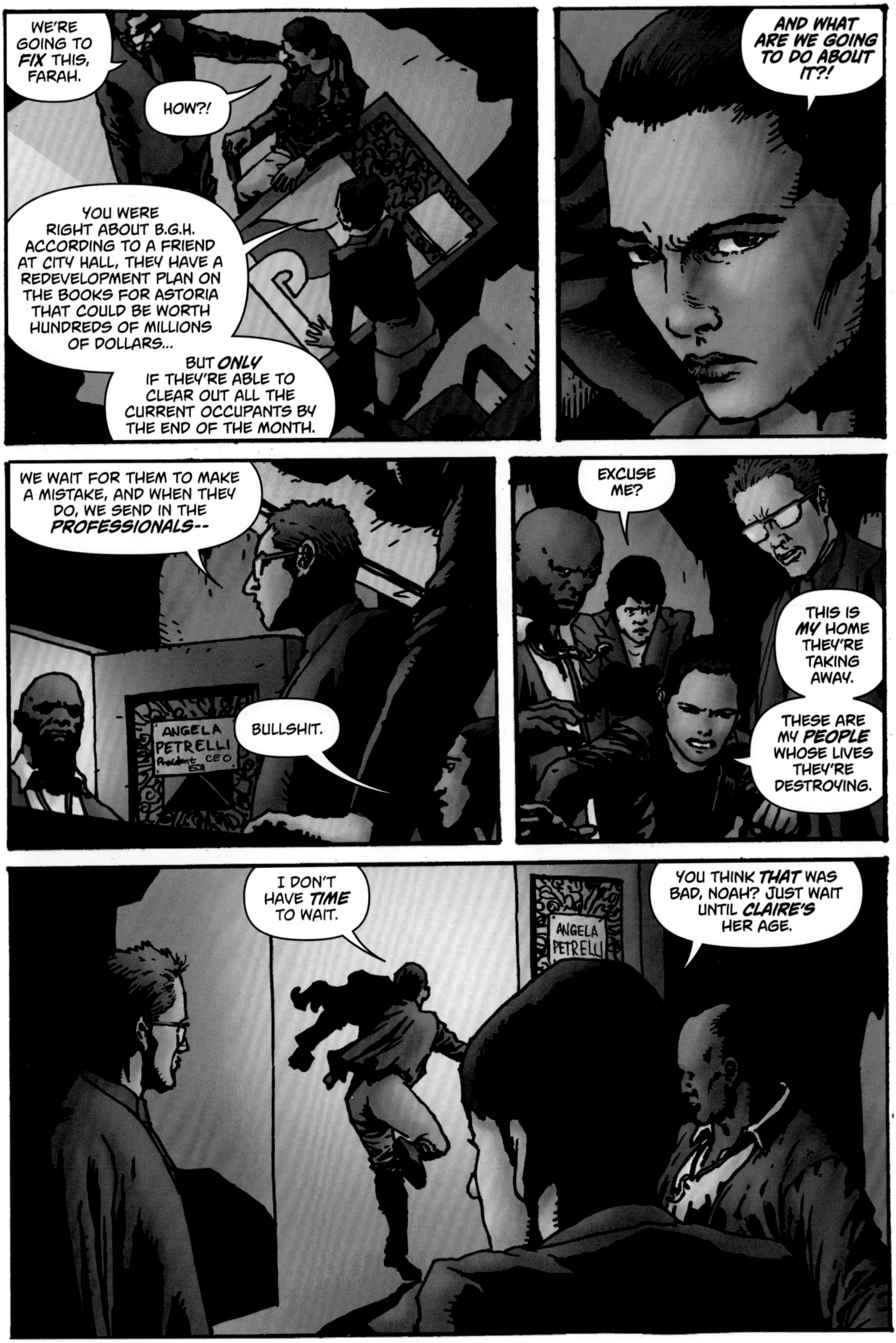
WE'RE GOING TO FIX THIS, FARAH.
HOW?!
YOU WERE RIGHT ABOUT B.G.H. ACCORDING TO A FRIEND AT CITY HALL, THEY HAVE A REDEVELOPMENT PLAN ON THE BOOKS FOR ASTORIA THAT COULD BE WORTH HUNDREDS OF MILLIONS OF DOLLARS...
BUT ONLY IF THEY'RE ABLE TO CLEAR OUT ALL THE CURRENT OCCUPANTS BY THE END OF THE MONTH.
AND WHAT ARE WE GOING TO DO ABOUT IT?!
WE WAIT FOR THEM TO MAKE A MISTAKE, AND WHEN THEY DO, WE SEND IN THE PROFESSIONALS--
ANGELA PETRELLI President CEO
BULLSHIT.
EXCUSE ME?
THIS IS MY HOME THEY'RE TAKING AWAY.
THESE ARE MY PEOPLE WHOSE LIVES THEY'RE DESTROYING.
I DON'T HAVE TIME TO WAIT.
ANGELA PETRELLI
YOU THINK THAT WAS BAD, NOAH? JUST WAIT UNTIL CLAIRE'S HER AGE.

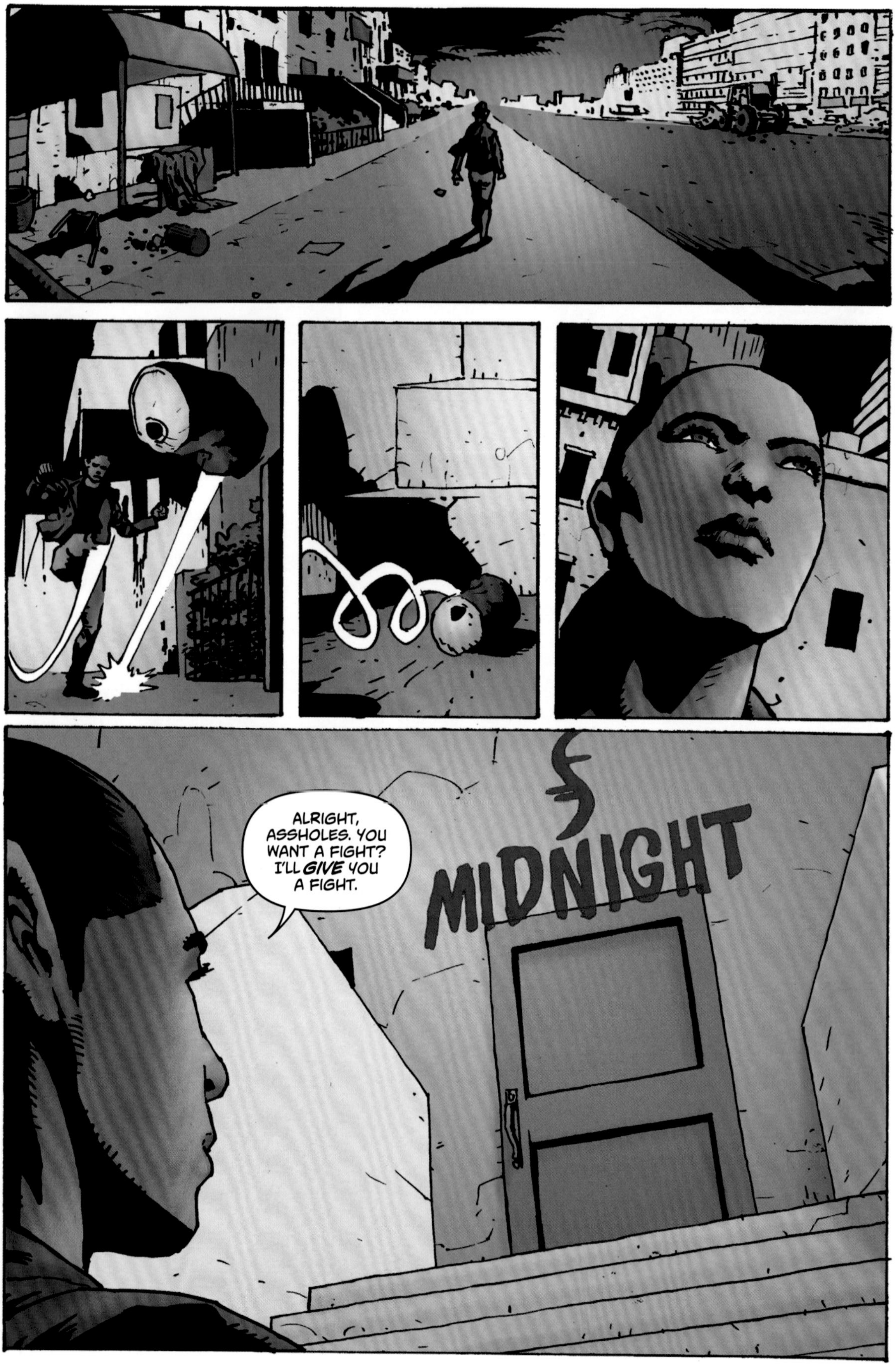
ALRIGHT, ASSHOLES. YOU WANT A FIGHT? I'LL GIVE YOU A FIGHT.
MIDNIGHT

THE ASTORIA PLACE COMPLEX, WITH ITS STATE OF THE ART ENTERTAINMENT FACILITIES, HIGH-END RETAIL SPACES, AND MULTI-MILLION DOLLAR LIVE/WORK LOFTS PROMISES TO BE THE HOTTEST PIECE OF REAL ESTATE TO HIT THE NEW YORK MARKET IN YEARS, AND ITS IMPACT ON OUR FIRM'S BOTTOM LINE WILL BE FELT ALMOST IMMEDIATELY.

WITH ALL DUE RESPECT TO YOU, MRS. HAAS, AND TO YOUR LATE HUSBAND, SOME OF US ARE BEGINNING TO WONDER WHETHER YOU'RE REALLY READY FOR A PROJECT OF THIS MAGNITUDE.

READY...?

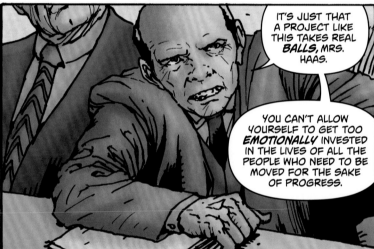

IT'S JUST THAT A PROJECT LIKE THIS TAKES REAL *BALLS*, MRS. HAAS.

YOU CAN'T ALLOW YOURSELF TO GET TOO *EMOTIONALLY* INVESTED IN THE LIVES OF ALL THE PEOPLE WHO NEED TO BE MOVED FOR THE SAKE OF PROGRESS.

AAAAAGGGHHHHHH!

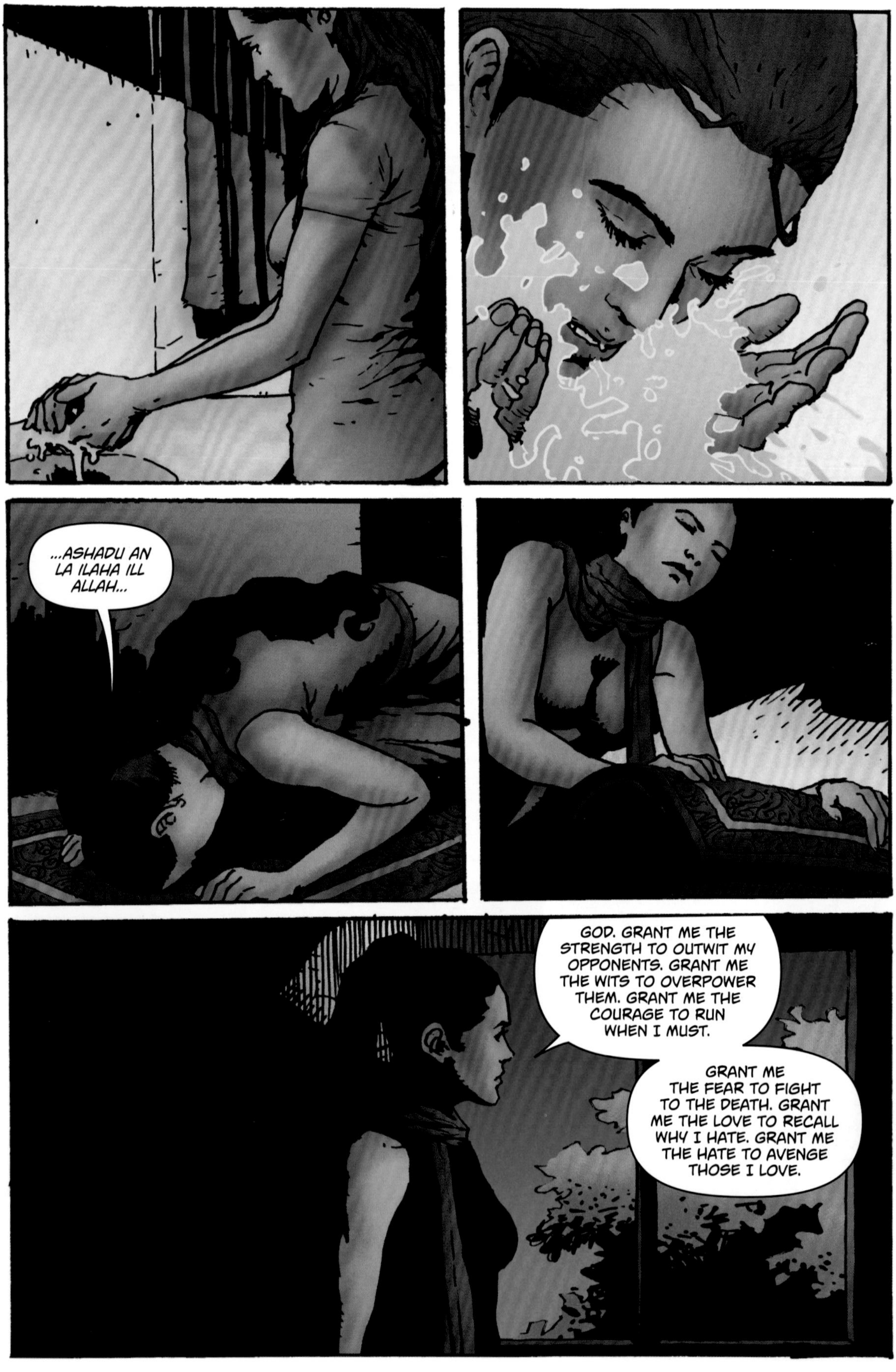
...ASHADU AN LA ILAHA ILL ALLAH...
GOD. GRANT ME THE STRENGTH TO OUTWIT MY OPPONENTS. GRANT ME THE WITS TO OVERPOWER THEM. GRANT ME THE COURAGE TO RUN WHEN I MUST.
GRANT ME THE FEAR TO FIGHT TO THE DEATH. GRANT ME THE LOVE TO RECALL WHY I HATE. GRANT ME THE HATE TO AVENGE THOSE I LOVE.

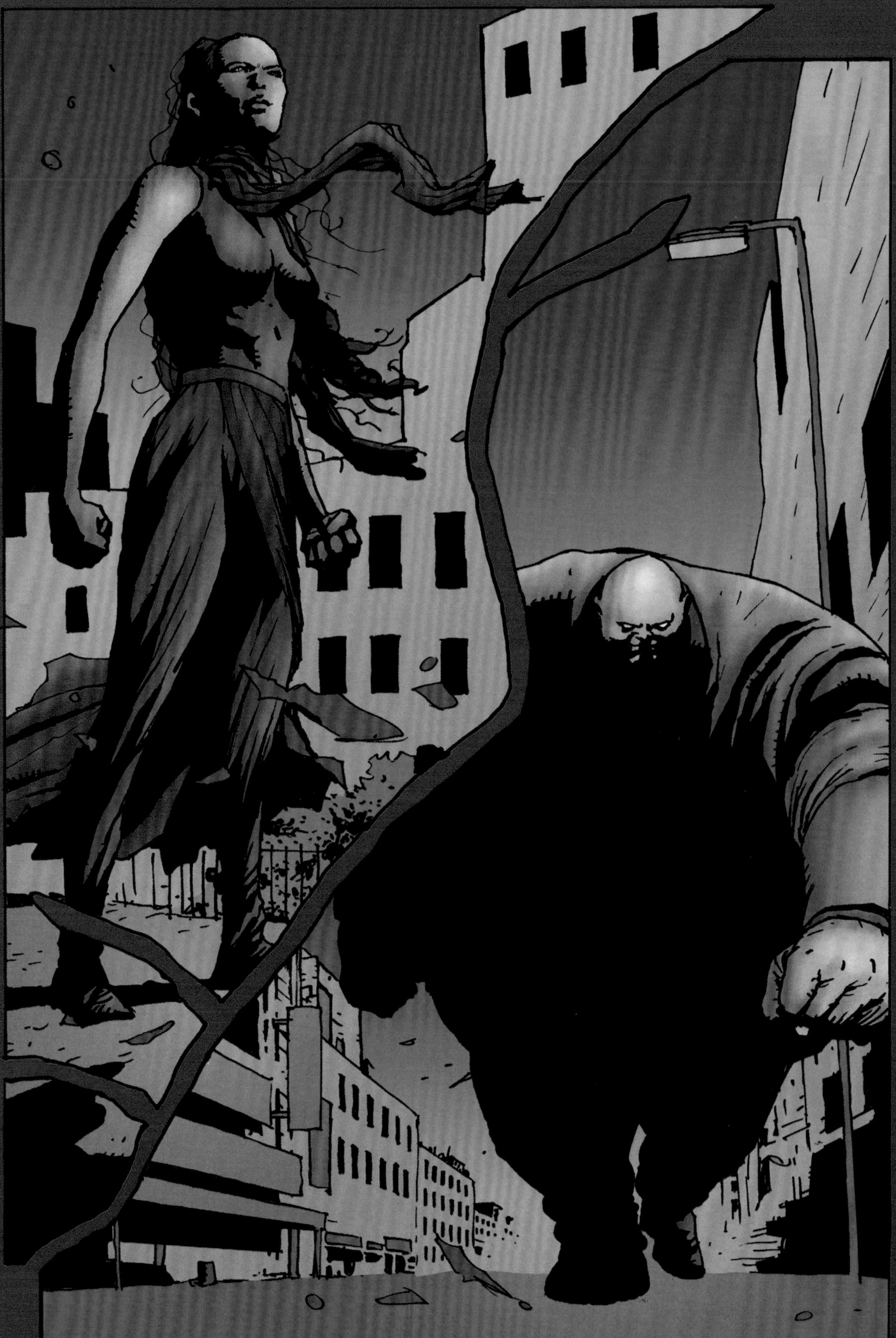

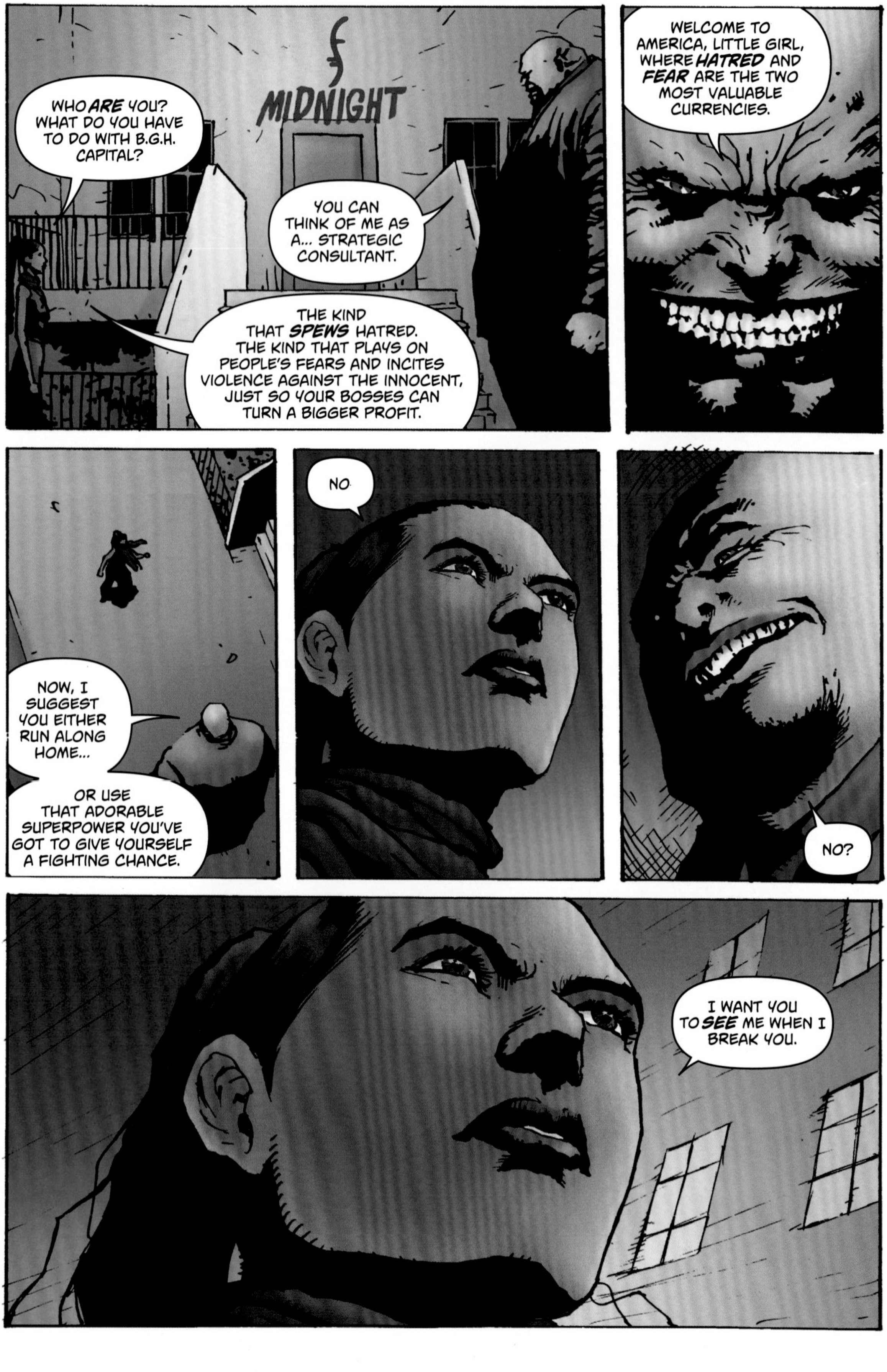
MIDNIGHT
WHO ARE YOU? WHAT DO YOU HAVE TO DO WITH B.G.H. CAPITAL?
YOU CAN THINK OF ME AS A... STRATEGIC CONSULTANT.
THE KIND THAT SPEWS HATRED. THE KIND THAT PLAYS ON PEOPLE'S FEARS AND INCITES VIOLENCE AGAINST THE INNOCENT, JUST SO YOUR BOSSES CAN TURN A BIGGER PROFIT.
WELCOME TO AMERICA, LITTLE GIRL, WHERE HATRED AND FEAR ARE THE TWO MOST VALUABLE CURRENCIES.
NOW, I SUGGEST YOU EITHER RUN ALONG HOME...
OR USE THAT ADORABLE SUPERPOWER YOU'VE GOT TO GIVE YOURSELF A FIGHTING CHANCE.
NO.
NO?
I WANT YOU TO SEE ME WHEN I BREAK YOU.

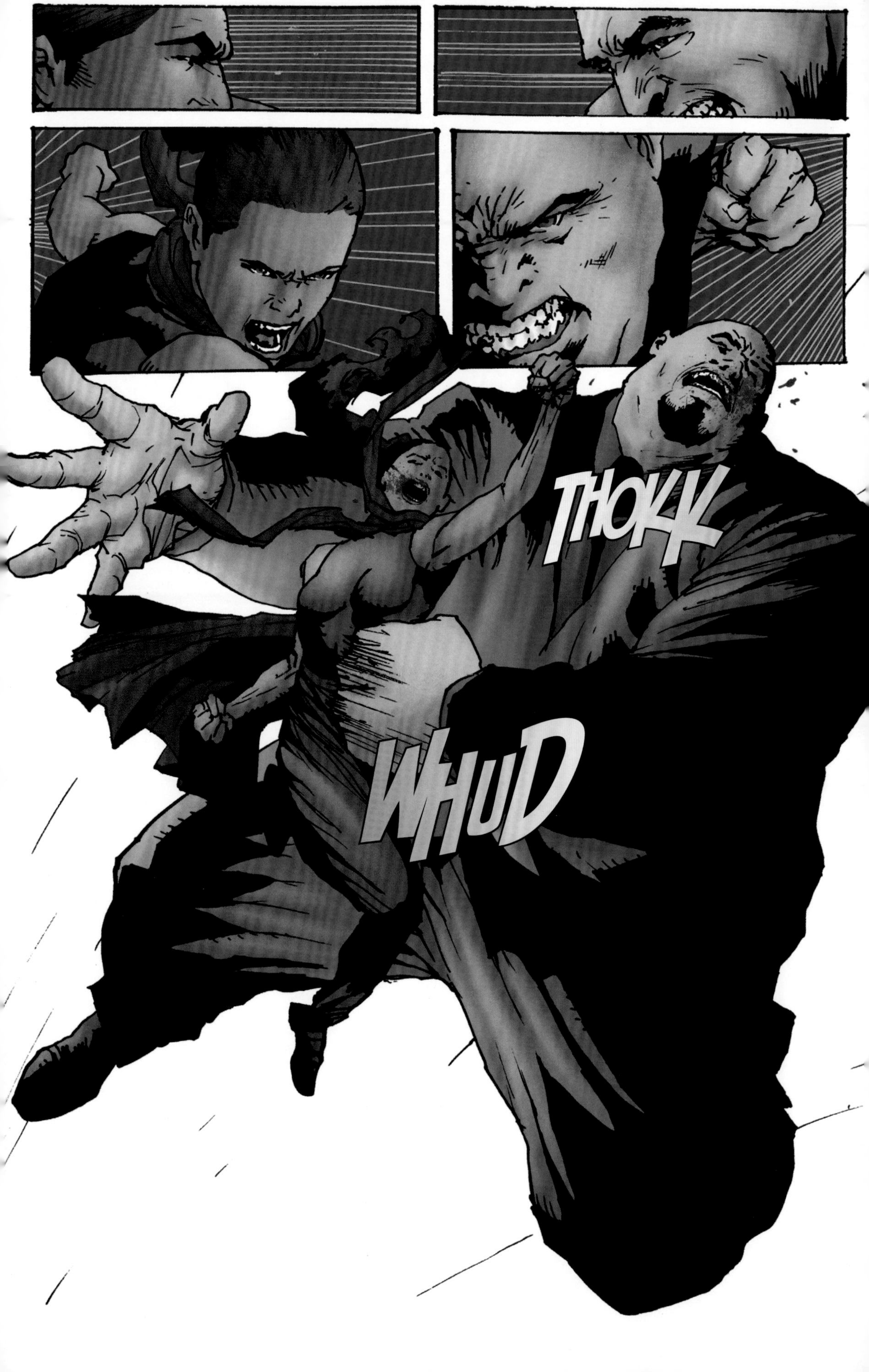
THOKK
WHUD

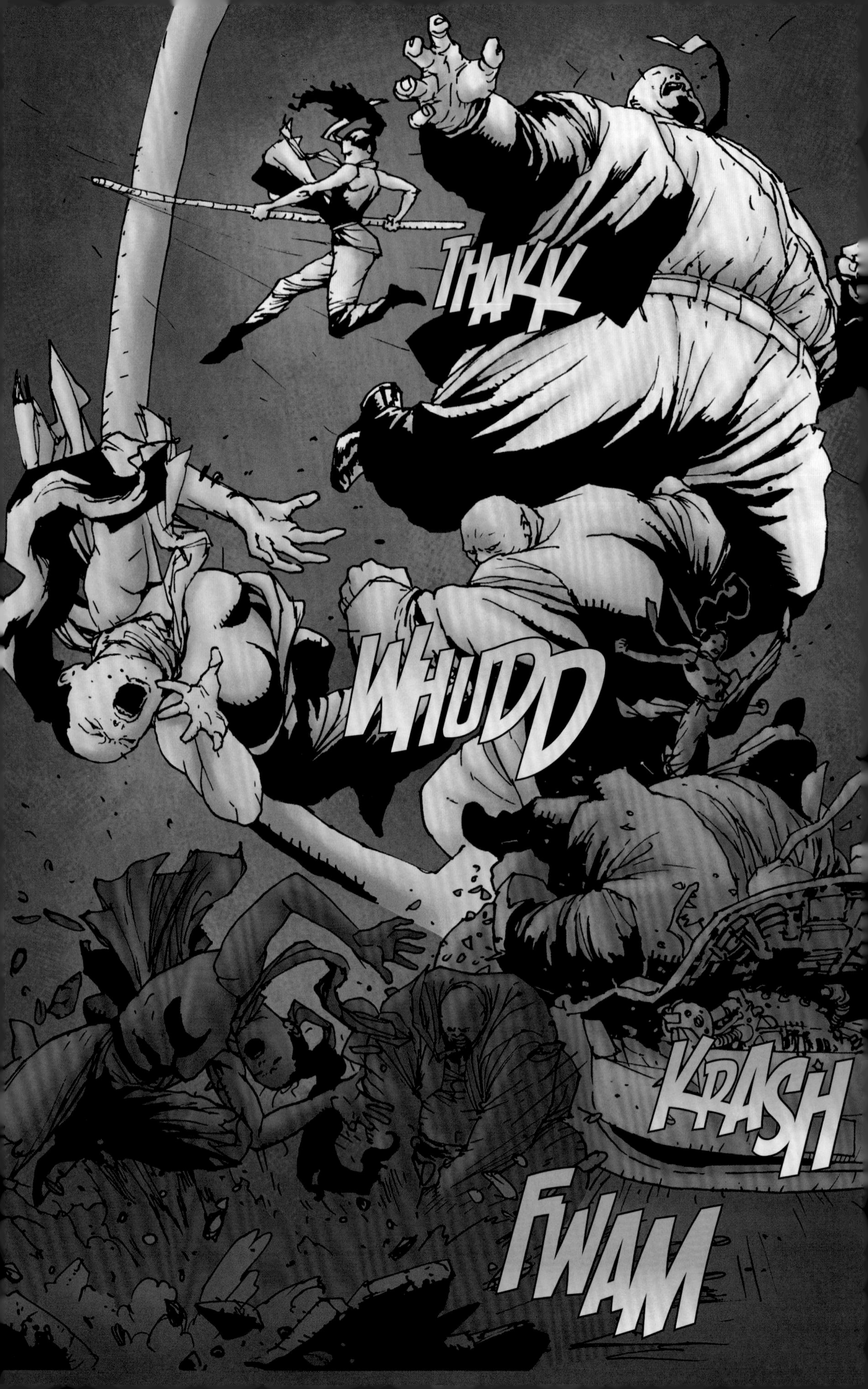
THAKK
WHUDD
KRASH
FWAM

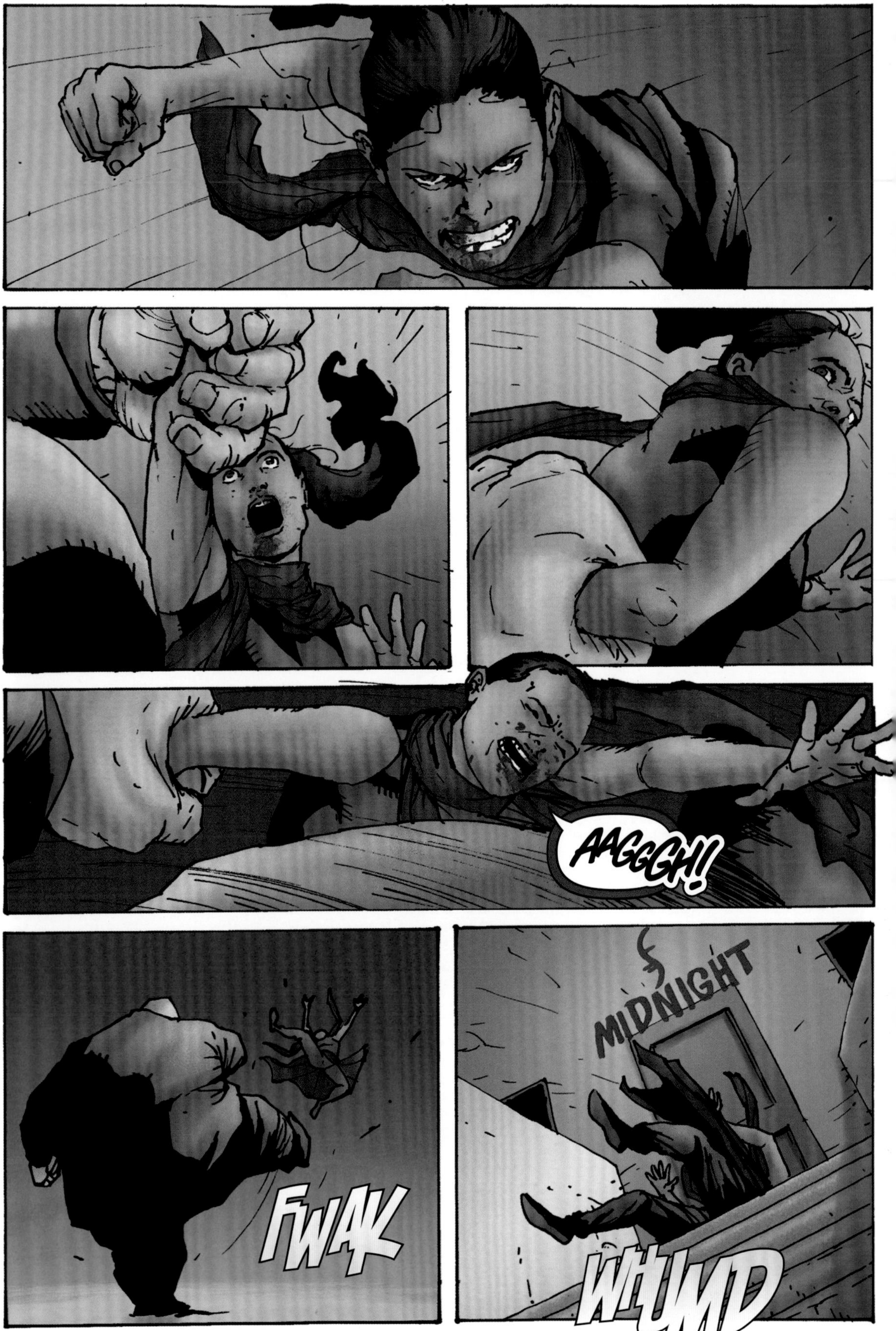
AAGGGH!
FWAK
MIDNIGHT
WHUMP

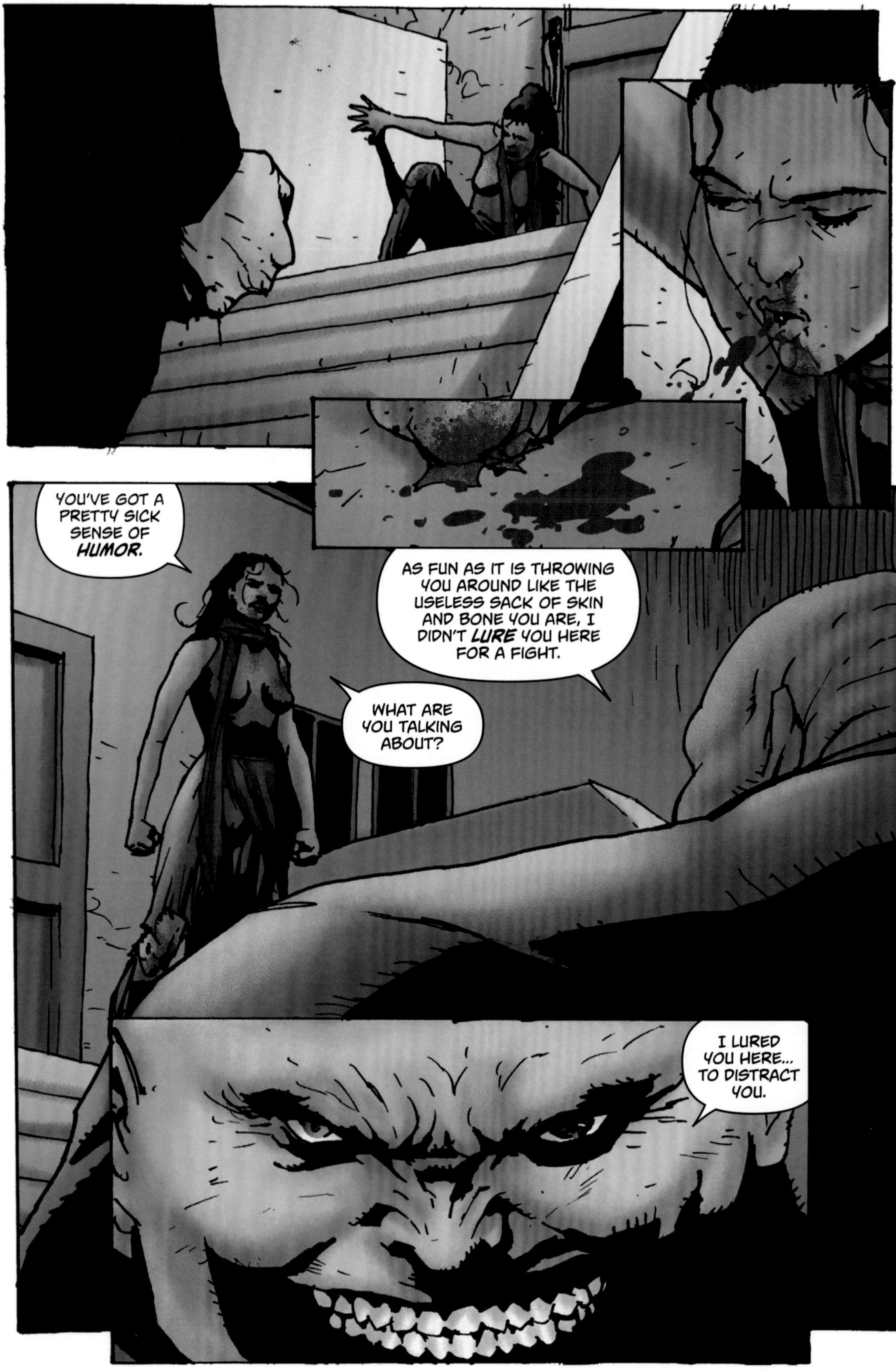
YOU'VE GOT A PRETTY SICK SENSE OF *HUMOR.*
AS FUN AS IT IS THROWING YOU AROUND LIKE THE USELESS SACK OF SKIN AND BONE YOU ARE, I DIDN'T *LURE* YOU HERE FOR A FIGHT.
WHAT ARE YOU TALKING ABOUT?
I LURED YOU HERE... TO DISTRACT YOU.

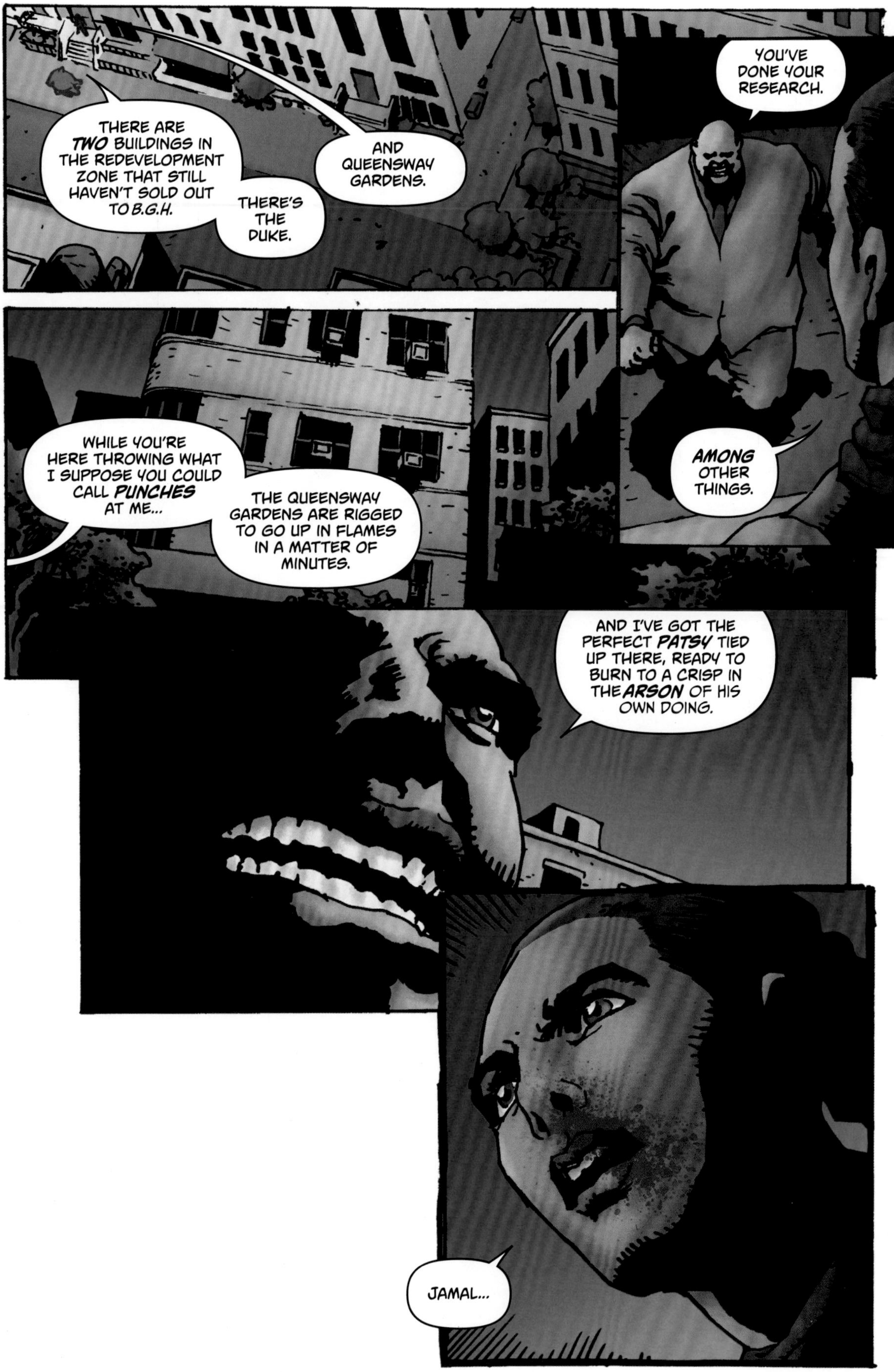
THERE ARE *TWO* BUILDINGS IN THE REDEVELOPMENT ZONE THAT STILL HAVEN'T SOLD OUT TO *B.G.H.*
THERE'S THE DUKE.
AND QUEENSWAY GARDENS.
YOU'VE DONE YOUR RESEARCH.
AMONG OTHER THINGS.
WHILE YOU'RE HERE THROWING WHAT I SUPPOSE YOU COULD CALL *PUNCHES* AT ME...
THE QUEENSWAY GARDENS ARE RIGGED TO GO UP IN FLAMES IN A MATTER OF MINUTES.
AND I'VE GOT THE PERFECT *PATSY* TIED UP THERE, READY TO BURN TO A CRISP IN THE *ARSON* OF HIS OWN DOING.
JAMAL...

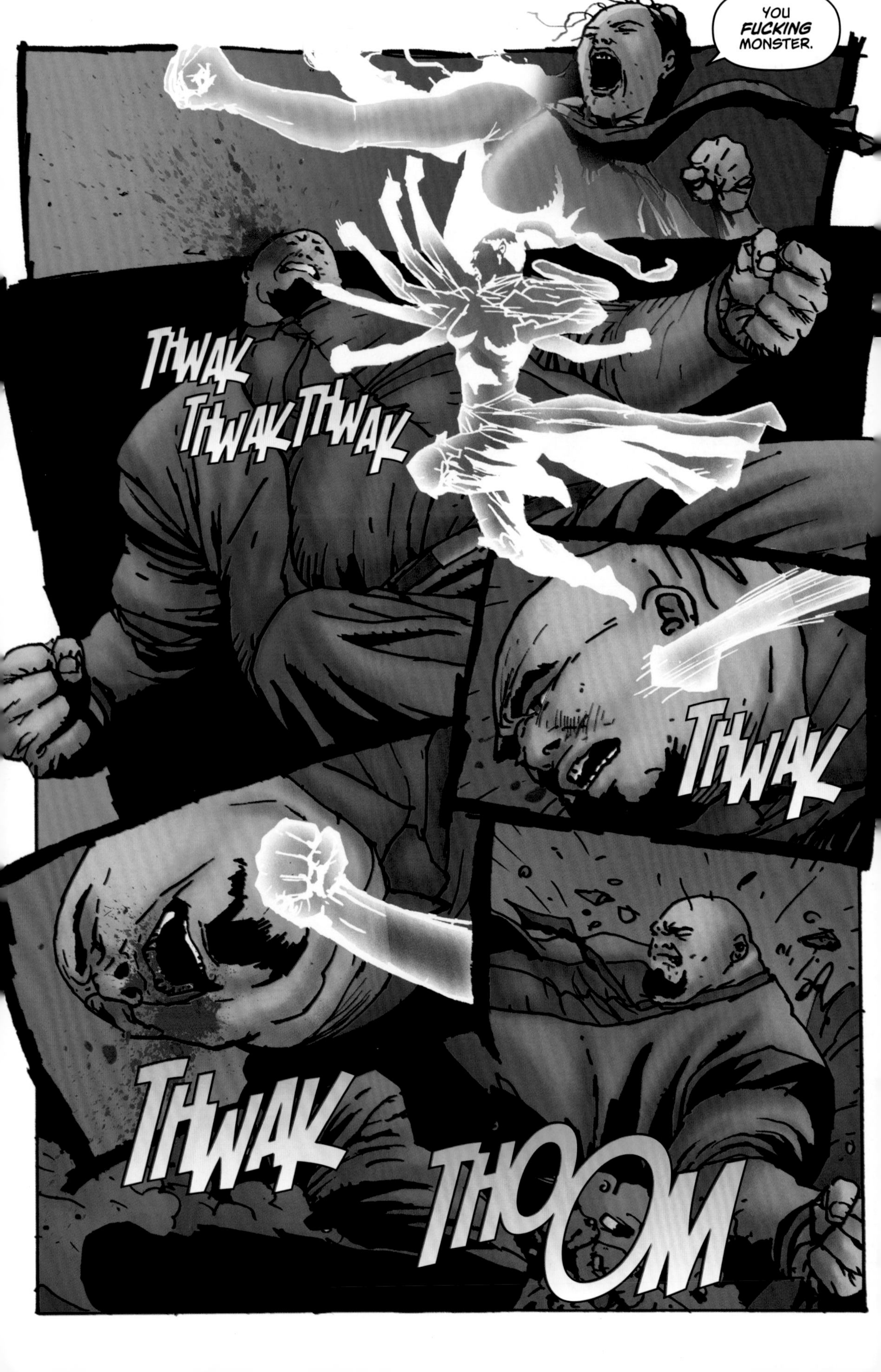
YOU *FUCKING* MONSTER.
THWAK
THWAK THWAK
THWAK
THWAK
THOOM

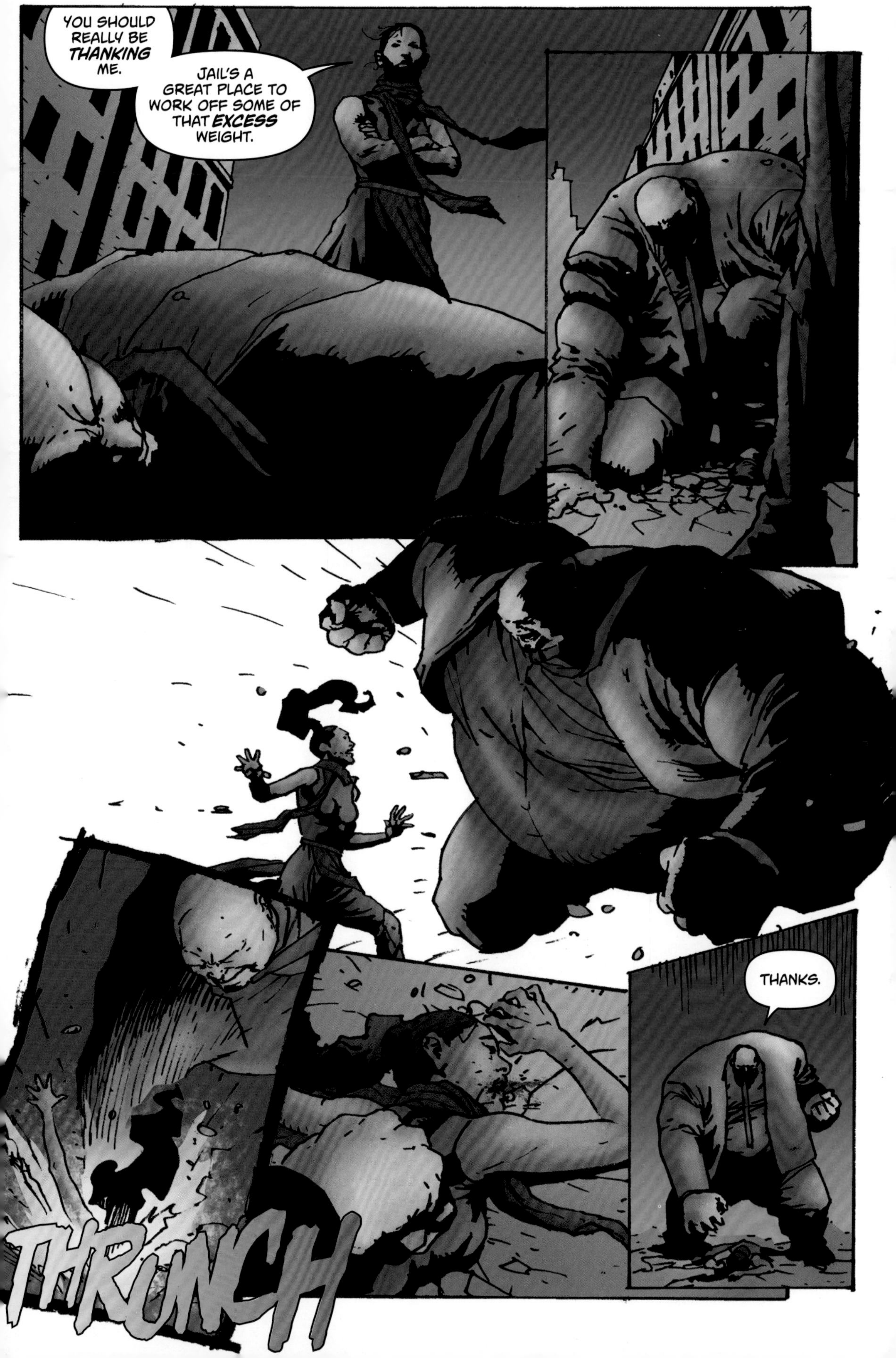
YOU SHOULD REALLY BE *THANKING* ME.
JAIL'S A GREAT PLACE TO WORK OFF SOME OF THAT *EXCESS* WEIGHT.
THRUNCH
THANKS.

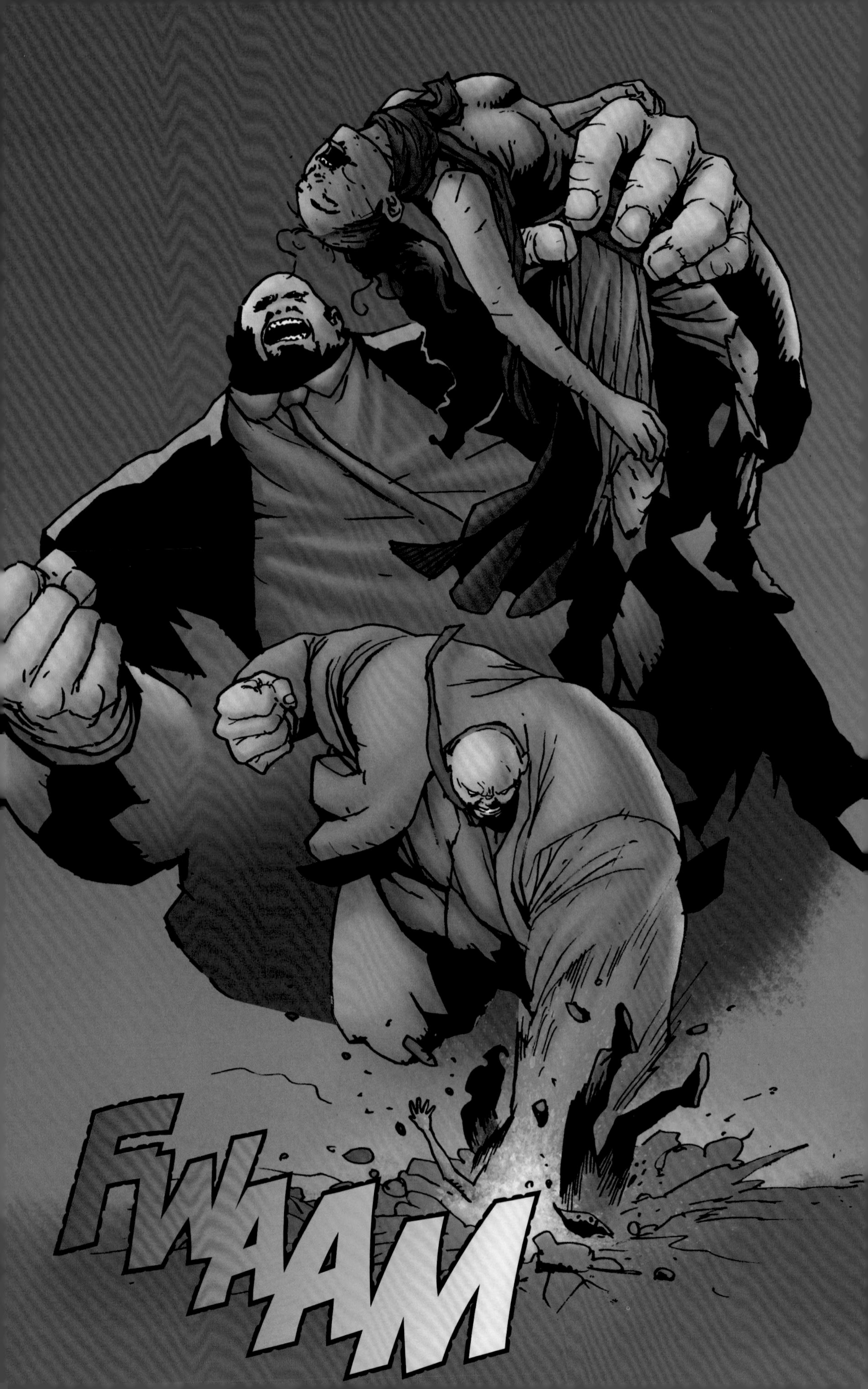
FWAAM

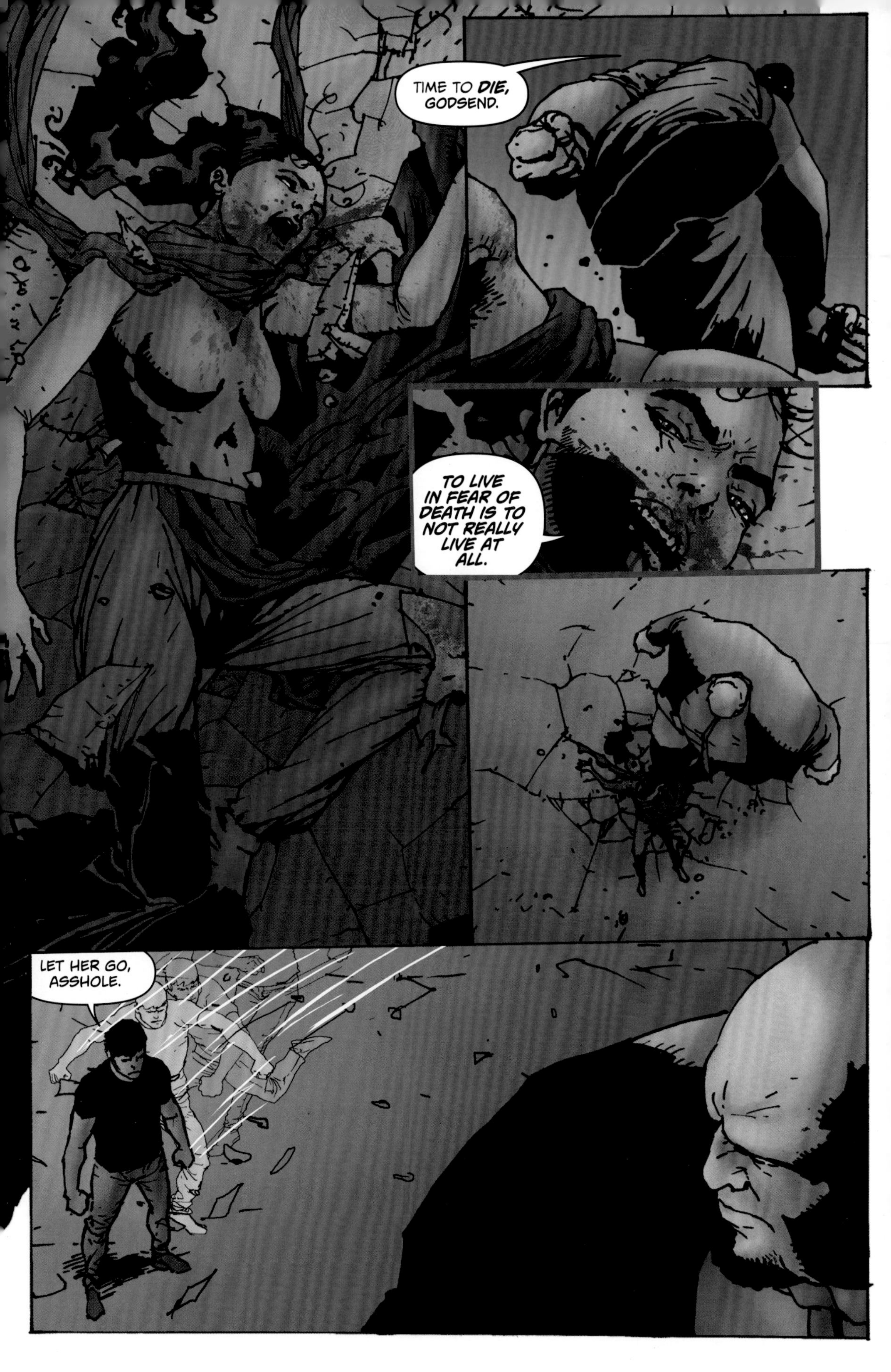
TIME TO *DIE*, GODSEND.
TO LIVE IN FEAR OF DEATH IS TO NOT REALLY LIVE AT ALL.
LET HER GO, ASSHOLE.

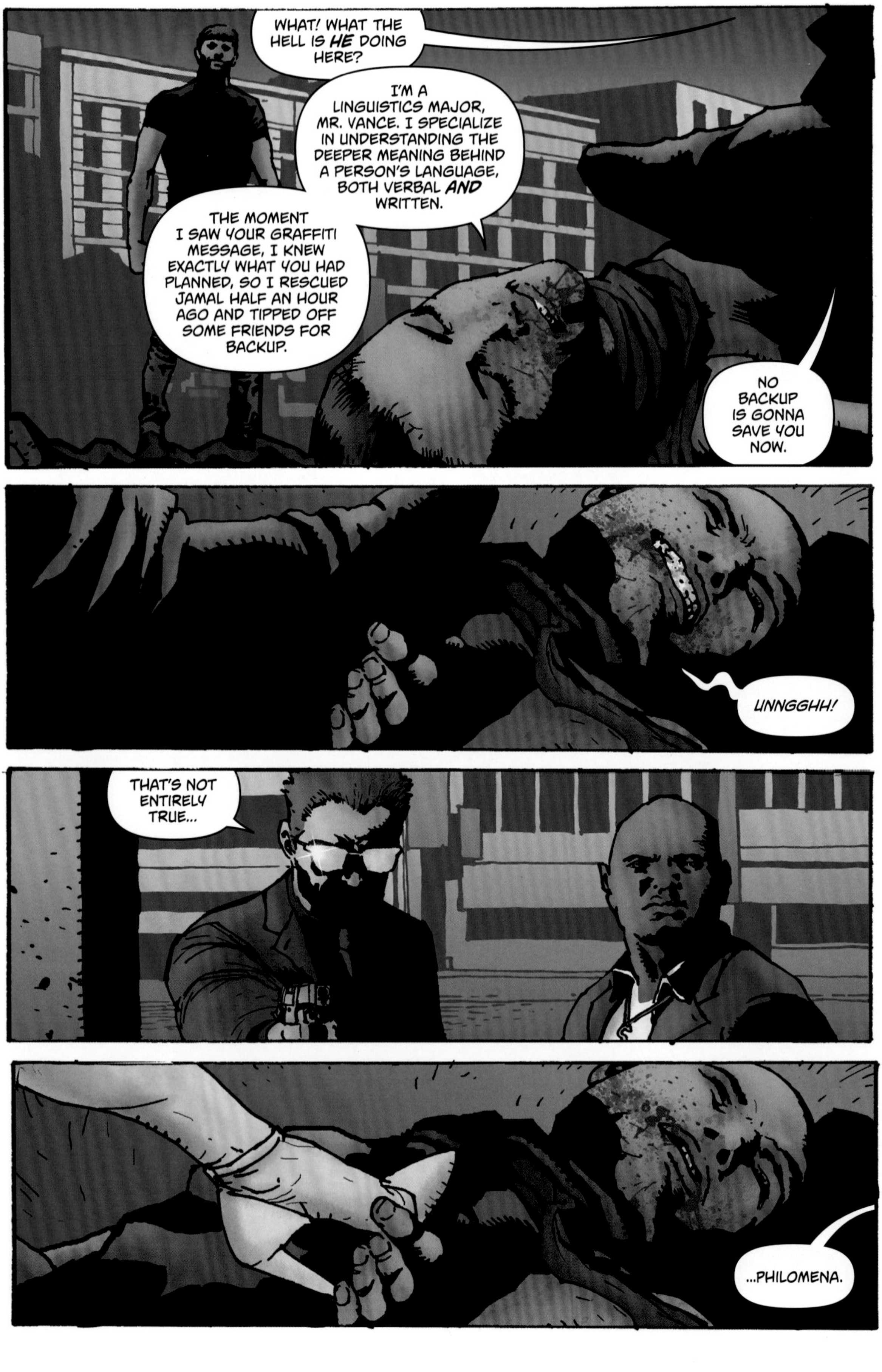
WHAT! WHAT THE HELL IS HE DOING HERE?
I'M A LINGUISTICS MAJOR, MR. VANCE. I SPECIALIZE IN UNDERSTANDING THE DEEPER MEANING BEHIND A PERSON'S LANGUAGE, BOTH VERBAL AND WRITTEN.
THE MOMENT I SAW YOUR GRAFFITI MESSAGE, I KNEW EXACTLY WHAT YOU HAD PLANNED, SO I RESCUED JAMAL HALF AN HOUR AGO AND TIPPED OFF SOME FRIENDS FOR BACKUP.
NO BACKUP IS GONNA SAVE YOU NOW.
UNNGGHH!
THAT'S NOT ENTIRELY TRUE...
...PHILOMENA.

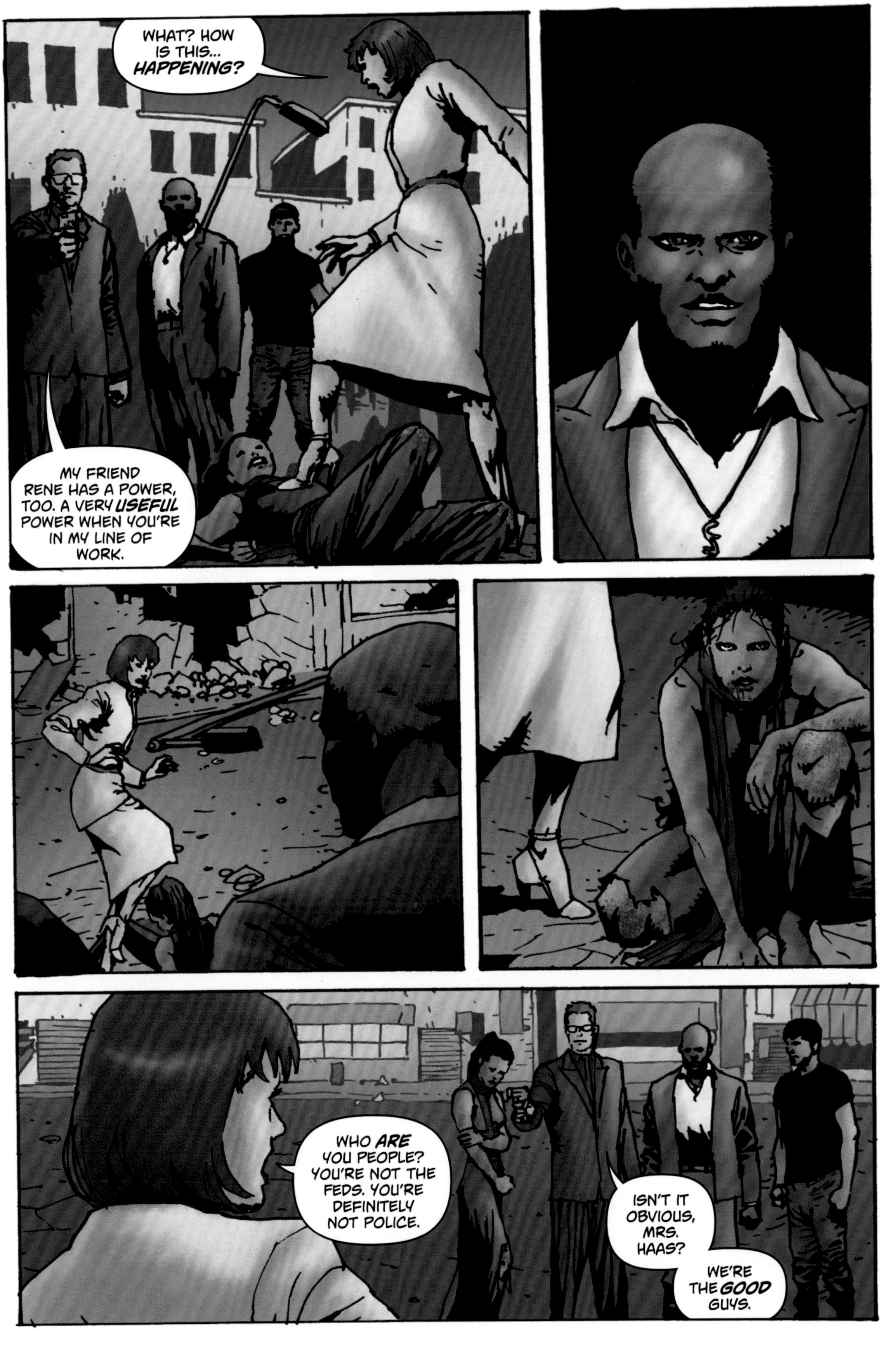
WHAT? HOW IS THIS... *HAPPENING?*
MY FRIEND RENE HAS A POWER, TOO. A VERY *USEFUL* POWER WHEN YOU'RE IN MY LINE OF WORK.
WHO *ARE* YOU PEOPLE? YOU'RE NOT THE FEDS. YOU'RE DEFINITELY NOT POLICE.
ISN'T IT OBVIOUS, MRS. HAAS?
WE'RE THE *GOOD* GUYS.

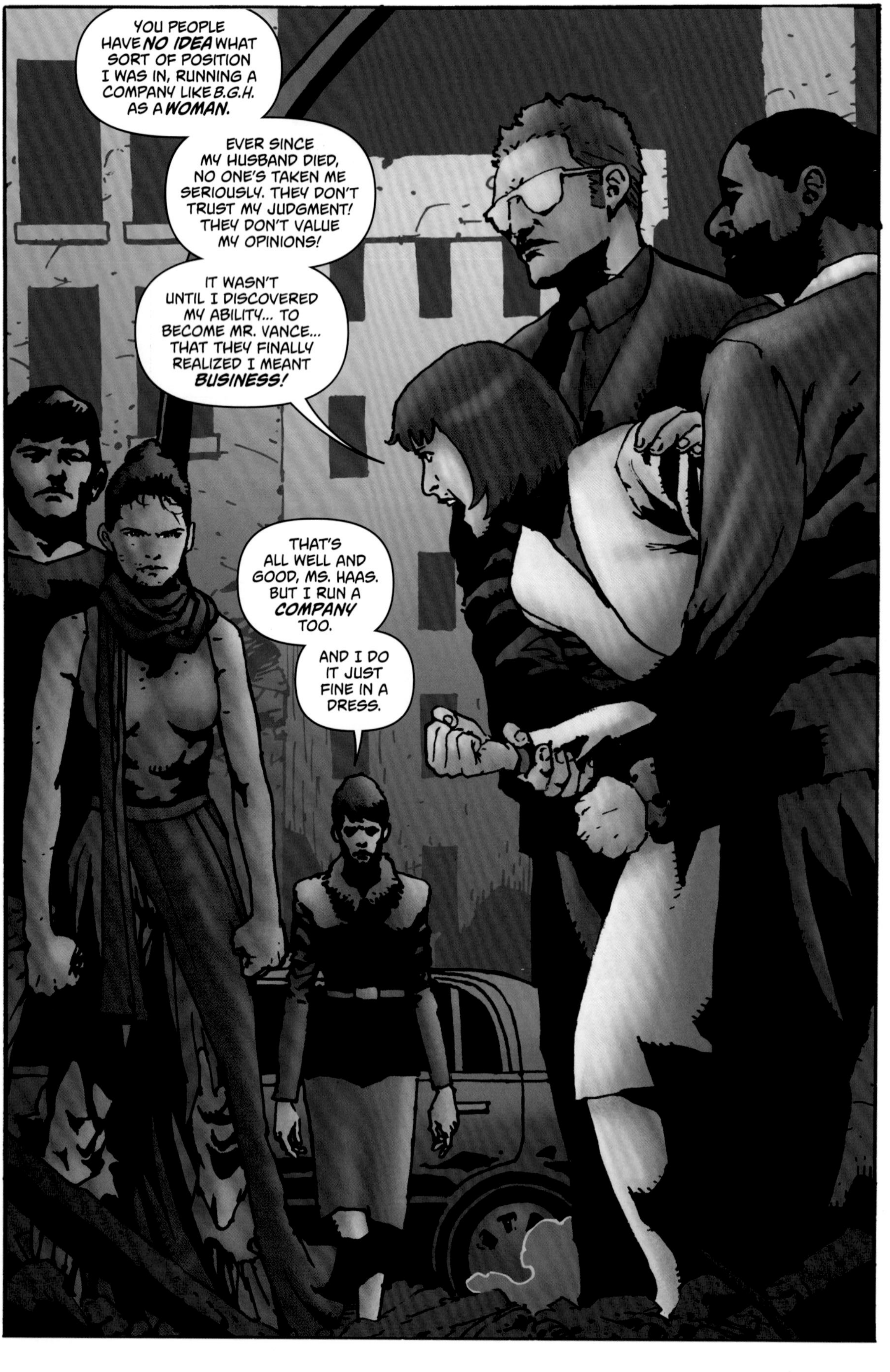
YOU PEOPLE HAVE NO IDEA WHAT SORT OF POSITION I WAS IN, RUNNING A COMPANY LIKE B.G.H. AS A WOMAN.
EVER SINCE MY HUSBAND DIED, NO ONE'S TAKEN ME SERIOUSLY. THEY DON'T TRUST MY JUDGMENT! THEY DON'T VALUE MY OPINIONS!
IT WASN'T UNTIL I DISCOVERED MY ABILITY... TO BECOME MR. VANCE... THAT THEY FINALLY REALIZED I MEANT BUSINESS!
THAT'S ALL WELL AND GOOD, MS. HAAS. BUT I RUN A COMPANY TOO.
AND I DO IT JUST FINE IN A DRESS.

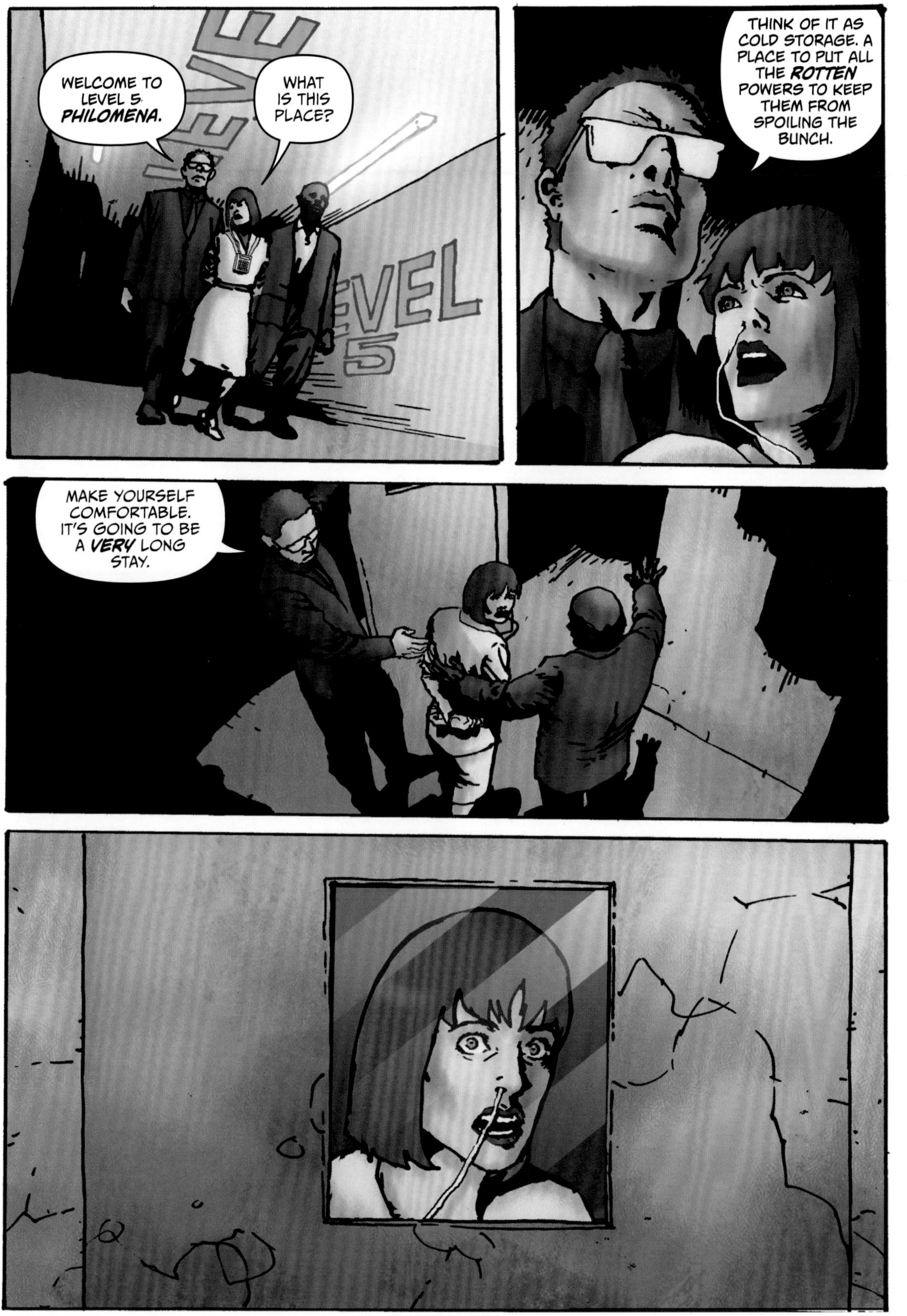
WELCOME TO LEVEL 5, PHILOMENA.
WHAT IS THIS PLACE?
LEVEL 5
THINK OF IT AS COLD STORAGE. A PLACE TO PUT ALL THE ROTTEN POWERS TO KEEP THEM FROM SPOILING THE BUNCH.
MAKE YOURSELF COMFORTABLE. IT'S GOING TO BE A VERY LONG STAY.

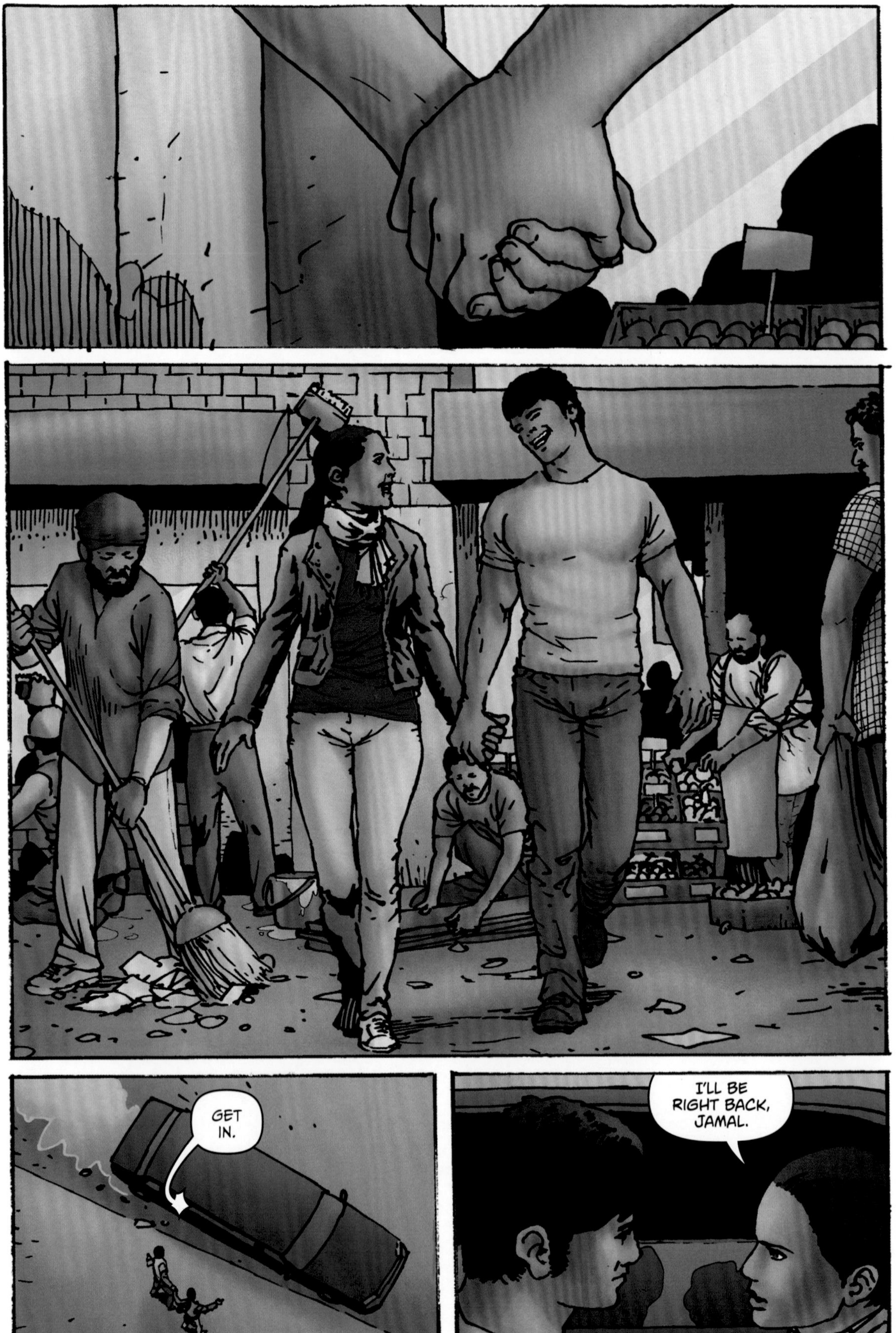
GET IN.
I'LL BE RIGHT BACK, JAMAL.

YOU DID WELL, MS. NAZAN.

I DIDN'T DO IT FOR YOUR *PRAISE*.

I ADMIRE THAT SPIRIT. YOU REMIND ME OF MY SON, *NATHAN*.

I HAVE A STRONG FEELING THAT THIS *WON'T* BE THE LAST TIME PRIMATECH CALLS UPON YOUR SERVICES.

I'M NOT MAKING ANY PROMISES.

WE'LL SEE ABOUT THAT...

WHAT IS THIS?

OPEN IT.

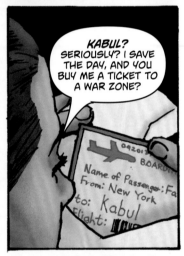

KABUL? SERIOUSLY? I SAVE THE DAY, AND YOU BUY ME A TICKET TO A WAR ZONE?

Name of Passenger: Fa
From: New York
to: Kabul
Flight:

THE TICKET'S NOT FROM ME, FARAH. IT'S FROM YOUR *PARENTS*.

THEY'RE *STILL* ALIVE, AND I'M TOLD THEY'RE READY TO SEE YOU NOW.

END OF VOLUME ONE

DANIEL LINDERMAN

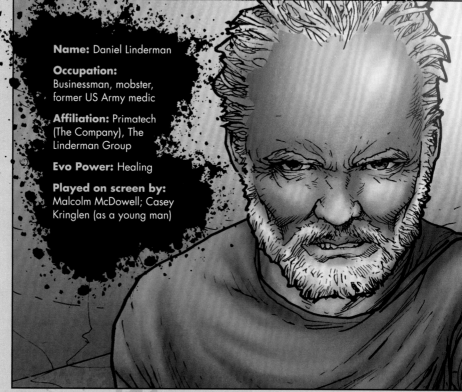

Name: Daniel Linderman

Occupation: Businessman, mobster, former US Army medic

Affiliation: Primatech (The Company), The Linderman Group

Evo Power: Healing

Played on screen by: Malcolm McDowell; Casey Kringlen (as a young man)

Farah's first mission in *Heroes Godsend* is to spring the mysterious Daniel Linderman from a high-security prison. But who is he? Find out more in our guide to the man with healing hands…
By Tolly Maggs

Seemingly a harmless and slightly eccentric businessman, Daniel Linderman is actually a ruthless manipulator and one of the founding members of Primatech, also known simply as "The Company." The organization's goal is to locate evolved humans, and teach them to use their powers for good, or to terminate them if they prove too dangerous to handle.

Linderman established and assumed the role of the head of a major business empire in both the hotel and gambling industries under an umbrella organisation known as The Linderman Group. His cunning and influence have helped him to become an infamously feared mobster. Through manipulation and favors owed to him, Linderman's influence has such a far reach that he can even decide the outcome of elections.

With this kind of power at his disposal, Linderman has plenty of politicians and other notable individuals in his pocket.

Linderman is respected and feared by his peers – and for good reason. If negotiations don't work out the way he wants them to, Linderman has many options at his disposal to deal with anyone who gets in his way, whether it's through kidnapping or even murder. No matter what strategy he chooses, he has more than enough pawns to do the dirty work for him.

On top of all of this political and influential power, Linderman has the extraordinary ability to heal any living thing simply by touching it. Needless to say, this power is highly sought after. Furthermore, despite the fact he uses immoral means to get what he wants, Linderman still believes he is fighting for peace and to heal the world. He does, however, think that some lives are expendable when it

comes to the greater good of mankind.

In his early years, Linderman served in the Vietnam War as a field medic with the rank of Corporal. It was there that Linderman befriended his brother-in-arms Arthur Petrelli, a fellow evolved human. It wasn't until years later that Linderman and Petrelli were once again brought together, along with 10 other evolved humans, to form The Company. Their aim was simple: to put together a group that could use their evolved human abilities to help mankind.

Eventually, however, the group's dynamic deteriorated, and Linderman felt his work was unfinished.

Ultimately, Linderman has a plan to save the world, no matter what the cost. But first, his healing power is needed to save another potential savior of the world…

HEROES

GODSEND

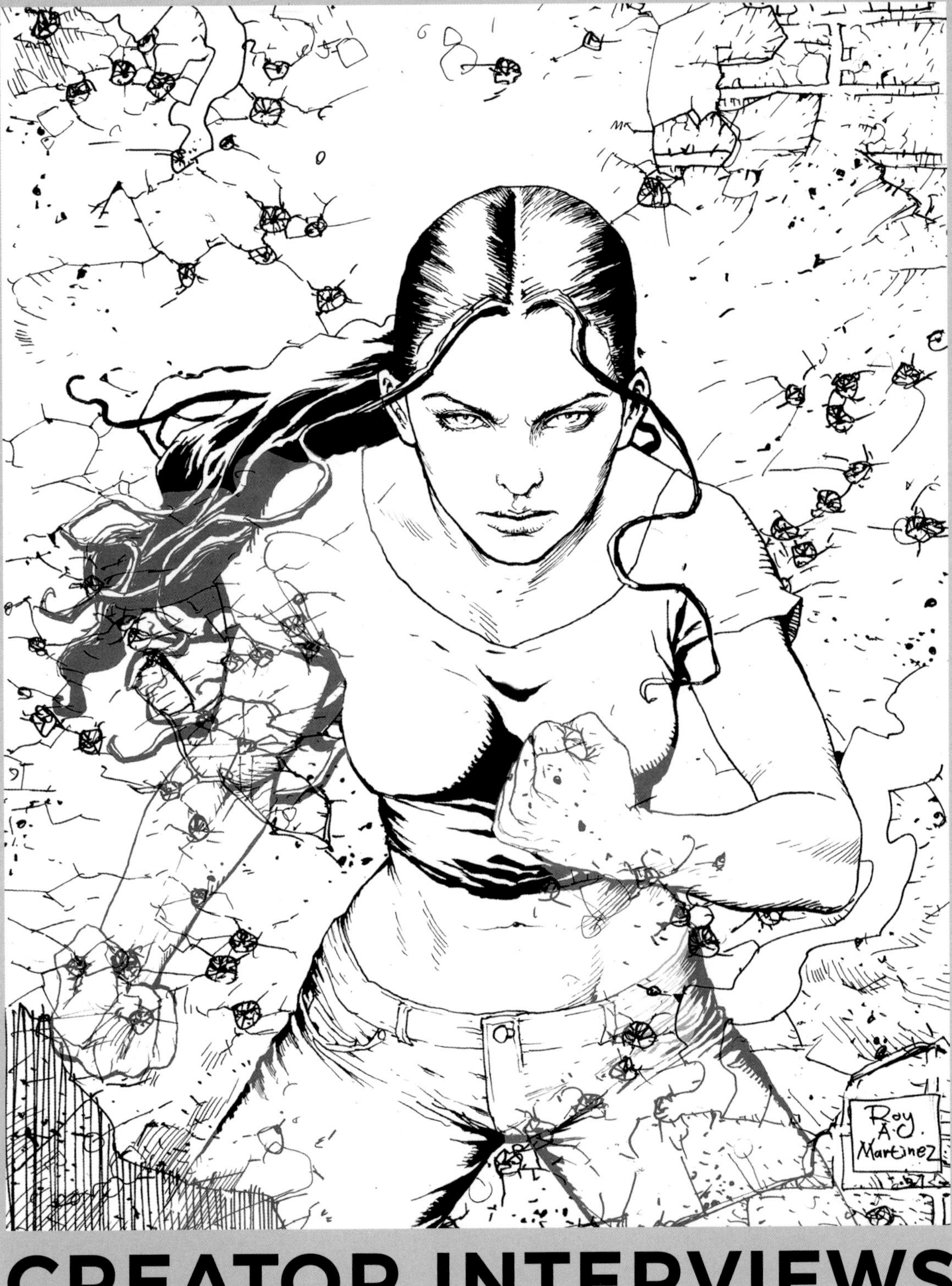
Roy A. Martinez

CREATOR INTERVIEWS

AN INTERVIEW WITH WRITER JOEY FALCO AND

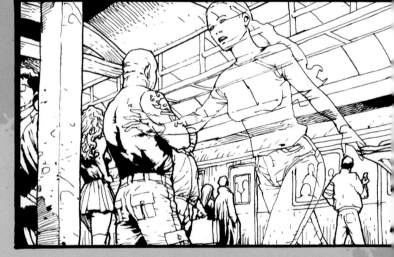

Can you tell us a bit about yourself and your work?

Roy Allan Martinez: I started my comics career in the local comic industry in the Philippines. After a year or so, I started drawing for Marvel, DC comics, etc.

Joey Falco: I was a staff writer on *Heroes Reborn*, which was my first gig in a TV writers' room and the realization of a lifelong dream.

Who are your comic influences – Roy, for your art, and Joey, for your writing?

Roy: Lan Medina, Jim Lee, and Milo Manara. One of the most influential comic books which inspired me to be an illustrator is *Kilabot Komiks*.

Joey: Joss Whedon, George R.R. Martin, Billy Wilder, Stephen Sondheim, Paddy Chayefsky, Quentin Tarantino, J.K. Rowling, Arthur C. Clarke, Alan Moore; and *Heroes/Heroes Reborn* series creator Tim Kring has been an amazing mentor over the past year.

Joey, how would you describe *Heroes: Godsend*?

Joey: It's a classic superhero origin story in which a young person loses her parents, develops a power, and uses it to fight back against an unjust world. Only Farah Nazan isn't a white farmboy growing up in Kansas or a white playboy growing up in Gotham. She's a Pakistani Muslim, so that's kinda cool.

What made you decide to write a story about Farah?

Joey: When I was assigned to write the fourth episode of *Heroes Reborn* and had the opportunity to create a brand new character who would be protecting Malina, I knew right away that I wanted her to be a strong Muslim woman – something I've almost never seen in the

ARTIST **ROY ALLAN MARTINEZ**

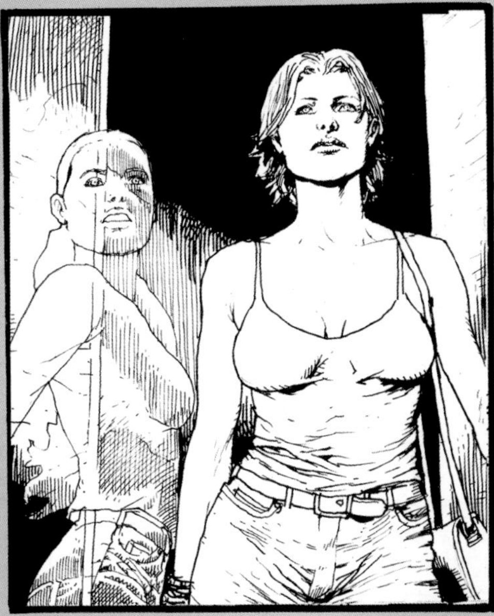

superhero genre. I had always had Farah's origin story in the back of my head while we were writing the show, so when the opportunity arose to explore it in a comic, I leapt at the chance.

Are there any other *Heroes Reborn* characters who you think would make for a good comic?

Joey: I think a lot of people have asked about the origins of M.F. Harris, the masochistic cloning operative of Erica Kravid. Has he always been so deliciously evil? When did he find out that he could produce clones by lopping off his own appendages? And do the "M" and "F" stand for what I think they stand for? Other than that, I would love to use the comic medium to explore what Matt Parkman was up to between the end of the old *Heroes* and the start of *Heroes Reborn*. How exactly did everyone's favorite telepathic cop go down such a dark path, to the point that he started acting like his own father...?

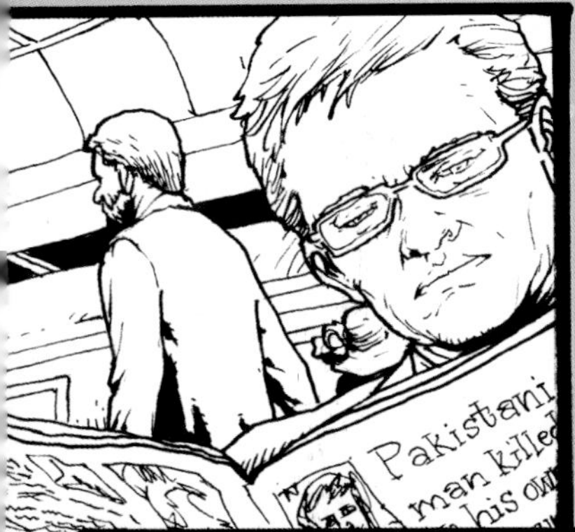
Pakistani
man killed

What advice would you give to aspiring comic artists and writers?

Roy: Make sure you learn anatomy, backgrounds, perspective and lighting.

Joey: Don't let a particular medium pin you down. We're living in an unbelievable time in which a writer can find an outlet for their words in film, television, theater, traditional books, self-published ebooks, comics, webisodes, videogames, blogs, and every form of social media under the sun. I read an entire book on Twitter last year. It's insane. So with this many options, no writer should limit herself to one of them and declare defeat when that first TV pilot doesn't sell or that first play doesn't get produced. Try something else!

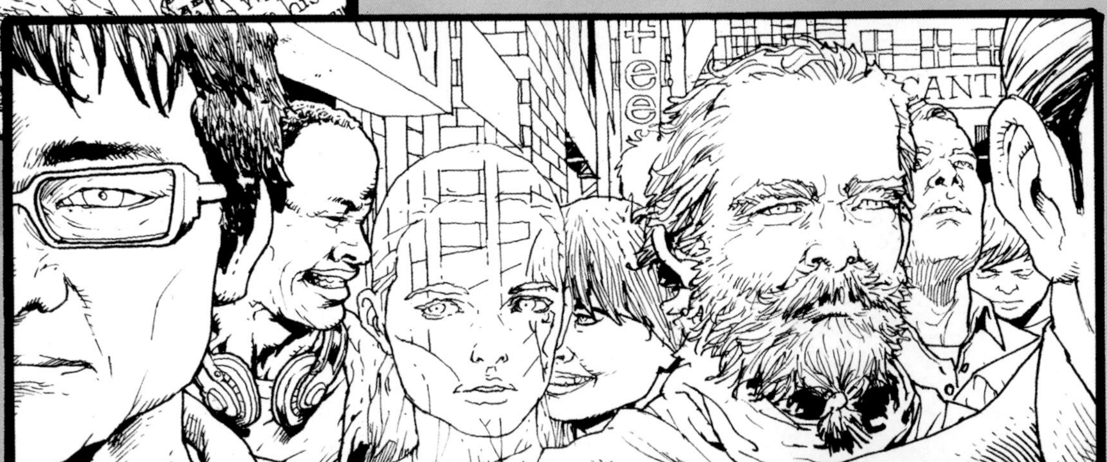